ADVANCE PRAISE FOR

Boots on the Ground, Flats in the Boardroom

"Identify your 'leadership soul' here! I found mine through this highly motivating, unique, unmatched collection of life-changing, real stories of women leaders in a male-dominated world. As a passionate, fearless, determined, non-white woman leader/engineer who embraces challenges with joy, I am awed by these amazing professional/personal experiences of wisdom, strategies, power, passion, spirit, and courage. This is a revolutionary historical collection of inspiration that will continue to grow with YOUR story! To be inspired and to inspire, a chain reaction has started its journey . . ."

NOOPUR JAIN, PE, SE
Project Manager/Structural Engineer

"Bravo! A long overdue and instructive read, a tutorial in trailblazing. Demonstrating grit and grace, these pioneering women in transportation deserve our attention, respect and praise. I've no doubt a new generation of women will aspire to reach the same heights after reading this book."

AYANNA PRESSLEY
Boston City Councilor At-Large

"These are inspiring stories of bold women who were both visionaries and implementers—seers and do-ers—in the critically important world of transportation. They should motivate the next generation of women leaders to follow in their courageous footsteps."

ALAN WEBBER
Co-founder, *Fast Company* magazine

BOOTS *on the* GROUND
FLATS *in the* BOARDROOM

Transportation **women** tell their stories

BOOTS *on the* GROUND
FLATS *in the* BOARDROOM

Grace Crunican and Elizabeth Levin

© 2015 by LEVIN-CRUNICAN LLC

For information, address
LEVIN-CRUNICAN LLC
342 Bunker Hill Street, 5A
Charlestown, MA 02129

Library of Congress Cataloging-in-Publication Data
Library of Congress Control Number: 2015913362

ISBN-13: 978-1-516-90361-0

ISBN-10: 1-516-90361-7

FIRST EDITION

CreateSpace Independent Publishing Platform
North Charleston, SC

Typeset in Scala and Scala Sans
by Dutch type designer Martin Majoor

DEDICATION

This book is dedicated to three women: Violet Gang Raum and CoraLee Cunningham Crunican (our mothers), and Carmen Turner, the former General Manager of the Washington Metropolitan Area Transit Authority (WMATA).

Born in 1912, **Violet Gang** graduated from Wellesley College in 1934 as a French major. She then earned a law degree from the University of Southern California Law School. During the war she served as a Los Angeles Assistant District Attorney. In 1945, she took a break from work to raise children. When her husband, Bob Kopp, was diagnosed with cancer, she went to work at Gang, Kopp, and Tyre (now Gang, Tyre, Ramer & Brown), an entertainment law firm where her brother, husband, and sister-in-law were partners. Bob died at age 42. Violet, a widow, raised three young children while working. She exemplified the values of a loving family, caring for others and being a working mom.

Born in 1924, **CoraLee Cunningham** graduated from Pacific University with a degree in business administration in 1947. Throughout her college years she worked at the local phone company. She continued to work after marriage to Mark Crunican and throughout her three pregnancies. Crunican eventually retired from General Telephone after 42 years of service, at one point holding the highest position held by a woman in the company. She taught Grace the joy of work, family, and community service.

Carmen Turner worked her way through many transportation jobs in the Washington, DC, area. Eventually, she rose to the position of General Manager of WMATA in 1983. Not only did she have to overcome the gender bias of the time, she also had to conquer racial biases, as a strong African-American woman. Intelligent, elegant, and poised, she was the proverbial Ginger Rogers of transportation, doing everything that Fred Astaire did only backwards and in high heels. She also never forgot to help those climbing the ladder behind her.

ACKNOWLEDGEMENTS

This book happened because of the participation of many special people.

We deeply thank the women featured in our book. They generously told us their stories, revealing many candid moments. For that, we are grateful. We hope that each of you enjoys the power of your own story and the collective power of all of these stories to advance women.

We thank the dedicated team of professionals that helped us prepare the book. They include our gifted advisor, Alexandra Spencer, who was always there for us; our talented main writer, Arthur Schurr; our contributing writer, Paul Napolitano; our careful editor, Erika Grotto; and our devoted production manager, Crescent Wells, who helped us through endless changes. Each of you helped bring us neophytes through the difficult and unknown aspects of authoring a book. You made the book possible.

We would also like to especially thank our families, whose support has always mattered. More specifically:

From Liz – I want to thank my husband Chuck Levin, my two sons Ben and Dan Levin, my daughter-in-law Michelle Levin, my grandsons Will and Josh Levin, and our wonderful extended family.

From Grace – I thank my children, Sarah and Andrew Crunican, my brothers Bruce and Dan Crunican, and my extended family and friends that have surrounded me with support and challenged my thinking.

Finally, we want to thank each other. The book was a huge undertaking and we had no idea whether we would finish it. We inspired and complemented each other, the way a partnership should work.

CONTENTS

There is a special place in hell for women who do not help other women.

—Madeleine K. Albright

Chapter 1

THE POWER OF STORIES

Why write a book? For us the reasons were simple and compelling. We knew strong, powerful women who had succeeded in traditionally male-dominated arenas. We wanted to provide examples of women role models and leaders. We wanted to capture the story of early female transportation leaders before their stories faded away. And we knew their stories would contain fascinating tales, examples of leadership, unbelievable stories of human behavior (both good and bad), and advice that would benefit young, mid-career, and even senior women—as well as some men. But that's not all.

We also wrote this book with specific audiences in mind. First, we wanted to develop this book for the many women and few men who attend the professional development sessions at WTS International conferences. WTS International, originally known as the Women's Transportation Seminar, is an organization dedicated to building the future of transportation through the advancement of women. Many of the subjects in this book have appeared at WTS podiums around the nation, answering questions about how we all did what we did, got where we got, and overcame obstacles in our way. We saw a real need for conversation about the combination of career and personal decision making and the intersection of personal and work values, dynamics, logistics, and politics.

Women at different levels in their transportation careers are our second major audience. That covers mid-level professionals, women just entering the profession, and those young women still in school. We want them to know—we want you to know—that there is a place for you, a path forward, and people to talk with and support you. You are not alone in your journey. You don't have to repeat the mistakes we made and the lessons we so painfully learned. We are here to help. But there are other audiences that also are a natural fit for this conversation.

Professional women in nontraditional roles, such as engineers, lawyers, those in the sciences, etc., have much in common with the journeys presented here. Men who are stereotyped in non-traditional roles for their gender will also find kinship and helpful information here, too. Finally, students in management classes will see a range of leadership and management styles for examination and study, and they'll find these stories intriguing.

Ultimately, while the stories in the book are from transportation women, at their essence these are human stories about determination, struggle, leadership, perseverance, survival, luck, and moxie. They apply to a broad range of both women and men. And they represent the collective wisdom of decades in the trenches of both the public and private sectors in the US. They present a picture of the way things were and the way things are today.

When we started our careers, things were different. The landscape featured few to no women leading state departments of transportation, major transit systems, or national transportation firms. Women serving on boards of directors were rarer still. But there were some. In 1976, California Governor Jerry Brown appointed Adriana Gianturco to head the California Department of Transportation. Joan Claybrook became the first woman to head a modal administration within the US Department of Transportation when, in 1977, she began her term as head of the National Highway Traffic Safety Administration. And as mentioned in the dedication, Carmen Turner took the reins as General Manager of WMATA in 1983. These women were trailblazers. However, even though a few women advanced, it did not mean that there were established role models for women beginning their careers at that time. In fact, quite the opposite was true, making their accomplishments all the more stark. Aspiring career women had virtually no role models at the time, no icon or indication that leadership would or could be the norm. There were other pioneers, though, many of whom speak to you in this book.

Going into this project, we as the authors were aware that we each had unusual role models very close to home. Our mothers had both graduated from four-year colleges. Both were professional women—a businesswoman and a lawyer. Though we had personal role models in our upbringing, many of our subjects did not. So we understood the power of role models and wanted to capture the stories of our colleagues who have become role models for the many young women in the transportation industry today.

Since we began our careers, much has changed. Women do lead agencies, authorities, and corporations. But the numbers in no way represent true equality. In some instances, we are no better off now than we were back then. As we write this book, boards of directors of most US architecture/engineering firms have at best one or two female members. There are many still with *no* female board members. Thus, while women have made progress in this male-dominated industry, that progress seems woefully inadequate. That, too, is why we felt compelled to tell how our subjects were able to navigate that landscape and surmount incredible obstacles to come out on top. And we chose these women for very specific reasons.

For inspiration and structure, we turned to the invaluable *The Managerial Woman* by Anne Jardim and Margaret Hennig, a book we both read at the beginning of our careers. It outlined the lives of 25 women who had risen to the top of companies by the 1970s. For our book, we chose 18 women. We tried to get a diverse group representing different transportation modes, geographical and racial diversity, and at least a few women from the private sector.

At least one of us knew or knew of each woman selected, and felt that her story would be valuable. We were by no means perfect in our selection: too many from Massachusetts, too many

Democrats, and too many public sector women. But there was always a method to our madness. For example, both Massachusetts Governor Mike Dukakis and his Secretary of Transportation Fred Salvucci encouraged talented women to seek high positions in their administration. They gave many brilliant, highly skilled women a foothold from which to launch their careers. And the women flourished in such a welcoming and supportive environment. Many other women and men also provided such opportunities, and we tried to acknowledge them and their contributions whenever possible and appropriate.

Of course, there were many other women we could have chosen, many others we considered. Space and time could allow us to do only so much. This is just a snapshot of some of the pioneering women that made a difference. But these 18 women made their way to leadership positions, mostly without role models and institutional support. Some were not as visible as others. Some made the front pages of newspapers around the country. But all of them made it a very long way from where they began. And all of these women succeeded in either nontraditional ways or in nontraditional positions, or both. Frequently, they were the only women in the room—whether it was a classroom, boardroom, or construction field office.

Our interview process was fairly straightforward. One of us and one of our writers interviewed each woman. We wanted each woman to tell her story with minimal interference. Our writer then edited each woman's story, using her own words, until we all agreed on the story. We did not attempt to expose our subjects for any particular weaknesses or embarrassments. By the same token, we did not seek to glorify anyone. This is not historic documentation. It is also neither an academic study nor an analysis of their careers and lives. Simply, it is each woman's version of her journey through life, with an emphasis on her career. We chose to include our own stories in the book, not an easy choice. But we felt it was important that if others shared their personal stories then we should be willing to do the same, warts and all.

The name of our book, *Boots on the Ground, Flats in the Boardroom*, reflects our experience of being in places where women did not used to go. It also reflects forward movement (boots on the ground) and the fact that we—and most of the woman in this book—consider ourselves change agents at the highest levels (flats in the boardroom).

We hope you enjoy these stories and find that they strengthen and shape your own.

Thank you,
Liz Levin and Grace Crunican

JANE GARVEY

September 11 was actually a beautiful day, "severe clear" as the pilots say. I was in US Department of Transportation (USDOT) Secretary Mineta's office. And his Chief of Staff burst in and said, "Madame Administrator, Mr. Secretary—we need to see you right away!" We leapt up to see what was going on. On CNN, we saw smoke coming from the World Trade Center. Then my beeper went off. I called the Federal Aviation Administration (FAA) Control Center and they said, "We have a hijacking—an American plane." I said, "Is it the plane that went into the World Trade Center?" They said, "No." So I rushed back to the FAA building and it all unfolded from there. . . .

Jane Garvey has made history. But her beginnings in transportation were quite simple. She opposed a Massachusetts highway project along with a group of neighbors, and won. She got noticed. In 1983, Governor Michael Dukakis brought her onto his transition team after he won election. Next she became an Associate Administrator for the Massachusetts Department of Public Works (DPW), where she took on the Charlestown North Area Project, an antecedent to the Central Artery Project or the Big Dig. It was a huge success.

Garvey combined extraordinary political skills with expert advice and climbed the transportation ladder. In 1988, she became DPW Commissioner, where she served with distinction. Then in 1991, she moved to aviation, where she became the first woman Director of Boston's Logan International Airport. Her next step would be national.

Garvey joined the Federal Highway Administration (FHWA) as Deputy Administrator. She would rise to Acting Administrator and gain acclaim for developing the Innovative Financing Initiative. In 1997, President Clinton chose Garvey to serve as the 14th Administrator of the FAA, where she navigated successfully both the Y2K transition and the 9/11 terrorist attacks. She left the FAA at the end of her term in 2002. She then joined JPMorgan and headed up its US Public/Private Partnerships (P3s) advisory group. Recently, she served on the Transition Team for President Obama, focusing on transportation policies. Today, Garvey is the North American Chairman of Meridiam Infrastructure.

In addition to her work with Meridiam, Garvey serves on several corporate boards and commissions, including United Airlines and MITRE. She is also the Chairman of the Bipartisan Policy Project. Garvey has also received numerous awards, including the National Air Transportation Association's Distinguished Service Award, the National Council of Public-Private Partnerships Leadership Award, and WTS International's Woman of the Year Award. In 2002, the American Road & Transportation Builders Association accorded her its highest honor, naming her to its list of "The Hundred Leaders in Transportation in the 20th Century."

This is her story.

A Circuitous Route to Transportation

Jane Garvey entered the world of transportation out of necessity.

"I got involved with a group of citizens who opposed a highway project in Western Massachusetts in the mid-1980s. We thought it changed the character of the community. Working against the highway project piqued my interest in the role that transportation played in society. And we'd go to public meetings and raise questions about its necessity and whether the design standards were right. It was the first time I witnessed the intersection between transportation and community, and the enormous impact transportation can have."

It was a valuable lesson. Garvey would spend much of her career at the nexus between transportation and community. And it worked.

"The outcome was very good. The project moved forward, but in a very modified way. To the Highway Department's credit, they listened, worked with the community, and reached a compromise. We might have preferred no project at all, but the compromise worked out well."

It proved to be a turning point for Garvey. She went from being a community activist and teacher to believing that her future belonged in government service.

Joining the Team

Garvey joined Governor Michael Dukakis's transition team when he won election in 1983. Because of her work there, Massachusetts Secretary of Transportation Fred Salvucci asked Garvey to join the DPW as an Associate Administrator. Dukakis also believed Garvey brought something special to the job.

"Governor Dukakis was wonderful. He would say, 'We need geographic diversity. We need gender diversity, but we also need point-of-view diversity. And here is someone who brings that kind of perspective.'"

Garvey became one of three associate administrators. And it was here that she met her first professional mentor.

I Had Arrived

Garvey took to the work instantly. And she credits her boss for teaching her a great deal about leadership.

"We had a fantastic Commissioner, Bob Tierney. He was a Notre Dame graduate. He was an incredibly well respected and talented engineer. He knew engineering, government, and the private sector. He had been around transportation and engineering all of his professional life. Then he decided that he wanted to retire.

One of the great compliments of my career was that he strongly recommended to the Governor that I become the Commissioner. To have Bob Tierney, the quintessential, crusty Irish fellow with a great sense of humor—his wonderful way to motivate people—recommend me was high praise indeed."

Garvey became Department of Public Works Commissioner in 1985. She had been running DPW for a year when the powers that be handed her a unique challenge.

"'We have this project in Charlestown. And it's really associated with the Central Artery Project, but we don't want to call it the Artery, because we don't think this project will succeed. And if we call it the first part of the Artery, then we doom the Central Artery if the project fails. So we're going to call it the *Charlestown North Area Project.*' It turned out to be a great community success. I knew it was a success the day that I heard Secretary Salvucci and Governor Dukakis describe it as *Phase 1 of the Central Artery Project.* I knew I had arrived."

Working with Visionaries

Working with the community proved to be a strength for Garvey. But another aspect of her work appealed equally.

"I really took to public policy. I enjoy looking at an issue and figuring out the human dimensions of it. Again, I think it's because we had a Governor who was incredibly committed to the role transportation played. And he defined it in its broadest sense—not just highways, but transit and streetscapes, and so forth. I might not have enjoyed it as much if I had been in another state. But I describe my time there as the salad days of my career.

"Fred Salvucci was visionary in the same way as the Governor. I don't think Fred ever looked at an engineering drawing and didn't immediately say, 'What are the human implications?' Those were great lessons for somebody just starting out in transportation. So I was quickly drawn to and very much enjoyed the notion of building consensus and of bringing in competing issues on a matter. It was a great lesson to watch how Fred and the Governor created a coalition in support of the Central Artery that lasted far beyond their tenure. After they left, even though the project went to a diametrically opposed Republican administration with a very tough Secretary of Transportation, there was so much public support for it and so much outside support that they really had to stay the course. That was a great lesson to learn."

Garvey learned more invaluable lessons. And she discovered a particular appeal to state projects.

"Being Commissioner was one of the best jobs I've ever had. At the state level the projects that you build have such a direct impact. You went into communities and you changed downtowns. In those days there was a particular emphasis with that administration to try to figure out ways to revitalize places like Springfield and Holyoke and Lawrence, and so forth. So you could really see a direct impact and that was fun."

Getting to the Airport

Garvey did well as DPW Commissioner. But things were heating up in Boston with the Central Artery Project. And there was a key component that needed greater attention and a new leader.

"Becoming Director of Logan International Airport was another big leap, but not necessarily unexpected in the sense that it was when the Artery was being built. We had seen the Central Artery through the environmental phase, but not the construction phase. And it was moving forward into construction. The first part of construction involved building the tunnel under Logan Airport. But you had to keep the airport running during construction. They needed someone who knew how to deal with the project. The board thought that it might make sense to have somebody who was familiar with the Artery and who understood the team pretty well. I moved over with Governor Weld's blessing, and served as the Director of Aviation during that phase of the Artery project.

"Being the Aviation Director is really very similar to being the mayor of the city, because you have these concessions, businesses you have to deal with that were relying on a bottom line. You also had constituencies. And they remembered when the airport was taken over and there were women in East Boston with baby carriages trying to stop the bulldozers and so forth. So it is very much like running a whole city. We even have a chapel and a pastor!"

Garvey was the first female Director of Logan International Airport.

Management 101

Much like DPW, the Aviation Department was predominantly male. Management was a challenge. And in addition to the Central Artery Project, Logan was on the brink of a large modernization. Garvey had her hands full.

"How do you win these guys over? How do you deal with them? How do you try to move forward? I worked very hard at it and took it as a personal challenge. I think it turned out pretty well. We'd host meetings for the station managers. There were lots of meetings, lots of discussions, and lots of bringing them into things. Logan was beginning to think about a real modernization plan, so we would bring them in for some of those discussions, even when it wasn't necessary. That always goes a long way in maintaining and developing those relationships. In a way it's management 101. You've got to establish some connections. You've got to establish them early with people who were part of the community that you work with.

"I tried to use humor to defuse some situations, something I learned from Bob Tierney. I'm always hesitant to say gender is a factor, although I will say my experience suggests that more women are apt to say, 'Let's find common ground here. Let's find some way to move this agenda forward.' Whenever women were involved—from organizations like the League of Women Voters to community groups—there tended to be a more participatory process. I probably lean more toward that outlook, but I will tell you that there was no one better than Bill Clinton at doing that."

Becoming a Champion and Dealing with Patronage

Being the first female Director at Logan was no small challenge. But Garvey discovered strategies that transcend gender.

"At both DPW and Logan I had to find an issue, or two or three issues, that were important to our constituents that I could really work hard to resolve. At DPW, it was a question of saying, 'Look, they haven't had a budget increase for years. Nobody has been able to deliver that. With the Secretary's help, can I work with the legislature to get them a budget increase? And can we get them additional resources?' And we did. That was a pivotal moment, because people then saw me as a champion for them. That happened at Logan as well. The neighborhoods and the airlines had been shut out of some discussions. And I worked very hard to find a way to bring them into the early discussions on modernization."

But building consensus was by no means the only daunting challenge she faced.

"Some of the bigger challenges involved politics, where a political godfather would say, 'I need you to hire so-and-so for a position.' That was particularly true at Massachusetts Port Authority (Massport). It's very hard because these people are in positions of power. You have to deal with it head on and hope you have a reservoir of goodwill and that you can get them to understand, 'Look, this wouldn't be good for you, and this wouldn't be good for me. Neither one of us needs a story in the *Boston Herald*.' Other times you just say, 'We can't do that and here's why, but perhaps there's something else he's appropriate for that might work better.' This didn't always work, but you have to figure it out. But you definitely have to hold your ground on the areas that are really critical."

Massachusetts provided Garvey with great training for her next step.

"Do You Know Any Interesting Candidates?"

Bill Clinton took office in 1997. Garvey had her hands full at Logan. But she caught wind of her name being bandied about at higher levels.

"When Bill Clinton was elected, there was considerable discussion about Bill Daley being the possible Secretary of Transportation; the Daleys were very close to all of the Boston politicians. And the Daley people began to reach out to the Governor and other people in Massachusetts asking, 'Do you know any interesting candidates?' My name was put forward.

"Then Bill Daley was out, and the candidate for Transportation Secretary was Federico Peña from Denver. I interviewed with Secretary Peña and he was wonderful. He gave me a choice of Aviation or Surface Transportation. Congress had just passed a very significant piece of legislation called ISTEA, the Intermodal Surface Transportation Efficiency Act, which meant quite a bit of new money for transportation. More importantly, it really opened things up to include more intermodal issues and transit issues. I thought that might be a wonderful place to be and it turned out to be a really good decision for me. So I went in as the Deputy Federal Highway Administrator. The Administrator, Rodney Slater, was a really wonderful fellow who was also a great, inspirational leader and very close to the President."

Garvey was thrust onto the national stage. And she was completely prepared for it.

"That was another career leap. It was definitely a moment where you take a deep breath and just go for it. I talked to a lot of people at home about the consequences and the implications of a decision like that. There was just enormous support and encouragement from my family. That was key. I think at any point had my family said, 'This is just too much for us,' I probably would not have done it. I will always be grateful to them for their support."

Making a Federal Case from Boston Training

Garvey moved to Washington, and her life changed dramatically.

"Taking this job meant no more coming home in the evening. It was more like, 'You get in the department and you stay there.' My children were, by that time, already in college. But I did try to maintain connection. Sometimes it didn't work as planned. I decided to surprise my son up at Bates College in Maine. I went to his room and saw a huge pyramid of beer cans. His response was that he forgot to mention that his room had been named the recycling center—a line I've never believed. I went unannounced because I had guilt pangs from not being in touch. I thought, 'I'll surprise him!' I never made that mistake again."

Despite the parental gaffe, Garvey enjoyed the launching of her federal career.

"The early days of the Clinton administration were very exciting. There's nothing like that first campaign or administration. You attract people, and this was true for Clinton. He attracted people who had not been in Washington before. There was such excitement, such enthusiasm, and the promise of an intelligent, wonderful leader. And there was a good relationship in those early days with Congress. Rodney Slater was the kind of leader who liked very much to do the external stuff. He did quite a bit of speaking and was gifted at it. He did a lot of work with the Hill and was delighted to let others do other things. He was very terrific to work with. But there wasn't a day where I felt, 'Boy, I really got this made; this is a piece of cake.' It always felt that there was something else to learn. And I will say that Boston politics was probably was the best training you can get for DC."

"Go for It"

Garvey used her training well. And she saw an opportunity.

"Rodney wanted to work on the National Highway System. He was an Arkansas guy—interested more in highways, although he understood the importance of transit. I became fascinated with the financial piece, because I could see that the Highway Trust Fund was not going to be the same for a long period of time. We had to start thinking of different ways to do financing. So I said, 'I'd like to take on some of these new innovative financing techniques.' And he said, 'Go for it.' I recruited a couple of really great people—one from Wall Street and the other was Steve Martin, the Director of Innovative Financing for USDOT. And we created this little innovative financing team. They were fantastic, and they put in place a credit program that still exists today that is the backbone of many big, complicated highway projects. They helped us develop legislation to set up state infrastructure banks. And in the final days when I was leaving FHWA, they submitted legislation to create GARVEE Bonds, or Grant Anticipation Revenue Vehicle Bonds, which are securities issued in anticipation of federal funding. That was their goodbye present to me, which was terrific."

Layers

But life was not necessarily easy at FHWA. Challenges were plentiful. And Boston training or not, navigating the federal government can prove daunting.

"Lots of things didn't go as I hoped they would. I've tried to learn from them. One of the challenging things for anyone in an agency is that you are part of a larger organization. For example, let's say I'm the head of FHWA, but then I'm also part of the DOT. So if I'm fighting for a budget, I have to go first to USDOT. If USDOT buys it, *then* the Office of Management and Budget (OMB) has to buy it, and then the administration has to embrace it. There are all of these layers. You must recognize that you're part of a larger entity and take that into account as you develop an agenda."

Garvey would soon test her mastery of nuances at another level.

"FAA Jane"

Tests come in many forms. Soon Garvey would face tests on a historic level.

"In 1997, when Rodney Slater became USDOT Secretary, everyone assumed that I would become the next FHWA Administrator. I had been the Acting Administrator for a number of months, so I was absolutely convinced that was it. The staff had prepared, thinking it was going to happen. Even the constituency groups thought it was going to happen. I even prepared my family for a couple more years in Washington. But on an April morning I got a call from the Secretary's office to go upstairs. When I went in he said, 'I'd like you to take on the FAA.' I thought he said, 'FHWA.' I thought, 'Oh, the poor guy is so busy. He confused the two.'"

Garvey thought Slater had made a mistake. He hadn't. He wanted Garvey for the FAA. Garvey tried to talk him out of it.

"I really did. I would go back and say, 'No, listen, Rodney. I'm not a pilot. Yeah, I ran Logan, but that's not the same. Think of all the things I would get done for at the FHWA.' He would just smile and say, 'FAA Jane.' It was like dealing with a priest. I had friends who would say, 'There's this funny little blurb in Al Kamen's article in the *Washington Post* today and it mentioned you and the FAA. They must have gotten it wrong.' And that was the beginning of an incredible five-year journey at the FAA. Boston politics had prepared me quite well for working at the FHWA. But I don't think anything prepares you for the FAA and the way it is treated by Congress."

Soon, even testifying before Congress would pale in comparison to other challenges. But she had to address Congress first.

"I Don't Think You're Qualified"

Congress held its first public hearing with Garvey. She was so excited that she brought her family to the hearing.

"I went in to see Chairman John McCain. There is this protocol where you go and see the members before you start. And you have a chance to figure out who's going to be with you and who's going to be against you. I walked in and there were all of these news cameras there. They were set up because not only was I the first woman to head the FAA, but I was also the first person to have a five-year term. Previously, Administrators had served for 18 or 24 months. So I went into Senator McCain's office, very nervous, and said, 'Chairman, it's great to see you.' And he said to me, 'I don't think you're qualified, but you're the President's choice and he has the right to make that choice.'

"My heart sank. And when I got into the hearing it was clear that he had not read my résumé. But when he started to read it, he picked up on the Central Artery and Third Harbor Tunnel and then he went into a 20-minute harangue about Speaker of the House Tip O'Neill and Boston Democrats and all of that. It was incredible!"

But she got through it. And in a postscript note, Garvey reflects on the moment.

"John McCain became one of my best friends in Congress. He ended up hosting my going-away party with Senator Ted Kennedy. From quite an inauspicious beginning, we ended up being pretty good friends. You know, he's an interesting character. . . ."

Why Did I Say Yes to This?

The challenges were monumental. For example, though the Y2K problem—the issue that resulted from the digital practice of abbreviating a four-digit year to two digits—seems inconsequential now, before the year 2000 people feared that entire systems would crash at the turn of the century. For the FAA, it was extremely serious.

"It's a distant memory now, but back then it was a big issue. We would have a hearing every week about it and I would have to trot up to the Hill with our plan. And every week the Republican-led committee would give me a letter grade. And we always got a D, because they were convinced the FAA could not do anything right."

But Y2K was not the only threat. People questioned Garvey's experience.

"There was a tremendous amount of skepticism, because I was not steeped in aviation. And the FAA is a tough place. There were close to 40,000 employees—most of them air traffic controllers—with a broken-down relationship between the controllers and management. There were many days that I wondered, 'Why did I say yes to this?' But the three immediate challenges were the Y2K issue, the air-traffic control/management dispute, and capacity issues that were causing delays. That was what I spent the bulk of my time on when I was there."

Her time would soon be taken up by an unprecedented event.

9/11

On the Saturday before September 11, 2001, Garvey talked to former President Clinton and former Vice President Al Gore about leaving the FAA. They told her not to leave, because she was the first five-year-term FAA Administrator. When President George Bush appointed Norman Mineta Secretary of USDOT, Garvey felt relieved. She had worked with Mineta before and liked him. Little did she know what the job would bring next. As she explained earlier, Garvey was in a conference room with Secretary Mineta when the first plane hit the World Trade Center on 9/11. She quickly orchestrated the FAA's response as news of the other planes in New York, Washington, and Pennsylvania followed soon after.

"A number of people at the FAA had spouses that worked in the Pentagon. So as I'm calling senior management teams together, we were learning about the Pentagon. One of the controllers in Boston, his wife was on one of the airplanes. Another thing was that we were not able to track every one of the planes. A number of transponders were off at the time. That has now changed in the regulations—you can't turn a transponder off now. And you look at these things afterwards and think, 'Gee, why didn't we require it before?' Well, that's because you wanted to be able to turn them off in case there were electrical issues in other parts of the system.

"I also had to call the CEOs of the airlines. And I remember hearing from the CEO of Delta that they had lost track of a couple of their planes and that they were trying to figure it out. One of the CEOs said to me, 'That's one of our planes.' It was incredibly surreal. It was controlled, but there was tremendous confusion as well. In addition to talking about evacuating, we also had to shut down the US airspace for the first time in history. That vision will always stay with me. I'd have to go and look at the exact number, but it was something like 4,993 planes in the air. By the way, it's interesting to compare it to other countries, where they have less than 100 at any given time. I had a screen in my room and I was watching all of the dots disappear until finally getting a call from the command center saying, 'Every plane is within 40 miles of a safe destination.'"

It was a difficult day, to say the least. But Garvey also remembers some of the positive moments that occurred.

"I felt a great sense of relief and some degree of pride that we had established such a good relationship with the controllers. It was seamless. The pilots, of course, also did a remarkable job of bringing the planes in. Another great story for me was the little community in Canada that took in all of the flights that had to land there because they couldn't get into the United States. They took all of the people in from the airplanes. I don't know if you've ever seen that photo where all of the planes that landed are all wing to wing."

But some moments override others.

"On 9/11 itself, USDOT Secretary Mineta had to get to an undisclosed location with Vice President Cheney. We had the concern about sending up F-16s and what that meant in terms of a flight that you may be fearful of. I will never forget as long as I live listening to the tapes of the plane in Pennsylvania and hearing the passengers rush the cockpit. . . ."

The events of that day heralded a new normal, particularly at the FAA.

Everything Changed after 9/11

Once the dust settled, people wanted answers. How could this have happened? Garvey knew she would be pressed to explain.

"There is always the tendency to point fingers and find blame after a tragedy of that magnitude, and as a Democrat in a Republican administration I might have been a good target. However, to the credit of a number of policy makers and some Congressional leaders, the focus and lesson of 9/11 became the fundamental need to share critical information among the intelligence agencies and ultimately getting that information to agencies like the FAA and Customs. It also led to a wholesale rethinking within the aviation community of how to deal with a new kind of terrorist, one who was willing to commit suicide to further their cause. Training of flight attendants and pilots all changed as a result of 9/11. No more emphasis on negotiating, but more on keeping them from the planes in the first place. And the lesson that individual Americans learned was the need for increased vigilance on the part of individual citizens."

"We had a conference call with the CEOs the next day about what we should allow on planes. What we do about knives? We had steak knives on the planes before 9/11. So, everything changed after 9/11. And that whole last year became focused on setting up the Department of Homeland Security, responding to Congress, changing the training, and so forth. But I got back on a plane before the weekend and came to New York. I met with the city folks—the New York Port Authority, our own people in the control tower, and folks in the regional office—and tried to keep morale up."

Garvey worked tirelessly to make needed changes and to keep the FAA focused on the future.

The Private Sector

In 2002, Garvey left the FAA when her term ended. Though she prized her time in government, Garvey now sees the private sector as offering the best of both worlds for her.

"I'm very fortunate in the position that I hold now, as the Meridiam Infrastructure North American Chairman, because it is as close to the public sector as you can get, while still being in the private sector. The work I do now allows me to work with public officials to build infrastructure projects and to see them from beginning to end. And that includes all of the lifecycle costs, which I find extraordinarily exciting and wonderful. Although I don't think there is anything quite as exciting as the public sector for shaping the agenda and for moving things forward, I'm happy to be working in the private sector now."

Everyone Does Politics

Garvey offers sage advice for people in both the public and private sectors.

"I have always been thrilled when people who are smarter than I am at issues are drawn to those issues. If you can get really smart engineers—and in aviation this is particularly true—that is the best formula, as you are never going to have somebody who knows it all. The issues are too complex and too complicated. Look at the present FAA Administrator, for example. He's not going to know about drones necessarily, but he will bring in someone talented who does know about drones. Being able to attract that kind of talent and being able to let them do what they do best is really important and critical. It's great when you can bring in folks who really complement what you do well."

Garvey also addresses another issue that crosses the public-private sector divide.

"Someone once said to me in a meeting, 'I don't do politics.' And I had to stifle myself from saying, 'Are you married?' because that is politics. But there is a little attitude that says, 'I don't do politics,' and nothing could be further from the truth. Everyone does politics."

She also cautions about the importance of maintaining the proper focus and developing a most important skill.

"Don't worry about your next step. Just to do what you are doing well, and that will speak volumes for you. And learn how to communicate. When I was at the FAA, I would ask engineers that I respected, 'What is the most important piece of advice that you would give others?' They always said, 'Communicate. No one is immune from the need to persuade.' As the President, you've got to persuade others. If you are an agency head, you have to have the ability to communicate and persuade. Work on communication skills. You must learn how to transmit the message that you want. That is really important. But the most important thing is to just do what you do well. That speaks volumes to others."

I Had a Child on Each Hip, or Literal Work-Life Balance

Throughout her career, Garvey faced many challenges. But one underlying element was key to surmounting all of those challenges.

"I was a community activist, a teacher, and a mother before I joined the government. At most of those highway meetings, I was carrying a child on each hip. And if you had asked me then, 'Are you going to pursue a career in transportation and government?' I would have said, 'No!' So joining the government was a challenge."

The challenge was even greater than many people realize. Garvey commuted to work from far Western Massachusetts to Boston for her job with the DPW, eventually renting an apartment in the city.

"When I joined state government, I was an hour and a half to two hours away from Boston. So I would get into the car very early in the morning with a number of legislators and their staff who were also from the Western part of the state and we'd carpool into the city. I don't want to make it sound like I didn't enjoy it, but it was definitely a sacrifice."

Still she made it a point to be home on weekends and whenever possible. Family time was sacred. Garvey also knows she was not the only one to make sacrifices for her career.

"Ultimately the credit—and I really mean this—goes to my terrific husband. We've been married 43 years, but it's only seven if you count the amount of time we've actually spent together. We can't decide if that has been the secret to our success. It may be. But he was incredibly supportive and encouraging. My kids remember a great deal of what happened when I joined the government. They were probably around 10 and 11 and I used to tell them, 'We have no room for broken bones or severe colds.' They were terrific about it, too.

"But there is a wonderful story about my son. I told him I was having trouble keeping up with everything, and he said, 'Why don't they put you in a slower group?' He had been going through a challenging time at school and they had put him in a slower group, so he thought they should do the same for me. Sometimes I think he may have been right!"

Above all else, Garvey is a realist. And that is an important perspective she offers to young people today.

"Throughout my career there were always trade-offs. I talk a lot about that when I meet with young women. So you have to go into it with your eyes wide open and recognize that there are going to be trade-offs that you've got to really accept and work with."

That is the philosophy Garvey continues to live by today.

Chapter 3

ANN HERSHFANG

I look at something that isn't going right and I think, "I'll call. I'll organize the street. I'll do something." I'm an advocate. It's a burden and a pleasure. And I don't think of myself as a risk-taking person, but I am to the extent that I put up my hand and volunteer for things and I'm willing to try things that I don't know how to do. I get elected to be president of things, and I never can quite understand why. But I say yes. And it turns out to be a good thing.

Ann Hershfang expected a more conventional life, but defying expectation would feature prominently in her career.

Hershfang began her career as a preschool teacher and an editor. Then in 1970 she joined the League of Women Voters. Around that same time she created a South End community organization that sought to prevent the extension of an interstate highway into the South End. Though seemingly inconsequential, the committee provided a launching pad for her transportation career and a platform for her advocacy. And she got noticed. Only four years later, Massachusetts Governor Frank Sargent appointed Hershfang the first woman on the seven-member Massport Board, where she served with distinction for seven years.

In 1983, then–Massachusetts Secretary of Transportation Fred Salvucci chose Hershfang to be Undersecretary of the Massachusetts Executive Office of Transportation and Construction (EOTC). She would serve in that capacity for the next five years, a critical time in Boston transportation. Next Hershfang became one of three board members on the Massachusetts Turnpike (Masspike) Authority, overseeing the major east-west route in the state from 1988 to 1998.

While serving on the Masspike Board, Hershfang also co-founded the first pedestrian advocacy group in the US, Walk-Boston. Advocating for improved pedestrian and streetscape design, WalkBoston became the model for pedestrian groups around the nation. She serves on its board today. But her advocacy has extended to many organizations throughout her career.

She chaired the Transportation Research Board Committee on Pedestrians and was Section Chair for the Pedestrian, Bicycle, and Motorcycle Committees (1992–2008). In 2009 Governor Deval Patrick appointed Hershfang as Chair of the Oversight Council for the Massachusetts Accelerated Bridge Program. And she co-founded the Massachusetts Trails and Greenways Network, an umbrella organization that raised funds to create trails linking to transit, town centers, and schools. And that lists only some of her extracurricular activities.

WTS also figures prominently in Hershfang's career. She helped found the WTS Boston chapter, served as its President (1985–87), and presided over WTS International (1992–94). In 1998, WTS Boston created a scholarship in her honor. And in 1999, she was named WTS Boston Woman of the Year *and* WTS International Woman of the Year.

Hershfang received a bachelor's degree from Radcliffe College and a master's degree from Tufts University. She was also a Loeb Fellow (1988–89) at the Graduate School of Design at Harvard University.

Ann Hershfang *has* made a difference in transportation in Boston.

This is her story.

Buy a House, Enter Transportation

Ann Hershfang was not thinking about a career in transportation.

"I started out in the 1950s in a world that expected women to be nurses and secretaries and teachers. And the interesting thing as I look back on what a transportation nerd I've become was that I assumed that English and history were my areas. My brothers and father were economists. And when I took the college entrance exams, I scored higher in math than in English. Yet it never occurred to me that might be an indication of a direction as opposed to a fluke."

But fate intervened when she and her husband bought a boarded-up house at auction in Boston's then-troubled South End.

"By chance I read of a presentation at the Harriet Tubman House being given by a group called Urban Planning Aid (a federally funded advocacy and planning group). They were showing plans for the highways that were going to go through our neighborhoods. None of us had heard about them! And the highway was going to be at the end of my street, about a half block away. There was an Amtrak railroad track there. But I had never known that the railroad would go away and there would be a four-lane highway and a three-lane transit way and it would destroy a whole lot of houses at the ends of all of our streets. And it just blew me away!"

Hershfang went to the presentation.

"The head of the Harriet Tubman House said, 'Would anyone like to form a group to follow up on the highway plans?' He chose a few men and then suddenly my hand shot up. I didn't even really think about it. And we started working against the bypass and with the broader anti-highway movement, which became very large and significant."

Her involvement would grow.

Fred Heard Her Voice

Men comprised most of the scrappy and highly visible Boston anti-highway movement. But women were incredibly important, too, as Hershfang would demonstrate.

"I stood out, for one, by just being a woman. In the anti-high-way movement there were a lot of men. As in every other part of life, they never heard you. You'd be in a room and you'd say something and the conversation would go on as though you hadn't said anything. And nobody would pay any attention, or as I learned later, they would pay attention to what a woman said and then attribute it to some man."

Then someone heard her.

"Fred Salvucci, who later created the Big Dig Project, is one of the smartest and most able people in Massachusetts. And I had said something at one of the meetings and everyone ignored it. Fifteen minutes later, Fred said, 'Let's go back and discuss what Ann mentioned.' It was the first time I was noticed. It blew me away. And I was friends with Fred thereafter and we worked together on many things."

Hershfang stood out for reasons other than gender.

"I was determined. I have *always* been determined. But by standing out in the anti-highway movement, I was recommended for the Massport Board. And Republican Governor Sargent appointed me. I think Secretary of Transportation Alan Altshuler—who is a wonderful guy—recommended me. I asked him once about it and explained that I always assumed it was because I was a woman and he said, 'No it wasn't.'"

Through the movement's focus on Logan Airport's impacts, Hershfang also became aware of Massport Executive Director Ed King.

"He was very aggressive, hostile, expansionist, and mean. He block-busted East Boston. He had unbelievable contempt for the surrounding communities. "

Hershfang would confront Ed King soon.

The King and I

Because of a brave decision by Governor Frank Sargent, the anti-highway movement had won its fight to cancel the highway projects and limit expansion of Boston's Logan International Airport. Now Hershfang sat on the Massport Board as a Sargent appointee when Michael Dukakis defeated Sargent for governor.

"The first thing I did was join with three others—there were seven people on the board—who had been considering firing Ed King for a year or two. And we fired him four to three. It was the biggest political action in Massachusetts that year. People called to persuade me to change my vote, people I didn't know in the Boston business world. But they didn't call me. *They called my husband!* It was really amazing."

Hershfang cites King's repeated disregard for and hostility to neighborhood concerns as the basis for his firing. He was "hostile to the region." But King had strong supporters and the firing did not go unopposed.

"The President of the Senate and the Speaker of the House tried to convince us not to fire him. One of the joys of being with an authority is that you have your own revenue. You don't have to ask anybody for anything. You can do whatever you want with it. So King hired everybody's brother and son. He was big on jobs. He was big on influence. He was big on gifts. He just bought everybody off. They loved him."

Hershfang faced more than anger from patronage employees. She faced a raft of negative press from King supporters. But it didn't stop there.

"There were threats on my life after the firing of Ed King, and there were state troopers out in front of my house for a couple of days afterward. It was my first entry into the official, respectable transportation world."

Affirmative Action

Things settled down and Hershfang set to work with Massport Chairman Jay Fay, "a terrific person," starting with changing the staff, the first task at hand.

"We had to replace King's top staff, because they were so devoted to the guy. One of my greatest satisfactions is that we did a lot of affirmative action hiring. The Director of Planning, the Director of the Seaport, a whole bunch of top-level women and minorities were hired. We totally changed the authority from being a place for political patronage into a place where there was good administrative management, opportunities for people, and concern for impacts on surrounding communities."

Reversing many of King's policies, Massport achieved remarkable progress on many fronts. But one element stands out—a new Master Plan.

"We stopped taking homes and moved some from under a flight path to an adjacent community, created an amazing noise abatement program, and started our first *payment in lieu of taxes*, a scheme that compensates surrounding local governments for some or all of revenue lost from non-taxable institutions like Massport, which was an independent authority. I think our first payment was some $6 million or $7 million a year. Today it is a lot more and dwarfs other payments in lieu of taxes to the city."

Return of the King

Hershfang views her time on the Massport Board as a golden age. But all good things must come to an end. When it did, she had to take stock: "What to do next?"

"It was the most incredible change in an agency and the biggest achievement of my career. But there was never a crystallizing moment where I knew transportation was it. However, after those seven years, it didn't occur to me to do anything else. I wasn't going back to editing. I wasn't going back to preschool teaching."

Hershfang had two years left on her term when Ed King defeated Michael Dukakis for governor. But when her term ran out, Hershfang was once again unsure what to do next.

"I was sort of at loose ends. Alan Altshuler thought I should get a law degree, because that kind of qualifies you for just about anything. It's good training. Or he thought I should go into community organization. Neither of them appealed to me. So I just sort of vegetated and brought up my children. And then Dukakis won the next election in 1982! I worked very hard on his election, as you can imagine."

Dukakis, Salvucci, and the Big Dig

Fred Salvucci asked Hershfang to help manage the transition between the King and Dukakis Administrations. Then he asked her to work with him at the EOTC. But there was a snag.

"Salaries for state jobs required that you have a certain amount of experience, and I didn't have it. So I had to be Undersecretary because that was the only position that had no requirements. I had no problem working with Fred. We didn't always agree, but we respected each other. And he included me, as Undersecretary, because presumably if something happened to him I would have become Secretary. So he kept me in the loop of everything that was going on at the time."

And there was a lot going on. Arguably the father of the Big Dig project (officially known as the Central Artery/Tunnel Project), Fred spent much of his time initially reversing what King had undone, to ensure federal funding and project viability. That left Hershfang to oversee many of the other programs at EOTC. And there were some surprises.

"Up to this point my experience with females—the League of Women Voters, Massport agency heads, WTS—had been very collaborative. I expected that to happen in Fred's office. He had done a wonderful job with affirmative action and had hired a lot of high-level women and minorities. But it didn't; it wasn't collaborative. And it really struck me. A couple of the high-level women in his office whom I expected to be friendly at least and even collaborative, were not. They were much harder to deal with than the men. It was quite a surprise and a disappointment."

Too Close to Home

Hershfang served as EOTC Undersecretary from 1983 to 1988. She accomplished much. But at home once again a challenge arose.

"We had defeated the South End Bypass highway, but there's this rail right of way they were going to do something with. There was this very complex design process for what would be done with the space. And I was very involved in how it was done and whether it would be covered."

Covering the open rail right of way was never a given. In fact, she and Salvucci had differed on the concept, and she let him know in very explicit terms that she was not happy about it.

"I called Fred and said, 'I'm so angry at you. I thought you'd be sympathetic, and you weren't! And I really hope you change your mind.' Years later at the opening of the Orange Line, I said to Tony Pangaro, Manager of the Southwest Corridor Project, building the train and transit lines and designing the park along the right of way, 'I am so happy. I was thinking maybe that conversation with Fred Salvucci was influential.' And Tony said to me, 'No. You didn't convince Fred. You convinced me. *You* were responsible for getting it covered in the South End.' I can't tell you how satisfying it was, because it made my neighborhood."

Changing Directions, Literally

Hershfang loved her work. She valued the opportunity to help shape the city, especially when it was close to home . . . again.

"Ken Kruckemeyer, other South Enders, and I created a plan to change the street directions and widths in the South End to discourage through traffic. It had been a through-traffic corridor from the Southeast Expressway to Back Bay and the Prudential Building and from downtown out to the southwest. Fortunately, Boston had a forward-looking woman—Emily Lloyd—heading transportation, and the city endorsed our plan!

"We got streets narrowed. We got streets turned against each other. So you can't drive across the South End now. And everybody thinks it's just those wacky Boston streets*! Nobody has any idea that we did it.* In fact, when it first happened, the city didn't do anything about it. So these streets were turned around overnight and drivers were driving across and they couldn't continue. So we had to go out ourselves to the intersections and hand out flyers explaining to people what had happened. But these changes are what made the South End! That's why all of those restaurants are there today. Tremont Street is narrower. Columbus Avenue had two lanes of traffic removed. The sidewalks are wider. And that's why they're so pleasant. I still give tours showing what we did."

My Way and the Highway

After Hershfang's successful stint at the EOTC, Governor Dukakis appointed her as one of three board members overseeing the Masspike. It was a very unique time and opportunity.

"Dukakis was a wonderful, wonderful Governor. He had so many good people working for him. He was so honest and government-oriented. He wanted to be Governor to do useful and worthwhile things. He didn't care about patronage. He didn't care about power. He was just an amazing Governor and I didn't realize it until I experienced a couple of other Governors, like Bill Weld and his successor Paul Cellucci. And the Transportation Secretaries after Fred were appalling, ranging from useless to mean and cruel. I didn't realize what an amazing experience I had had."

But her work at the turnpike seemed less challenging than at EOTC. As she put it, "it's just a road." Still she could not resist the Hershfang need to pioneer. She cites two programs in particular. The first was painting the bridges along the turnpike in bright colors, which also had a teaching aspect. An artist named Adele Bacow worked with high school students and Masspike engineers to create painting designs for bridges. Hershfang also created a very forward-thinking landscape management program—a.k.a. "let the grass grow"—through the work of Geri Weinstein. Hershfang recognized good ideas and acted on them. And she was about to do that again.

WalkBoston

She had worked in virtually every transportation mode. So Hershfang went back to transportation's roots, the oldest mode—walking.

"We got together our friends, who are all, of course, transportation nerds, and sat down at Jake Wirth's, the restaurant, and plotted out this new group. We got 40 members with the first letter. And we started the first pedestrian advocacy group in the US, WalkBoston. We don't demonstrate or do things like that. We look at plans, and we make alternative recommendations. We're very technical and very persistent in terms of advocacy. But the most significant, the largest thing we did was take on the design of the Rose Kennedy Greenway."

The Rose Kennedy Greenway is a mile-and-a-half long linear urban park that stretches through Boston's Chinatown, North End, Financial District, and harbor communities. The greenway is a direct result of the Big Dig. Hershfang and WalkBoston wanted to make sure its design was handled properly.

"We started by having the designers of the Central Artery Project go on a South End walk with us. We walked them all through the South End and showed them the street direction changes. And they got really fired up."

But it didn't quite work as planned. So Hershfang maneuvered further.

"Boston Mayor Tom Menino and his transportation guy were designing five travel lanes in each direction on top of the depressed Central Artery—ten lanes total. But I knew that Fred cared equally about the pedestrian-friendly aboveground part as he did about the underneath. He wanted to restore downtown Boston. Happily, the Central Artery designers sneaked us information about the expanded road changes, because they, too, really cared about how it looked. WalkBoston got together and worked with them. And we created our design and arranged a press conference to present it.

"The Mayor had been at a meeting with some North End waterfront people about some other issue and they said to him, 'Oh, by the way, Mr. Mayor, did you know that your walk to the sea from Faneuil Hall across to the harbor is going to be ten lanes wide?' And he looked at his transportation commissioner and said, 'WHO IS DOING THIS? CHANGE IT!' So we gave him our plan and they designed their plan around our plan.

But it was one thing to have a hand it its design. It was quite another to preserve it.

"When I was at EOTC our legal counsel, James Aloisi, suggested to me that the greenway should be named the Rose Kennedy Greenway, because Senator Ted Kennedy would protect its funding and design. And Senator Kennedy said yes. He loved that it would be named after his mother! She grew up in the North End. And the elevated Central Artery had been named after John Fitzgerald, who was his grandfather. So I wrote a letter to the legislature, and they passed the bill officially naming it the Rose Kennedy Greenway."

It seemed settled, or so everyone thought.

"About five or six years later, Aloisi said to me, 'You know Ann, I can't find this legislation anywhere.' That may have been because Governor Bill Weld and Director of the Massachusetts Turnpike Authority and Manager of the Big Dig James Kerasiotes decided to name it something else. I forget what. Then suddenly this legislation naming it the Rose Kennedy Greenway pops up out of nowhere. And the *Boston Herald* asked Kennedy where it came from. His reply: 'Oh, Ann Hershfang and WalkBoston.' Very nice for WalkBoston! But it did protect it. So it was brilliant. Jim Aloisi has very smart ideas, always has."

Today Hershfang remains deeply committed to WalkBoston.

"One thing that I really love about my career is that I can see the results of what I've done every day and everywhere. I helped design the park across the street. I helped create the Southwest Corridor at the end of the street. There are sidewalks all over the South End and all over Boston that I had some impact on. And when I drive out the Masspike, I look at everything. When I go to the Port Authority, I look at everything. I love being able to see the results of things that I've done. And they're there. That's one thing about construction. It's there for years and years and years. It's a real legacy."

Kerasiotes, the Big Dig, and the Night of the Living Shred

Hershfang has a very strong moral compass. But she did come up against others whose compass didn't always point north.

"When I came in at the EOTC, Kerasiotes was Undersecretary of Transportation in the outgoing administration and he briefed me, very well, I have to say, on the talents of the staff. One of the startling things that he said was that the General Counsel was corrupt. It took me a while to get my head around the fact that he seemed to know that and they had kept him. The General Counsel eventually did go to jail. I don't remember his name. But what he and they did when they left was take *all of the files*. That really stunned me.

"When we came in we didn't know that there had been a lot of money, approximately $2 million, set aside for special grants to different cities and towns. And after King had lost reelection they gave all of that money out. A hundred thousand here, two hundred thousand there—and *they took all of the records*. So we had no idea who had gotten the money or where it had gone."

But this went beyond confusion.

"There's a state law that says you have to save all of your government files. But later when Kerasiotes became Turnpike Chairman, his lawyer had a shredder in his office! I'm sitting there talking to him and there's this shredder! So clearly they're shredding. After Kerasiotes left—he was fired—their computers were broken. Files disappeared.

"What was lost will never be known, sad because Fred had done such a good job of saving and organizing all the records. And Kerasiotes never cared about the projects we were doing. But that was the thing. It was such a contrast to my experience with Fred. Kerasiotes expressed little interest in the issues. He only had interest in the power and the patronage. And he gave money out broadly."

The Big Dig provided another stark contrast.

"The Big Dig was Fred's baby, and he had spent years getting it going. Fred had very carefully strategized who would manage the design and construction. He was planning to hire some oversight guy who would make sure the managers did the job right. But Kerasiotes didn't do that. He told the designers to cut corners. And of course it was poorly managed, and it started running out of time and out of budget. And he cut stuff. He cut details. He cut quality. He cut right and left. So when the Big Dig opened and things fell down, it wasn't surprising because he just willy-nilly cut the quality and the timing to achieve his 'on time, on budget' mantra."

Leadership: What I Should Have Done

Hershfang describes herself as a reluctant leader. But leadership positions always seem to find her.

"I have not been the perfect president. I didn't manage firmly enough, and I didn't have the strength of my convictions always.

For instance, when I was president of WalkBoston, we had hired our first executive director. And he turned out to be a self-centered, arrogant guy. We were sitting in the same office, yet he ignored me. It took me a long time, but I eventually moved forward and asked the board for a vote. The board would have done it earlier had I asked, but I was just wimpy about it.

"It was also true of WTS International. When I was president, I had a woman on the board who just didn't like me. She tried to undercut me. It took me quite a while to figure out how to move the board along regardless. I do have a skill for getting all those around the table to become part of the discussion. So I'm the sort of person that people choose to be their leader. But I'm not sure it's always a good idea. It always seems to take me a while to start leading."

Changing the World

Ultimately, though, Hershfang is a realist.

"I'm not smug or proud or anything—it's probably the way my parents brought me up—but I feel entitled to work on changing the world. I have not felt like a helpless victim. But I think a characteristic in the development of my career is that, while I've not been a striver or a planner or a strategist, things have come my way and it has been so much fun. It had its hard moments, but it's just been fun all of the way."

Chapter 4

SHIRLEY DELIBERO

I'm one of nine children, next to the youngest. And all of my sisters were married housewives, with the exception of one who became a schoolteacher. But growing up, I always wanted to be somebody. I used to say all of the time that I wanted to be a boss. I wanted to have a big job. I want to make lots of money. I don't know why . . . I wanted to be somebody. No one in my family was; the role models were all get married and have babies. I wanted to do more than that . . . I always had that drive in me.

When you say the name Shirley DeLibero, it resonates. Fan or foe, one thing is certain, you do not forget Shirley DeLibero. Self-described as firm, but fair, DeLibero hammered out an extraordinary career from humble beginnings in an industry that was little prepared to open doors for her. So she busted them down. Talking her way into a job with the Massachusetts Bay Transportation Authority (MBTA), DeLibero soon proved her mettle, despite some of the harshest work conditions anyone could face. And she was just getting started.

Rising through the MBTA, she moved on to WMATA, where she became the assistant general manager of Bus Services and managed the rail system from 1988 to 1989. DeLibero next served as Deputy Executive Director at Dallas Area Rapid Transit, overseeing operations and planning the light rail system. In 1990, she took the reins as executive director at New Jersey Transit (NJT), where she achieved award-winning success. DeLibero contemplated retirement, but the challenge of launching a light rail system (MetroRail) took hold, and she joined the Metropolitan Transit Authority of Harris County Texas (Houston Metro) in 1998 as CEO. The MetroRail system debuted in 2004. Today DeLibero is the president and CEO of DeLibero Transportation Strategies, LLC, a transportation consultancy in Massachusetts.

But DeLibero also made her mark in other ways. She served as chair of the Conference of Minority Transportation Officials (COMTO), chair of the American Public Transportation Association (APTA), and as a WTS International Advisory Board member. In addition, Houston Metro named its rail operations building after her and APTA annually awards the Shirley A. DeLibero scholarship. Shirley DeLibero changed the transportation industry.

This is her story.

Starting Out

Transportation was "the farthest thing" from her mind when Shirley DeLibero set out to look for work. But her mother had issued an ultimatum: "Get a job in the city where you're home more with your sons." So DeLibero answered a newspaper ad for a car-barn foreman at the MBTA.

"They were looking for a project manager to refurbish old Green Line streetcars. I interviewed for about an hour and a half. But I could tell that the Green Line superintendent was not really interested in me: 'Well, you never worked on streetcars.' And I said, 'No offense to you, but when you came here you had never worked on streetcars either. You learned them.' Just as I said that the chief mechanical officer—a guy named Dick Goodlatte—walked in and heard that part of the conversation.

"The original interviewer told me he would get back to me. But when Dick Goodlatte walked me out he said, 'I gotta tell you. I can't believe what you said to him.' I said, 'But it's true! He didn't have that experience; he learned it. I have a lot of transferable skills and I think I could do this job. And I could learn streetcars. I know how to read schematics. You're his boss, if you think I could do it you should hire me!'"

The phone did not ring. So DeLibero took action.

"I called Goodlatte and he said, 'This guy does not want you.' So I said to him, 'But do you think I can do the job?' He said, 'Yeah, I think you can. But I think it would be tough if I bring you on. You weren't his choice.' But I convinced him and I told him that I would have them eating out of the palm of my hand. So I got the job. And I have to tell you, I never had them eating out of my hand—eating my hand maybe, but not eating out of it."

Getting the job proved to be only a small part of the battle.

"It was tough. They were terrible to me. Every morning I came in there were obscenities *carved* into my wooden door. When I started I had a really thick door. By the time I ended up shaving all the obscenities off of the door, well, it was very thin by the time I left. And when I would walk through the car barn they would call me all kinds of names.

"They were very vocal about the fact that I was black—and they didn't say *black* then. And you could never find out who said it. I knew I was just going to have to be tough. I was at the MBTA from 1976 to 1981, when Robert Foster was in charge, and then Barry Locke. And it didn't look like there was any opportunity for advancement because of color or gender. As a superintendent, I was the highest-level minority there. I knew I wasn't going to get promoted. And I thought that if I'm ever going to be a General Manager or CEO, I've really got to learn all modes. So I was talking with some people in DC. And there was an opportunity . . ."

Expanding Knowledge and Meeting Mentors

Washington, DC, was different. Tasked with running three bus garages as the WMATA regional manager of Bus Services, DeLibero was far from the only woman and minority.

"It was like I had died and gone to heaven. There was a black guy that was the regional manager for DC. And there wasn't that racial animosity, because there were a lot more minorities in maintenance and operations than there were at the "T" (a nickname for the MBTA). And at that time, Carmen Turner was the head of Administration. She later became the first African-American female general manager at WMATA. Carmen was always very classy—totally opposite from me!

"I used to drag her out to the bus garages for staff meetings and she would come in her Ferragamo shoes and silk dresses and her pearls and I would say to her, 'You need to get some overalls!' But she was very classy. I'll never forget. One day I said, 'I am so *pissed!*' She was cracking up; she had never heard that word! She was very stylish and a very good general manager, but certainly not the way I was. My style was definitely like the guys. But I learned a lot from her. When I became the assistant general manager running all of Bus, she took me up to the Hill when she went to testify. She knew that someday I wanted to be a General Manager so she gave me opportunities to learn. She was definitely a mentor. And she told me I needed to clean up my language if I wanted to be a GM!"

DeLibero also credits then–Washington, DC, Deputy Mayor and WMATA Board member Tom Downs with helping her on her path.

"Tom Downs asked me if I was interested in a deputy job that was open in Dallas. He said a friend of his from college was the CEO. I said, 'Are you kidding?! I am not going to Texas!' He said, 'Well, you might just want to go talk to him. . . .' So I did, and it sounded great. I said to myself, 'If you really want to be a general manager someday, you've had bus, you've had some rail, you've had some light rail, now you need to get into the politics.' And this would give me the opportunity. So off I went!"

Learning Lessons

Dallas transportation officials wanted to build a light rail system. Soon after DeLibero arrived they floated a referendum to obtain federal financing.

"We lost, horribly! But the CEO and I convinced the board that we should do a starter line of 20 miles, and to build it with local dollars. I was only there three years. I wasn't there long enough to actually start construction. . . . Then Tom Downs called again—here we go!

"Tom Downs has definitely been my mentor. He was now the Commissioner of Transportation for the state of New Jersey. And he called me up and said, 'What do you think about coming to New Jersey?' And I said, 'I just got to Texas!' He said he had heard I was doing a great job and that he needed somebody to run New Jersey Transit. He also said there were no guarantees and a lot of competition for the job. But he thought I should give it a shot. And I went and interviewed and there were six of us, but I was the only female. And I got the job."

A Whitman Sampler: A Boss Who Hates You and a Management Style with Substance

Surveying the situation, DeLibero knew that NJT needed to do three things: improve on-time performance, improve customer service, and hold the line on fare increases. And she did it. On-time performance skyrocketed. Customer service improved. And fares remained steady for *her entire nine-year tenure*. She praises transit-friendly Democratic Governor Jim Florio for making transit a priority. But three years into her tenure, Florio lost his reelection bid to Republican Christine Whitman.

"Think about it. The governor that brought me in is gone. The commissioner that brought me in is gone. It's a Republican governor, a Republican commissioner that didn't hire me. I swear to God he was there to get rid of me, but it never happened."

Forced to go before the state legislature each year for her budget (despite not being a state agency), DeLibero proved that popularity was less important than other factors.

"They respected me. I don't think they ever liked me, but they respected the fact that I ran a tight ship and that we didn't have to raise fares. And that was what was important to them."

DeLibero earned their respect for good reason. Under her leadership, NJT increased ridership and won numerous awards, including several for outstanding achievement from APTA. But she still had to deal with a hostile Governor.

"I just kept doing my job. I put a good team together. I changed very few people. When we had groundbreakings or openings, Governor Whitman made sure she was there, and I was okay with that. She was the Governor. But people knew we were responsible. Like when we opened the extension going into New York, she made it very clear to me that she was going to drive that first train. And I said, 'Absolutely.' Of course I wanted to, but I knew my role. I kept telling my staff, 'We just have to do a good job. We just have to continue taking care of the public and make sure the trains run on time and the buses are out there.'"

DeLibero cites her no-nonsense, practical management style as one key to her success in New Jersey. But there was another fundamental element.

"I believe in hiring to my weakness. So when I first got there I evaluated the people I had, the senior management team. I never go and just bring a cadre of people. I always give the benefit of the doubt that there's talent there and let them see how it works with me. The only weak position was the budget director. So I brought a guy in from American Airlines. And he was my budget guy. And he was excellent. He was from the private sector, where everything was for profit. So I knew he'd be a stickler for line items and stuff. We did zero-based budgeting and I won some credibility there with the legislators, because I wasn't constantly asking them for money."

Taking Hits, Making Your Mark, and Meeting the Hammer

She was all set to retire. But the phone rang. Then–Houston Mayor Lee P. Brown, Houston's first African-American mayor, wanted to build a light rail system. In his second term (of three possible terms), he had three years left to build his dream system. And he wanted DeLibero to do it. DeLibero balked, but Brown was persistent.

"I ended up flying to Houston. And I gave the mayor ridiculous demands. I said, 'If I'm coming here—and Clinton was the president at the time making $200,000—I want $210,000. And I want five weeks' vacation, five weeks' sick time, and fifteen years added to my pension when I walk through the door. . . .' And everything I said he said, 'Yes.' So I said, 'Okay, I have to come.'"

41

DeLibero convinced Brown *not* to hold a referendum, given her experience in Dallas.

"We needed to give people something to look at before a referendum. Otherwise, it was never going to pass. People didn't want to get out of their cars. But in Houston, there's a big rodeo every year. And there's a parade. I convinced him to build a prototype of a rail car and have it in the rodeo parade. He thought I was nuts, but he went along. So we had a prototype built and we had 'Rail Is Coming' on it. You have all of these horses coming down the street and a big replica of a rail car with me and the board members on it coming down the street. Now that I think about it it's hilarious. But it worked! We got everyone excited about the rail line."

Next DeLibero called on then–US House Majority Whip Tom DeLay to seek funding for the line.

"He was known as 'The Hammer.' And he made it very clear that he was giving me *no money* for rail. Then he said this to my face—and I'll never forget it as long as I live—he said, '*Those people* can ride on buses. . . .' I said, 'Who are *those people?*' And he looked at me and realized what he had said. Then he replied, 'The transit dependent.' So I said to myself, 'Quick thinking on your part, buddy.' We never got any money, but we built the rail."

DeLibero redefined *fast track*. Her team broke ground on March 13, 2001. Mayor Brown drove the first light rail car on his last day in office, January 1, 2004. Honoring their effective working relationship, DeLibero describes the scene.

"As he drove the first train through, I said to him, 'You know, normally this is what I'm supposed to do.' And he said, 'Get over it.' It was wonderful working for him. He was very supportive and helped me do whatever I needed to make it happen. I could not have done it without him. But it wasn't without a lot of scars and getting beat up. I think I'm tougher for it."

She was. But that doesn't mean she forgets what she faced.

"Houston is the South. And people would say to me that they were worried people were going to come in and rob their houses if mass transit were implemented. And I said to them, 'When was the last time you saw somebody on the bus with a television! They pull up in trucks and haul things out. They don't come on mass transit!' They wanted to make sure that if we put bus stops in that they weren't in their neighborhoods."

But the greatest challenge was personal. And the attacks were relentless.

"They made fun of the way I talked; I still had my Boston accent with my R's. I think they gave me a hard time when I first got there because I was a woman. Then they figured the only reason I got the job was that the mayor was black and I was black. I had to show them that was *not* why I got the job. I got the job because I'm capable and competent. The first time I visited the editorial board one of the reporters asked me about myself. I talked about what a great job I did in Dallas and New Jersey. I talked about things I had accomplished. And he said to me, 'Well you're pretty cocky.' And I said, 'No. Cocky is when you don't have a track record to prove it. I'm confident.' And that's how I started my first visit to the editorial board. After that, it got easier.

"But they still went after me. They watched everything I did. I remember the reporters went and looked at all of my expenditures and my travel records. They looked at my company car to see if I used it personally. They looked to see if any of my expense accounts had drinks on them. I was under a microscope. But I had nothing to hide. So if they wanted to look at that, I let them look."

Ultimately, DeLibero triumphed. In fact, Houston Metro named its operations center after her, something she recalls with great pride, satisfaction, and humor.

"I didn't even have to die to get a building named after me!"

Going Home

In Houston, DeLibero achieved what many thought was impossible. Then, after moving back to Boston, she did the impossible again.

"I finally decided in June (2014) that I was working no more. My kids helped me with that. They said, 'Mom, you're 76. We're going to get a call one day saying, 'We have this lady at the airport and she doesn't know where she's been or where she's going, but she says she's your mother.' And my accountant showed me that I was *losing* money by working. But I just love the industry. But I can still love the industry and do things. I'm on two APTA committees. I belong to WTS. I'm on the COMTO Advisory Board. I can still give back, which is what I want to do."

Walking a Mile in Her Shoes

DeLibero is sanguine, always. And it is one key to her success. But there is more to it.

"You have to be a risk taker. When I mentor people now, I tell them that I don't think I would have had the career I've had if I didn't move around. A lot of people don't want to move. They're in their comfort zone. To be successful you've got to get out of your comfort zone. You've got to take risks. And this is where the confidence comes in. I always surrounded myself with people that knew what I didn't. But a lot of people I mentor have a fear of that. They're worried that people will show them up and that's crazy."

DeLibero knows she makes it sound easy. She also knows it's not easy, ever.

"The unfortunate thing in my career is that I never had a good balance between home and work. My job became my life. My kids were important, but when I moved to Washington, DC, I remarried. My husband was a CPA and he didn't want to move to Washington. He gave me an ultimatum—your career or me. And off I went to Washington. That's tough. But by the time I went to Washington, my children were older: one was finishing college and the other one was in college. But that's a hard thing for folks, the balance of your personal life and your work."

DeLibero believes that work-life balance is not the only calculation young professionals must make.

"Today you not only have to be educated, you have to be politically astute. Jobs today are more political than they've ever been. I was just in Washington at the APTA leadership meeting. I was talking to the head of a transit authority, and he said that now three-quarters of his time is spent dealing with politics. He said he has to make sure he has a good chief operating officer, because that's who's watching everything while he's out there trying to quell the storms. Kids today need to understand the whole political side of the business."

As if politics weren't enough, DeLibero was blindsided by another important transportation element.

"I was surprised how strong the unions were! That was a shocker. The union was on my case all the time. They said I was trying to bust the union, but I wasn't. It was just that some of the rules got so ridiculous at times. That was the toughest thing for me to wrap my arms around. At the time when I was at the MBTA, I had 31 unions. Now they're down to about 23. I tell folks now that are thinking about being general managers that they need to know labor and labor law. There's a lot more to running a transit authority now than just kicking tires and checking air pressures. Boston was really good for me, because all of the unions *after* Boston were a piece of cake."

She also believes in the value of "management by walking around."

"People want you to know who they are, that they're not just a number on a timecard. So I always had my staff meetings out in the field. Each garage always had a Christmas party and I went to all of the garages and wished everyone a Happy New Year. But you've got to do that. In order to be successful people need to know who you are.

"I was just in Washington, and a bus driver beeped his horn, waved, and shouted, 'Hello, Miss DeLibero!' He still remembered me! I hope this new generation realizes that you need to be out and about. Before the young person meets with a union guy, they should know what people do. If they don't, they're going to be looked at like some college kid who doesn't know his ass from his elbow. The first thing they should do in the job is make it their business to go out to the facilities. My motto is, and has always been, 'If you take care of the people, they will take care of the product.'"

The Final Word

"One of the best things to do when you get in one of these jobs is to negotiate a good contract. Now I can live on my five pensions and be happy! You want to make sure that you have money and don't *have* to work until you're 80 years old."

Chapter 5

JOAN CLAYBROOK

So in 1966 I interviewed with one member of Congress who I really admired, and we had a great interview. I felt really good about it. Then he said, "You know, I just don't think this is going to work." I said, "Why not?" He said, "We're just guys here. We're very rough. We use rough language and I just don't think you'd fit in." I said, "Would you like to hear the cuss words I know?" He said, "No. I just don't think it would fly." I was so taken aback by that. He later became a senator and did great work, but that was a shockaroo.

For Joan Claybrook, determination is as essential as oxygen. Groomed for politics from an early age in her father's campaigns for the Baltimore City Council, Claybrook joined the legislative policy division of the Social Security Administration (SSA) as an intern in 1958 just before her senior year at Goucher College in Baltimore. She returned full time after graduation. Six years later her boss recommended her for, and she was awarded, a fellowship in Congressional Operations by the American Political Science Association and moved to Washington, DC.

Claybrook first joined the staff of Congressman James Mackay, a newly elected Democrat from Atlanta, Georgia, the new South.

It was her first foray on Capitol Hill and into auto safety. It was also her first exposure to the dynamic Ralph Nader and his book *Unsafe at Any Speed*. After five months of helping Representative Mackay initiate his auto safety bill, she joined then-freshman Senator Walter Mondale's staff under her fellowship. An epic fight in Congress was under way to get the auto safety bill passed. The discovery that the largest corporation in the world, General Motors, had hired gumshoes to tail and get dirt on Ralph Nader to discredit him jolted the Congress and played a large role in getting the auto safety bill enacted into law in September 1966. Continuing her work on auto safety, Claybrook was next hired as a Special Assistant to Dr. William Haddon, Jr., the first-ever Administrator of the newly created National Highway Traffic Safety Administration (NHTSA).

Claybrook was working at NHTSA when President Richard Nixon was elected in November 1968. That is when she applied to law school at Georgetown University and started at the night school in the fall. In the summer of 1970, Claybrook resigned from her post at NHTSA to spend the summer in Baltimore, her hometown, to "relax" and read books. Relaxing didn't happen. She began working for Paul Sarbanes, a state legislator running for Congress. He won and offered her a job on his staff. At the same time, Ralph Nader also offered her a job. She decided to join Nader to be an advocate outside the government and then embarked on a historic trip to Japan in 1971 to look at the Japanese auto companies, while Nader lectured on the environment and citizen action.

In 1971 Nader formed Public Citizen, a nonprofit consumer rights advocacy group. Two years later, under the auspices of Public Citizen, and with Nader's guidance and support, Claybrook founded Congress Watch, a nonprofit Congressional watchdog group, which she ran for four years. Then in 1976, Jimmy Carter was elected President. When he took office in 1977, he appointed Claybrook Administrator of NHTSA. Claybrook ran NHTSA from 1977 to 1981, when Carter's term ended. In 1982 she returned to Public Citizen and served as its President until January 2009, when she stepped down.

Many civic groups have recognized Claybrook for her public service. She received the Philip Hart Distinguished Consumer Service Award from the Consumer Federation of America. She was named Foremother by the National Research Center for Women & Families. The Georgetown Law Center recognized her with the Excellence in Public Service Award. She also received Honorary Doctor of Law degrees from Goucher College and Georgetown University, as well as an Honorary Doctor of Public Service from the University of Maryland.

Joan Claybrook made indelible contributions to public safety, particularly through auto industry regulation. She is, in part, responsible for many safety elements that people take for granted today. Recent studies by the US Department of Transportation have shown that over 600,000 lives have been saved in the United States because of the work of NHTSA since the 1960s, as well as millions of injuries prevented.

This is her story.

Being Groomed for Politics from an Early Age

No one background is perfect training for politics, but Claybrook's upbringing is about as good as it gets.

"My father was a bond lawyer in Baltimore. Bond lawyers get people to come together and agree to build new schools, sewer systems, or public projects. My mother was very avant-garde. She hated rules and never made us go to bed at a certain time. We went to bed when we were tired. She never made us eat food we didn't want. My father said, 'You have to clean your plate!' My mother said, 'Then they can choose what they want to eat from what I've cooked.'

"On Monday nights, I would go watch the Baltimore city council on which my father served, and then we would talk about it at dinner. When I was almost 10, he ran for city council, and I helped him campaign. My mother was his campaign manager. I used to walk the streets of Baltimore as a human billboard with great big signs. So that is how I learned about campaigning and elections, from the bottom up. We stood at the polls from dawn to dusk on election day, and I would ask people to vote for my father. I got very tuned into politics at an early age."

But politics were not the only area where Claybrook was precocious.

"I got married when I was 19. My father was opposed, saying 'You'll never finish college.' I said, 'Oh yes I will.' I'm sure that's when I decided to finish college. I had to prove him wrong. So I transferred from Connecticut College for Women and went to Goucher College in Baltimore and graduated."

"Determined" is a descriptive that would routinely be used to describe Claybrook's character.

From School to Work

Though Claybrook was groomed for politics, necessity forced a change of plans.

"In the summer of my junior year of college we really needed money. So I went to work at the Social Security Administration. I was accepted after applying for about 50 jobs. All they wanted were secretaries and I was *not* going to be a secretary. My father had a secretary who was 60 years old. I asked him why he had hired her. He said, 'Because she can't get pregnant. I'm sick and tired of training secretaries. Then they get pregnant, leave, and I've got to train the next one.' A lot of men felt that way!"

She joined the legislative and policy division at SSA, and she loved it. "It was a fabulous job, and they asked me to come back after I graduated from Goucher, so I did."

Entering Transportation

Change was in the air in many ways in 1966. Claybrook applied for and accepted an offer for a fellowship in Congressional operations, an opportunity that brought her to Washington, DC.

"I went to work for Rep. James Mackay, a Congressman from Georgia. He wanted me to work on auto safety, but I didn't know a thing about it. He gave me *Unsafe at Any Speed* by Ralph Nader and told me to read that as an introduction. I learned that cars weren't as safe as manufacturers could make them and that occupants died as a result. Mr. Mackay wanted to introduce legislation. So I went to the legislative draftsman in the House of Representatives, but he was unable to draft a decent bill. A staff person from Senator Vance Hartke's office called, saying that Hartke wanted to cosponsor our bill because his sister had been killed in an auto crash. I said, 'That would be fine, but we need a skilled legislative drafter.' He said, 'We'll get you one.' So we got together with Blair Crownover, who turned out to be a fabulous draftsman and he put together our bill. Mr. Mackay and Senator Hartke jointly introduced the first auto regulatory bill in the United States of America. Years later I learned that Crownover was in Ralph Nader's class at Harvard Law School."

The Auto Industry Notices

Mackay wanted to meet with Nader. Claybrook arranged it. Naturally, Nader strongly favored federal legislation. Nader's book shook the auto industry and helped to galvanize the companies to oppose any Federal legislation.

"General Motors's Chief Counsel hired a gumshoe to tail Ralph Nader to get dirt on him to get him to shut up. When Nader discovered he was being investigated by General Motors and made it public, suddenly he became a hot issue. At the same time he kept talking about legislation needed to make cars safer. Senator Abraham Ribicoff, Nader's senator from Connecticut, held a massive hearing in the huge Senate caucus room. Every television, newspaper, and magazine was there. Ribicoff made General Motors CEO James Roach apologize to Ralph Nader for tailing him. They found out that it was General Motors because Ribicoff called AMC, Chrysler, Ford, and General Motors and asked if they were tailing Nader. Three said, 'No,' and one, General Motors, said, 'No comment.'"

The intensity of the hearings would escalate, putting Claybrook right in the middle of a contentious legislative battle. She could not have found a better learning experience.

"Bobby Kennedy was on the Ribicoff subcommittee. The auto companies were scared to death of what Kennedy would do to Roach, because Kennedy was a cutthroat interrogator. So

General Motors hired Ted Sorensen, a lawyer and presidential advisor to John F. Kennedy. General Motors had sent a prostitute to approach Ralph, but he brushed her off. And Bobby Kennedy went after them."

While all this was brewing, Nader wanted new amendments to an auto safety regulatory bill sent to the Hill by the Johnson Administration, which would be the basic bill considered by the Congress. He particularly wanted criminal penalties for CEOs and other executives who didn't obey the law, and recall of unsafe cars or ones that violated safety standards. He worked closely with Claybrook.

"Ralph was working on the amendments one weekend in May 1966 with a University of Virginia law professor, but had to go out of town and asked if I would help get a package of amendments prepared. That was a huge job. It took us all day Saturday, all night Saturday, all day Sunday, and all night Sunday, and early that Monday, too. I had to report to work on Monday to Senator Mondale for the second part of my fellowship. So I gave the package of some 25 amendments with an explanation of each to Mr. Mackay and Senator Hartke. Senator Hartke put it in the Congressional Record. Now everyone in the world knew about it and the auto industry went berserk.

"They hired a shrewd lawyer named Lloyd Cutler to get rid of the criminal penalty proposal. Cutler came to see Mondale. Cutler knew I had been working on the House side, where the auto industry had already nicknamed me 'The Dragon Lady.' Even though I had only been in Washington for six months! He walked into Mondale's inner office where I was sitting and said, 'What are you doing here?' I said, 'I work here,' and he almost had a heart attack.

"Then the bill was considered by the Senate Commerce Committee, where it was 'marked up' with the changes the Senators wanted before it went to the Senate floor for debate and passage. Senator Mondale was not on that committee, but Hartke was. And he wanted me to attend because I knew so much about the bill. But I made the terrible mistake of wearing a bright yellow dress."

Finding the Leak

Claybrook was not trying to make a fashion statement, but her dress got her noticed.

"It was a hot summer and we were all wearing light clothes. I just wore the lightest dress; I didn't think anything of it when we went down to the markup. There were about 40 people there, all men. But that morning in the *Washington Post*, Drew Pearson had written a column divulging how every Senator was going to vote in the secret committee meeting. So most of the Senators wanted to know who leaked this information to Drew Pearson.

"They ranted and raved for about an hour. All of a sudden the Chairman, Senator Warren Magnuson from Washington State, looked up at me. I was standing at the other end of the room taking notes in this bright yellow dress. He looked straight at me and said, 'Why are you taking notes!' I was the most junior person in the whole room. I didn't even know who Drew Pearson was until that morning! So I said, 'I'm taking notes for Senator Hartke. He's late.' He snapped, 'Don't take any more notes.' The suggestion was clear; he fingered me as the leaker. After the markup the staff came to me and said, 'You can't come to any more of these meetings.' I was furious!"

Claybrook soldiered on. Eventually, she was vindicated.

"About 25 years later, the Senate staff counsel, Michael Pertschuk, admitted to me that Magnuson had leaked the information to Drew Pearson. Magnuson was looking for a way to stop the discussion. I understood all of that. I never thought it was personal. It was all about the issues and the politics."

Despite the accusation, Claybrook would soon see the fruits of her labor.

The Bill Comes Due

Claybrook worked tirelessly on the bill. Now she would see it advance to the Senate floor.

"They finished the markup. Mondale wanted me to go, because he had a section dealing with recall notification and he wanted to be sure it got included. The bill went to the Senate floor. The big debate was about the absence of criminal penalties. Hartke tried to add it on the Senate floor, but we lost. It just wasn't going to happen. The auto industry had done its work. But because they focused on criminal penalties, they paid less attention to the rest of the bill and got no changes except for some language in the committee report.

"Then the bill went over to the House. After public hearings and a markup, the bill came up on the House floor and there was another debate on criminal penalties. This time a relatively unknown representative from Massachusetts named Thomas 'Tip' O'Neill proposed it. But we lost again. Ralph was disappointed, but otherwise they were pretty strong bills. Then it went to a House-Senate conference, where a knock-down, drag-out fight occurred. The auto industry was all over the place, trying to change or stop the bill."

Before the law passed, auto companies had never sent out formal, public recall notices. But someone in Detroit leaked this information to Ralph Nader.

"After GM was caught following Ralph, he started getting calls from industry people from Detroit. One guy told him that the auto companies were doing secret recalls. Ralph went to Ribicoff and Ribicoff wrote a letter to every manufacturer and said, 'I want a list of all of the recalls you have done since 1960.' Ribicoff had a report assembled, printed, and held a big press conference. Oh my God, the press went crazy. The auto manufacturers could not believe it."

These activities brought great attention to the issue and to Claybrook's boss Walter Mondale. She would soon make great use of that attention.

Mondale Was Delighted

Mondale had been appointed to the Senate when Senator Humphrey of Minnesota ran for Vice President on Lyndon Johnson's ticket. In 1966 he faced his first race for the Senate. Claybrook would use an important strategic alliance to help him in the fight.

"Mondale was looking for something high profile to do, and that is when he came up with this idea of public notification about auto recalls. The issue was hot. I was working extraordinary hours and Mondale's office just loved me. But before I started in Mondale's office, I had made friends with the press over on the House side. The grumpy House staff guy wouldn't give the press any documents. But as a staff person to Rep. Mackay, I could go in the back room and use the Xerox machine. I went back there and made 10 copies of all of Mr. Mackay's materials and handed them out to the press."

It was not a carefully crafted plan. It was more a common courtesy. But it ended up proving to be a great investment.

"I thought it was mean that they wouldn't give the press information. I didn't realize what long-term relationships I was going to build as a result of that. But when the bill passed the Senate, *Washington Post* staff writer Morton Mintz called. So with Mondale's press guy, I wrote a statement for Mondale saying, 'I'm delighted that this bill has passed. . . .' It was on the front page of the *Washington Post*! It was the first time Mondale had even been quoted in the *Washington Post*, much less on the front page. When Mondale came back to town he was extremely pleased about the attention to his work."

After passage in the House, the auto safety bill went to conference with the Senate bill and was signed into law by President Lyndon Johnson, just as Claybrook's fellowship was over. It was quite an achievement and Claybrook played no small part. Mackay rewarded her efforts.

"Mr. Mackay took me to the signing ceremony—the only one I've ever been to—and I got a pen and that was just very special. But then I had to find a job. Otherwise I had to go back to Baltimore and the Social Security Administration from whence I came."

She did not return to Baltimore. In September 1966, Claybrook started working for Dr. William Haddon Jr. as his special assistant at the National Highway Safety Bureau (NHSB), renamed NHTSA in 1970. There would be more changes soon.

Driving to NHTSA

"I worked like a dog for Bill Haddon. He was brilliant but not very political and he did not like schmoozing with people. He didn't really get along with anybody on the Hill. He was a physician, an epidemiologist, a scientist, a thinker. He was not a schmoozer, so I did a lot of that work. He also hated lawyers—hated lawyers! In his view, lawyers would never give him a straight answer. So I would negotiate with the lawyers over all matter of things. He wasn't sure what to do in many situations. None of us was sure what to do, but I was willing to pick up the phone and ask."

Claybrook makes it sound easy; it was anything but.

Making NHTSA Count

Many auto industry safety measures are taken for granted today. But Claybrook and her colleagues fought staunchly to realize them.

"We issued the first auto safety standards in January 1967. There was a ruckus about each of them. CEO Henry Ford had a big press conference saying the proposed safety standards were going to kill the auto industry. They mocked up a model car that showed all of the horrible things they would have to do to their beautiful cars in order to comply with the standards, which of course was malarkey.

"We recalled millions of cars and made the information public despite the opposition of the industry, initiated research and data programs, issued highway safety standards for state compliance with a grant-in-aid program, formed two major advisory committees, crash tested some cars, and Haddon issued almost 50 motor vehicle safety standards and some consumer information standards during his two-and-a-half-year tenure. The structure of the agency as Haddon organized it is still the same today. It was an amazing experience."

Then the political landscape shifted.

"The night Nixon got elected, I decided to apply to law school, because I figured that Haddon's days were numbered and my civil service career was probably nearing its end, too."

She was right, almost.

"Nixon took office and Haddon resigned in anticipation of being fired. His deputy, Robert Brenner, became Acting Administrator. But he needed me, too. He was an engineer, and he was even less astute about politics than Bill Haddon. Anyway, I loved him; I loved them both, and I worked really hard for a year while I waited to see if I got admitted to law school."

She would attend Georgetown at night. During the day, she continued to fight the good fight for auto safety.

"In the spring of '70, we had gotten an airbag rule proposed. The airbag manufacturers showed us that these incredible devices could save thousands of lives. So we put out an Advanced Notice of Proposed Rulemaking and had a big public hearing. The new Secretary of Transportation, John Volpe, was a very nice guy, but I was concerned his staff would never tell him about airbags. I staffed the Secretary's auto safety advisory committee so I got the advisory committee to ask Volpe to come down for a meeting and we put on a briefing on airbags. We bypassed his staff and got to him directly. He fell in love with airbags. I just knew that if he understood what they did and saw the crash test results, that he would just be enthralled because he was such a decent guy."

Volpe championed airbags. But Claybrook saw her NHTSA days were numbered.

Taking Time Off . . . or Not

Claybrook remembers when she resigned from NHTSA the first time.

"I left soon after the bombing of Cambodia and the new Administrator Douglas Toms arrived. He was a very decent guy from Washington State, but I was ready to move on."

In the summer of 1970, Claybrook returned home to Baltimore to "relax." Though a noble goal, it was just not in her nature.

"My parents went to a fundraising event for Paul Sarbanes, a state legislator running for Congress. He asked me, 'Why don't you come by the office and just see what we're doing?' He was very smart. I ended up working for him 15 hours a day for the whole summer. It was a very tough campaign. He was challenging the Chairman of the House transportation committee, who had strong financial support from the transportation industry."

Sarbanes won by 2,500 votes, as Claybrook entered her second year of law school.

I Earned My Pay on That One

Claybrook worked hard to catch up in law school. She had missed the first three weeks helping Sarbanes win his campaign. But she also needed a job.

"Paul offered me a job, shortly after Ralph Nader did. Nader had just won a lawsuit for invasion of privacy against General Motors. He asked me to work on auto safety. I decided I would rather do that than work for a freshman member of Congress, which I had already done with Mr. Mackay. Right after I got there Nader scheduled a trip to Japan. My assignment was to visit with the Japanese auto manufacturers. I had a wonderful experience, particularly meeting the elderly Mr. Honda. It was early 1971, and there had been a horrible rollover scandal about the Honda N360, which was his first car."

Claybrook learned that Japan had no requirements for recalls of defective cars—much like the United States before 1966. But Japanese companies now had to recall defective Japanese cars in the United States. Claybrook saw an opportunity.

"I said to Ralph, 'We ought to write a letter to somebody, maybe the Prime Minister, and demand that they recall cars in Japan that they were recalling in the United States.' He loved that idea. We arrived in Osaka and I had to use an ancient typewriter—the most recent one they had in English—to type a two-page letter. It took me all day long. We made some copies. Ralph held a press conference back in Tokyo, and it was a bombshell. Then we hand-delivered the letter to the Prime Minister's residence. Ralph loved it. I earned my pay on that one."

That Would Be Fine

Claybrook turned her attention back to law school. At the same time, Nader founded Public Citizen, a public-rights advocacy group. And then he funded a yearlong study of Congress and persuaded Claybrook to head the part of it doing profiles of every member of Congress running for reelection in 1972. It was a grueling 18-hour-a-day job that lasted until late October 1972. Claybrook skipped law classes until the reports were released, and then in a deal with

Nader, worked full time on law studies for the rest of the semester to catch up so she could still graduate in 1973.

"For Public Citizen, Ralph had hired a litigating attorney to head up the litigation group and a doctor to head up the health group. I said to him, 'You need to have a lobby group because lobbying is as much of a discipline as litigation is. There are rules for the House and Senate. How do you get a bill introduced? How do you get it considered? How do you get it through?' So he said, 'How would you like to head it up?' I jumped at the opportunity."

Claybrook was completing her senior year of law school while she began taking the reins of the new entity.

Keeping Watch over Congress

Under the auspices of Nader's Public Citizen, Claybrook hired five lobbyists—two women and three men—and created a new lobby group called Congress Watch.

"We were the more avant-garde part of Ralph's operation. At Congress Watch, we worked on about five or six pieces of legislation. We were all new lawyers. I had just graduated. We worked on the Consumer Protection Agency bill, something Ralph really wanted enacted. It had been considered but did not pass the prior year (before we formed Congress Watch), during which Ralph had a knock-down, drag-out fight with the representative who was the Chairman of the Government Operations Committee."

Claybrook worked tirelessly behind the scenes and helped the bill pass the House 394 to 5. The bill then went to the Senate, where Committee Chairman Ribicoff held hearings. Other committee members included New York's Jacob Javits and Chicago's Charles Percy, the "nicest guy."

"We started working on the Senate bill, but soon hit a brick wall. A senator named Allen from Alabama was the industry's man to stop the bill. He knew every trick and rule. West Virginia's Bobby Byrd was the Senate Majority Leader and one of the most knowledgeable senators. There was a filibuster, an action that obstructs the legislative process. We had four cloture votes. Cloture is a procedure for ending debate and forcing a vote to be taken on the bill. On the fourth cloture vote we missed by one vote because

Massachusetts Senator Teddy Kennedy was at a luncheon and got back late. Then Byrd brought it up for an unusual fifth cloture vote. One of the industry votes apparently was trying to mislead us; he had voted with us on the fourth cloture but he really didn't intend to if we had enough votes for it to pass. When we thought we had 67 votes, we really only had 66 because he switched. Byrd was furious. And we never got 67, but I really felt good about what we achieved even though we lost the bill."

It was this experience that persuaded Byrd that the 67-vote filibuster rule was too onerous to allow the legislative process to work, and he succeeded in getting it changed to 60 votes, where it is today. It's hard to get 60 votes, but a lot easier than 67, or two-thirds of the Senate.

Claybrook and Congress Watch worked on many issues, including auto safety, trade, public funding, corporate reporting, and energy policy. But once again, with the election of a new President, things would change for Claybrook.

Taking the Wheel at NHTSA

Jimmy Carter won election in 1976 and took office in 1977. He was considering naming Washington Congressman Brock Adams as the next Secretary of Transportation. Claybrook knew Adams's key staffer, Woody Price, from 25 years earlier when they were teenagers.

"He was tough. He called me up and he says, 'Brock Adams wants to talk to you about being the [blankety-blank] head of NHTSA, but I told him he's a Goddamn fool.' I went to meet with Adams. We had a wonderful conversation. His chief counsel was a woman, Linda Heller Kamm, who had recommended me for the job. Brock was very big on hiring women and so was Carter."

Kamm and Claybrook knew each other well, but had had a falling out several years earlier.

"She and I had a horrific disagreement in 1974. She worked for a Congressman from Missouri named Dick Bolling. He had fought with Ralph about the Consumer Protection Agency bill and tried to stop it. But in 1974, Bolling proposed that the committees of Congress be reorganized. One consequence was that all jurisdiction over energy policy would be in one committee rather than three. I agreed with Congressman Philip Burton who led the effort to defeat Bolling's proposal supported by others such as the AFL-CIO. Why should we give the energy industry such an advantage?

"There was this huge fight and Linda defended Dick Bolling's proposal. We won, so she was really angry with me. We didn't speak for two years. Finally a friend of ours said, 'I'm going to have a dinner party, inviting you both, and I want you to be civil to each other.' So she had this make-up dinner party and it turned out to be very instrumental, because within a couple of months after that Linda recommended to Brock Adams that I be the next NHTSA Administrator. Much of what goes on in Washington is personal *and* political; a lot of it is about friendships."

Claybrook served as NHTSA Administrator from 1977 to 1981, issuing landmark vehicle safety standards for air bags and fuel economy, publishing a popular consumer car book, encouraging states to enact child restraint use laws, and more.

She Becomes a Public Citizen

After leaving NHTSA when Carter lost reelection, Claybrook was asked by Ralph Nader to return to Public Citizen as its President. She served from 1982 to 2009, covering a wide array of issues from campaign finance to regulatory reform. But some issues took prominence.

"When I came back to Public Citizen, efforts to curtail federal regulation, misnamed 'regulatory reform' legislation, were being pushed hard by industry. These efforts would have taken jurisdiction away from agency heads and brought key agency decisions under the jurisdiction of the Office of Management and Budget. It was my idea to go to the different members of the important Congressional committees and tell them, 'This bill will take jurisdiction away from you. Key final decision-making authority is going to go to OMB.' They immediately understood that—jurisdiction is one of the hottest issues on the Hill. So they all went and testified at the Rules Committee against the bill and that killed it."

In another instance, Claybrook won over a staunch foe by doing her homework.

"Mississippi Senator Trent Lott became the Chair of the Transportation Subcommittee that oversaw auto safety—much to my horror because I had had huge fights with him over campaign finance reform. He would not let us testify about SUV rollovers. We went to Alaska Senator Ted Stevens and with Hawaii Senator Daniel Inouye invited Lott to a meeting with us. We took just two sheets of paper: one showed a rollover-prone SUV illustrating what needed to be fixed, and the other listed how much it would cost to fix each element. It worked. Lott thanked us at the end of the meeting and put the two sheets of paper in his breast pocket.

"The industry had a really boring engineer make their presentation. After ten minutes, Lott says, 'You've got five minutes left and we must leave to vote.' The engineer says, 'Well, it's going to cost a tremendous amount of money, too much money.' Lott reached into his pocket and said, 'Well, maybe you should hire Joan Claybrook, because she has some really good cost figures here.' Lott took charge of the bill and he was the best legislator I ever worked with. The bill went through and was signed into law. He said to me afterwards, 'I bet you like me a whole lot better, Joan, since I passed your bill.' And he was right."

Claybrook was remarkably successful in Washington, and with good reason. But her philosophy for success applies equally outside of the Beltway.

Being Effective in DC

When it comes to examining people or legislation, Claybrook pulls no punches.

"You have to assess what your strengths and weaknesses are and be very brutal and frank about them. Then find other ways to handle something when you have weaknesses. One story I love occurred when we were fighting with the inter-city motor coach industry. The inter-city motor coach industry was barely regulated. So they kept coming up with new excuses against safety regulation. One was that it would cost them millions of dollars. It occurred to me one day, 'How much does this really cost them? How many people really travel on intercity buses?' We looked up the numbers and figured out that the many safety requirements proposed in the bill would only cost $0.10 a ride. We started promoting that and the industry went crazy. They couldn't rebut the math. When you are in a battle you have to explain the key issues in an accurate, appealing way that the public and members of Congress can understand and support."

Claybrook is renowned for doing exactly that.

Not Having Children

Claybrook often sounds like she is all business. In actuality, she is quite social and believes strongly in good work-life balance. She loves to cook, and often entertains. In addressing non-work issues, she is equally frank.

"Put your family first, especially if you get married, get pregnant, and raise a family. I do regret not having kids. But on the other hand I have two brothers, and four nephews who are just like my kids. They are very loving. They are now 45, 43, 40, and 37, with four grand nieces and nephews. I've traveled to Mexico, San Francisco, Russia, and the Baltic with one over a number of years, to Scotland and London with another one, to India with another, and to Africa with two of them together. One of them lives in Washington, DC, and I see him and his new baby frequently. He was in the Peace Corps in Africa. When he came out of the Peace Corps in 2008 he was not well. He was really harmed by taking an anti-malaria drug. He came to live with me for a year, and we help each other all the time. I'm just very close to all four of them. That's my life and I love being with them."

That is her life. But through her work in Congress and in transportation, Joan Claybrook has had a profound effect on many other people's lives throughout the world.

JOLENE MORITZ MOLITORIS

I will remember it in Technicolor and forever. I had on my red suit. The double glass doors leading into the Federal Railroad Administration (FRA) were straight ahead. The joy of my first day at FRA, the first woman ever to serve as FRA Administrator! It was a dream come true! I should have been terrified! Life and death issues to solve! A complex male-dominated industry. How could I help make the difference I believed was possible? Yet I knew in every fiber of my being that we would save lives. We would make railroading safer! I didn't have every answer in my pocket. But President Clinton and Secretary Peña of the USDOT had empowered us. Together Team USDOT, Team FRA, and the railroads and rail labor would make rail safety history!

Jolene Molitoris has an indomitable spirit. Countless times she has faced impossible tasks. After she completes them, she only wants to know what's next. Consider the start of her career. Fourteen years after she received her master's degree, she demonstrated her extraordinary resolve and took an entry-level position at the Ohio Rail Transportation Authority (ORTA) in 1978. In only three years she became its Deputy Director. Two years later she was the ORTA Executive Director managing all freight and passenger rail programs in Ohio. Next she became Deputy Director of Rail for the Ohio Department of Transportation (ODOT) when Governor Richard Celeste folded ORTA into ODOT. It was an auspicious start. But the next step was even greater.

In 1993, President Clinton nominated and the Senate confirmed Molitoris as the first female Administrator of the FRA. But Molitoris made history in many ways besides gender. After making her mark on the federal level, she entered the private sector. From 2001 to 2005 Molitoris served as President and CEO of GeoFocus, a Florida-based real-time information systems provider. In 2007, Ohio Governor Ted Strickland appointed Molitoris Chair of the Ohio Rail Development Commission, then Assistant Director at ODOT, and then the first female Director of ODOT in its 105 years. She led the department for two years. Today she is President of US Railcar and Principal of Molitoris Associates.

Molitoris has been honored many times for her service to the transportation industry. Most notably, WTS International named her Woman of the Year in 1996. And in 1999, *Railway Age* listed her as one of 16 great 20th Century Railroaders. That same year the National Ethnic Coalition of Organizations bestowed on her its prestigious Ellis Island Medal of Honor.

This is her story.

It Was Time

Jolene Molitoris had a conventional life. She had earned a bachelor's and a master's degree in communications, married, and had two children. Then one day, something changed.

"I put my two children on the school bus, and I suddenly knew. *It was time.* I was looking for a professional challenge that really made my motors run! There was a new agency, ORTA, created after the deregulation of the railroad industry. It was looking at everything rail—freight, passenger, and high-speed rail. This was new, groundbreaking, transformative kind of work. And since it was small, whatever needed to be done you could jump in and help get it done. It was so interesting! It was so important! This work indeed made my motors run!"

Molitoris speaks of the newly formed ORTA, which she joined in an entry-level position. Soon she would gain a distinctive reputation there.

Not Possible? Send Jolene

Molitoris rose to Assistant Executive Director in fewer than three years. Her rise was earned on efforts like this.

"They wanted to create a multistate, high-speed rail compact. To do this, each state had to pass legislation. And we got New York and Ohio, but for some reason Illinois was just hanging out. So they said, 'Go to Springfield and get this passed.' Did I know anything about Springfield or Illinois politics? No. And it was just crazy to try. *But I didn't know it was impossible.* And they said, 'Don't come back until it's passed.' So I packed my bag."

She found an ally, a leader in the legislature. And in the very last hours of the session, the leader worked his magic. The compact legislation passed. Molitoris had learned a lot about legislation from a master. It was an important legislative lesson she never forgot.

This was the first of many successful "impossible" missions.

"I'll Help You"

When Governor Celeste folded ORTA into ODOT, Molitoris became ODOT Deputy Director of Rail. As such, she attended a meeting of the American Association of State Highway and Transportation Officials (AASHTO), a traditionally male bastion.

"I was one of very few women attendees. There was a presentation on legislation important to short-line railroads, very important to Ohio. The AASHTO legislative director opined that the legislation was *dead.* I asked, 'Why?' from the audience. He disregarded this as a question from someone who simply didn't have his knowledge and expertise.

"When I got back to Columbus, I talked to Jackie Gillan, who was in Governor Celeste's Washington office, about this. She said, 'Are you willing to accept this?' I said, 'No,' of course. And she, being the fearless woman that she was and is, said, 'I'll help you.'

Following Jackie's guidance and skill, we worked hard together to educate Congress about how important this was to Ohio. At the end of the day, the legislation survived."

Transportation Opens Up

Molitoris always kept a tight focus on the task at hand. That's partly what made her so effective. But that focus would soon broaden.

"In the deputy slot at ORTA and before, I was working on high-speed rail mostly. So I did not fully appreciate freight. When I became the Executive Director, the entire panorama of transportation opened up, because I had all of the information that I didn't have before. I couldn't see it before. I didn't have the opportunity before. And I thought, 'Oh, my god! This is life-changing!' Transportation made the difference in history, the economy, people's lives, the job market—everything."

With a more strategic outlook, she set to work.

Knowledge Is Power

The 160-mile Panhandle Route was once part of the Pennsylvania Railroad. Initially, it was the main rail route from Pittsburgh to Columbus, splitting onto Chicago and St. Louis. Today the state-owned line provides vital rail links between Ohio commerce and key Eastern seaports. Yet at the time, some parties wanted to sell it. Molitoris viewed it as an important investment for Ohio. But not everyone was convinced she was the right woman for the fight.

"There were these very, very senior guys—rail guys who had been in this business a long time—who were wondering what I was doing there. But at some point they realized I would fight harder than anybody else and decided to share everything they knew about railroading and the project. I was so thrilled to be taken into their confidence."

Ohio with Molitoris and the ORTA team won the fight. Ohio still owns the Panhandle today, or at least a good bit of it. Gaining the trust of those senior rail officials was an essential part of a successful conclusion and said a great deal about her. And they returned the favor in kind.

"Later when I was sworn in in Washington as FRA Adminis-trator, five of those men—and they were in their seventies at the time—drove from southern Ohio to Washington. They presented me with a plaque during the ceremony. And when the event was over they got in their car and drove back. They didn't even stay for the food! And they drove because they couldn't afford to fly. It touched my heart. I still get goose bumps thinking about it."

Learning from the Best

Governor Celeste brought ORTA into ODOT under Director Warren Smith to make ODOT a more comprehensive transpor-tation department. Together Celeste and Smith also sought to integrate women and people of color into ODOT. It was not an easy process, and Molitoris learned greatly from the effort. When Smith came into the department, he made the Administration's diversity priorities for hiring and promotion clear to his staff. But not everyone was on board.

"A year went by and there was no significant progress. So Smith took his first lieutenant in charge of HR and told him, 'Any time there's an open position in the districts, you bring it to me.' And every time they brought one to him he didn't sign it. The districts were wondering what was going on. He never said anything, and he never shouted. The districts started in with their excuses, 'Gosh, we can't find anybody! We're looking! But we can't find anybody that's *qualified*!' Then, all of a sudden, they got it. They finally figured out that if they wanted to fill anything, they better send people the Director wanted to see as candidates. It's amazing, isn't it? You can find quality, qualified people.

"When the Governor moved Warren to another tough job in state government, I attended his goodbye parties in the districts. I stood there. I watched. And I listened to these very seasoned ODOT career employees say to him, 'Goodbye. Thank you. You were right. And we were wrong. See that woman there and that one there—those are the ones I would want to have with me to help me if I was in trouble. What lifelong lessons I learned from Warren's example!'"

Molitoris learned the value of having support from on high.

"Plenty of people didn't think I could do the job because I was a woman. But when you have the Director at your back and the Governor, or the President and the Secretary, and remarkable agency teams, you are empowered. The fact is I knew that support was there for me no matter how hard the challenge. It gave me the courage to set goals like zero tolerance for any safety hazard; without such strong support, perhaps I would have been more hesitant to pursue them."

Zero Tolerance for Any Safety Hazard

In 1993 Molitoris began her tenure as the FRA Administrator. And she had to create a list of goals for the USDOT Secretary's Office for that calendar year. Her list made waves.

"'You can't do that! You can't possibly get that done,' was what I heard. And I said, 'Well, we can try.' They came back with, 'But you might fail.' And I said, 'Isn't it better to try? And if you don't get all 20, maybe you get 16.' But they were really protecting me. They didn't want me sent to Siberia for not delivering on all of the goals."

But one goal shocked people. Molitoris had the nerve to set a goal of *zero tolerance*, no injuries or deaths from rail accidents in any year.

"That became my mantra. And they said that you absolutely cannot say that. You'll never get to zero. So I said, 'Well then, how many people do you think we should say can be injured and killed this year?' That definitely changed the conversation! But the fact is we had the seven safest years in railroad history during my tenure. We saved so many lives and limbs and sent people back home to their families whole and happy. The new approach to increasing safety was a partnership approach—between railroad management, rail labor, and FRA—with techniques focused on elimination of the root causes of safety hazards rather than a focus on fines. But Congress said I wasn't being tough enough, that I was being soft on the railroads. And I said to them, 'I understand your concerns. But this is the way to save lives and reduce injuries. I believe in this approach. Watch the numbers.'

"Near the end of my tenure, a man from one of the Senate offices came over and said, 'We owe you an apology. We gave you a terrible time. And now look at the numbers. The increase in safety is wonderful!' And I said, 'It's a tribute to everyone buying into the new approach and making it work. Because saving lives is what matters!'"

With that victory in hand, Molitoris girded for yet another battle.

The Rules of the Game

Rulemaking at the FRA is a tough process, as these rules have far-reaching rail industry implications. Changing the process itself would prove even more difficult.

"Previously FRA would have an internal development stage for a proposed new safety rule. Then FRA would put out a proposal. That's when the battles began. The railroads, the unions, no one seemed to like it, probably because they didn't have anything to say about it initially. So the FRA team created something new—its first consensus-based rulemaking process. Railroad management, rail labor, and FRA working together! No one thought it would work. But it did. It was a historic and dramatic change."

Molitoris says that only with everyone working together could this have happened. She credits all the labor, management, and FRA leaders who were key to this success. She especially recognizes Phil Olekszyk from FRA for his determination and skill in working with such a large group to guide the process and make it a reality. The Rail Safety Advisory Council continues its work to this day proving the value of consensus in improving safety for the rail industry. It also contributed to seven of the safest years in railroad history during the Clinton Administration. Molitoris derives great pride from these efforts.

"I have a photograph in my office today that I treasure. There are about 30 railroad men—and me. I'm the only skirt in the place. And the men asked the Secretary of Transportation, Federico Peña, if he could sign the first consensus-based rulemaking *on my birthday* in his office. It was a surprise; they never told me that's why we were going to his office."

Molitoris finished almost eight years as FRA Administrator, the longest serving FRA Administrator ever. After a stretch in the private sector and time on Ohio's rail commission, then–Ohio Governor Ted Strickland appointed her Assistant Director of ODOT and then Director to lead ODOT, only the second non-PE and the first woman to ever head the department in its 105-year history. She didn't waste a minute.

Here's an Extra Billion

Times were tough. But soon Molitoris faced an unusual funding situation, in a good way.

"ODOT got *a billion dollars* more than we budgeted for from the President's TIGER, the USDOT's Transportation Investment Generating Economic Recovery discretionary grant program, grant and stimulus money. There were stringent eligibility and time restrictions attached. So I created a TIGER Team right outside my office. I think the oldest team member was 40 years old. There might have been one that was 45. They were young and energetic and believed we could do it."

Tasking her young charges with learning the rules thoroughly, she ensured her team left no legislative stone unturned. But one young TIGER team member stood out.

"The first thing I said to my TIGER team was, 'Knowledge is power. Learn the rules inside out and all around.' And there was a young man named Drew Williams. And he took learning the rules so seriously; I think he memorized them. We'd meet with the regional office of the Federal Highway Administration. And they kept telling us we couldn't do this project in Cincinnati, that it wasn't eligible. Drew raised his hand and said, 'Director, if you don't mind, I would like to ask some questions of the FHWA people.' And he had his paper. And he started citing, 'Section 2, paragraph 3, line 4 says . . .'

"He had these regs cold. And we *still* didn't get the project approved. Then Drew came into my office and said, 'Director, if you will allow me, I will pay my own way to drive to Washington, because I believe *they* will know that I am citing the facts.' I think we ended up on a conference call. But the project was approved due to the determination and commitment of this TIGER Team member."

Her team didn't lose a dollar of the money or miss a single deadline.

Going with Your Gut Instinct

Molitoris possesses no shortage of determination. But there is another overriding intangible quality that has guided her from the start.

"I believe in a combination of information and intuition, gut instinct with lots of information and experience. And the places I came closest to making a substantive error happened when I didn't listen to my gut. So I always try to listen to my gut."

Molitoris always does.

Fire in the Belly

Everyone approaches her or his career differently. But some advice can benefit every aspiring professional.

"There is never a time when you know enough, never, especially today when things are changing so fast. Get information from every source, from people of experience, people from different industries who may have ideas that apply. It should be this driving force throughout life, not just professional, but also personal. Never, never, never give up on your dream, but learn what your dream is. It evolves. But ultimately you've got to have fire in the belly for what you're doing. If what you're doing is not exciting or making a difference in the world, move on."

Those are not idle words, but an active philosophy she implements every day.

Life Support Systems

"I was ODOT Deputy for rail when I met my beloved, phenomenal husband, David! This awesome man, I can't give him enough credit. I commuted for eight years from Columbus to Washington, DC, when I became FRA Administrator. And it never fazed him.

He'd pick me up every weekend that I could come home. He always had flowers on the table and soup on the stove. And the only thing he ever asked was, 'Do you want to do this? Is this making you happy?' He's one amazing human being. There's no way my career could have evolved without his incredible support."

But Molitoris is realistic. Even with a supportive spouse, the road can have bumps.

"It's never easy. Oh my goodness no. But what is easy that's worth doing? There are going to be times where things have to be addressed, when you have to speak up and step out, where you have to fight for things. And there are risks. But at the end of each day, as President Clinton told Secretary Peña, if we made the world better for one American, it was what he had asked us to do. It wasn't just a job. It was a mission. And it made me want to jump out of bed every morning! It doesn't get better than that!"

ANNE CANBY

You learn over time how to use your directness. I remember one time I was in a meeting with some cabinet colleagues—I was Secretary of the Delaware Department of Transportation (DelDOT) at the time—and some legislators, and the conversation was just going nowhere. I had hurt my foot, and I was using a cane. And I took the cane and slammed it on the table and I said, "Cut this bullshit and let's get on with whatever we're going to do!" And all of these people just sat back stunned. But I had just had enough. I just lost it totally. But it got their attention.

Anne Canby never dreamt of a career in transportation. Yet she has had a long and compelling career in the transportation industry. A European history major from Wheaton College, Canby entered politics first, working for former Congressman Pete McCloskey and then the National Committee for an Effective Congress. From there she joined USDOT during the Carter Administration, where she became Deputy Assistant Secretary for Budget and Programs.

In a most impressive progression, she went on to serve as Commissioner of the New Jersey Department of Transportation (NJDOT), Ex Officio Chair of the New Jersey Transit Board of Directors, Treasurer of the Massachusetts Bay Transportation

Authority, Secretary of the Delaware Department of Transportation, and President of the Surface Transportation Policy Project. Currently she is Director of the OneRail Coalition, an organization that advocates for investment in US rail infrastructure.

Canby has served on many boards and commissions, including the Executive Committees of the Transportation Research Board (TRB) and the American Association of State Highway and Transportation Officials; she currently serves on the Mineta Transportation Institute Board. She has also been acknowledged by many organizations for her leadership, including awards from WTS International and the 2006 Carey Distinguished Service Award from the TRB and Women Who Move The Nation award from COMTO.

This is her story.

Beginnings

Some people are born into transportation. Others come to it by design. Anne Canby's transportation route was, well, different. Canby came from the then-societal mindset where "most women my age thought they would find something to do for a while, get married, and raise children." Canby chose a different path.

"I just sort of fell into transportation. My path had *nothing* to do with transportation initially. I was working on Capitol Hill for Congressman Pete McCloskey. I left that and went to work for the National Committee for an Effective Congress in 1974 and we helped elect people to Congress. Sometime during all of that—I think it was 1976—I was in a meeting of campaign strategists and looked around the room and said to myself, 'Maybe I don't want to be like these guys, sitting in this room when I get to be their age!'

"So I used my political network to leverage a position inside the Carter Administration, and I had the great good fortune to land a job as an assistant to Mort Downey, who was the USDOT Assistant Secretary for Budget at the time. That is probably the best introduction to transportation I can think of. There was a steep learning curve, especially when you work for someone like Mort. He took home a bag with papers in it that were a foot or more thick, and you knew he read them every night. And I thought, 'I've got to keep up with him.' But I soon found out that was impossible. So I just tried to fill in where I could and learn."

And learn she did, lessons that would prove invaluable later in her career.

"I learned that there is more than one way to get something done. Figuring out how to go around resistance and move things forward is really important. For example, we were having difficulty with the Urban Mass Transportation Administration (UMTA) Administrator. He wouldn't move on an issue, so we put pressure on him from another direction. Mort contacted the OMB and, agreeing with Mort, they delivered the message from a higher authority. And that helped move the mark. This was a good lesson."

While there, Canby also found a true anomaly in the number of women in high-level positions. The administration featured the likes of NHTSA Administrator Joan Claybrook, General Counsel Linda Kamm, UMTA Deputy Administrator Lillian Liburdi (Borrone), and Public Affairs Deputy Susan Williams, with the roster rounded out by Ellen Finegold, Sarah Campbell, and Grace Crunican (an intern at the time).

In the Thick of It

A quick study, Canby soon found a new outlet for her lessons learned. In 1982, she took a position as Assistant Commissioner at the NJDOT. True to form, her tenure was anything but typical.

"Some months after arriving in New Jersey, Commissioner Lou Gambaccini decided to return to the Port Authority. We were at the end of Governor Brendon Byrne's term and there was a scramble to see who would replace Lou. Governor Byrne probably could have cared less about who would run the DOT, although I think he liked the idea of it being a woman. He mostly wanted someone to keep the lid on the jar. There was the Deputy, another Assistant Commissioner, and me, and the question was, who was going to get the job? I didn't even know if I wanted it, but the other people on the staff were saying that I had to do it, because the other two people can't. So I said okay. And *they* pushed hard on the Governor's office on my behalf. We had all of the interviews and the Governor actually picked me, and I became Acting

Commissioner. I then asked to be confirmed (so I could remove 'acting' from the title), and I was, as I knew this would be important for future job prospects."

Wanting to continue Gambaccini's efforts to secure stable, reliable transportation funding, Canby set to work. She quickly realized one aspect of employee engagement that needed to be addressed.

"Every employee in an agency helps create the image of the department—from the bus driver who doesn't tuck his or her shirt in to the maintenance people and how they fill the pothole to the toll collectors and how they treat rude customers. I had to help *them* understand that their image, their interaction with users, was part of what builds good faith and public trust. If the public feels good about you, they're more apt to support you. If they don't, they think, 'Why give them anything?'"

"When I was in New Jersey, I knew my efforts were working when a group of us from the DOT were driving along and we saw road workers just standing around with shovels in their hands. The Chief Engineer for the department blurted out, 'Those aren't our people!' It was comforting to see that my message had gotten through. Sometimes it's hard for the folks pushing snow or patching potholes to understand how they fit into the bigger picture."

Canby made her point. And the perceptual shift rippled through the department. But Canby also believed that if each worker represents the department, the department also has a responsibility to each worker. And she would get an opportunity to act on this belief again in a different department.

Lessons from Dover

Later in her career, Delaware Governor Thomas Carper appointed Canby DelDOT Secretary in 1993. She would hold the post until 2001. In her eight-year tenure, she gained national recognition for transforming the department. But she had some boots-on-the-ground issues to deal with initially.

"When I first got to Delaware, guys were plowing snow, and there were holes in the floorboards of their trucks! *Snow was coming up through the floor and into the cab.* What kind of a way is that to treat your employees? Mowing grass in hundred-degree temperatures! So we got them enclosed cabs and air conditioning so that they didn't get exposed to the heat and the grass in the summer if they were allergic and were protected from the snow in the winter. They hadn't had a regular equipment program ever! It was important to me to provide decent equipment so workers could do their jobs. How can leaders expect their employees to do a good job when they aren't provided decent working tools to do so?"

But Canby had big-picture issues to address as well. And her approach blazed trails on a number of fronts.

"Governor Carper wanted to raise the gas tax. So I said, 'Okay, we'll figure out how to do it.' Since all of us were pretty new to the workings in Dover and I had just moved back to the state, we had a lot to learn. We set up a team in Legislative Hall to work with legislators, identifying their issues, and dealing with questions. I worked closely with the co-chair of the critical committee, Senator Nancy Cook, a good example of women helping each other.

"A Democrat, Cook wanted to help the governor. She would send me little signals when I should go talk to people. And I would explain what we were doing. We put together a whole plan. We cut projects out of the capital program that were never going to be built, and the General Assembly approved raising the gas tax. And this may be the only time in history where the gas tax was raised and projects were cut from the capital plan at the same time. The Governor's office was a little amazed that we got it done, but we did."

But the legislative road was not always so smooth.

"DelDOT had always been run by someone who was much more political than me, but who had much less transportation knowledge or experience. My predecessor had been indicted and later went to prison. So when I came in, people in the department were ready to be less political—well, some of them anyway. But we did a lot of changing, and we didn't always just say yes to what the legislators wanted. Predictably, some of them didn't like that. And in the beginning of the governor's second term, there was a big newspaper story about right of way the department owned. The reason why they could even run the story was that we had taken the initiative to put all of our real-estate parcels into a database so we could figure out what we owned and dispose of them in an orderly way. The small parcels weren't doing us any good and it wasn't helping localities with their tax bases. But one member of the legislature wanted me gone, badly. So he kept feeding the right-of-way story to the press.

"Then it was revealed that the department also owned an office building and had been trying to improve it in order to sell it. And it was a real mess, since we weren't in the development business to begin with. So, the legislature formed a special committee to investigate, and the newspapers were just salivating over this. DelDOT this! DelDOT that! They can't do anything right! It became a feeding frenzy. They picked on me, too. And that wasn't the most pleasant experience in my life."

Canby knew she had to act. But what to do?

"It soon became a question of whether or not I could get the place organized and run correctly. So I sought a project we could do right, to show people we knew what the hell we were doing. That turned out to be a reconstruction of a short portion of I-95 in Delaware. Remember, 2000 was when the Republican Convention was in Philadelphia. I-95 is a critical highway link between Delaware and Philadelphia.

"After extensive work and many meetings with the public to work out the best strategy to accomplish the project, the option they strongly preferred was to close down I-95 in one direction at a time, tear it up, and rebuild it. It was faster, caused less disruption, and was less expensive. This plan made some people crazy, though. There was a big concern inside the Governor's office: should we do it? Should we not do it? Republican legislators were not at all pleased, but this is what their constituents wanted. Eventually, the Governor backed us. He said, 'Look, they've done their homework. They know what they're doing. Let's do it.' The project got done ahead of schedule and without any traffic issues. This really helped lift morale for the whole department.

"My main legislative opponent had probably never liked me anyway, so I don't think doing this project well made a difference with him. But a different legislator who spent a lot of time complaining about the department and me said, 'Well, when they do it right, you've got to recognize that they did it right.' So some of them got the picture."

But Canby's efforts were not limited to legislation and the roadways. She pushed for diversity in the department as well.

"Every year or so I would talk to classes at the University of Delaware. I would see who attended classes versus who was in my department in mid-manager roles. So I went back to a mid-manager meeting and said, 'Guys! If we want to hire the best and the brightest, guess what? It doesn't look like you, because that's not who's in the classes at the University of Delaware.' So we had a big push on diversity. Some people started learning Spanish so we could fill positions that were vacant with Latinos eager to work. Another group learned sign language to communicate with a coworker who was deaf. Leadership matters, and I'd like to think that my actions had an effect on diversifying our workforce; as the leader this was one of my roles—to facilitate that change.

"One of my great successes happened when I spoke to a class and met a young African-American woman. The next thing I know she shows up working in my Planning Department. Last year I was at the National Association of State Transportation Officials (NASTO) meeting up in New England and this woman came up to me and said, 'Do you remember me?' I said, 'Oh Shante, sure!' She was now Special Assistant to the Secretary. Little steps, but it was very heart-warming."

On the Personal Side . . .

Though raised during more traditional times, Canby was little vexed by the seemingly eternal professional conundrum for women—career versus family. For her it simply never became an issue.

"I didn't start my transportation career until I got married, when I was about 34 years old. My husband is a bit older and he had already had three children and wasn't interested in having any more. With my new job, the idea of having children just didn't seem to fit in with where I seemed to be heading. But it wasn't a big decision. I didn't sit up and say, 'Oh man, this is terrible! I'm never going to have any children!' We just both said that we didn't want children, and that was that."

Mentors . . . or Not

By most measures, mentors are invaluable. They are a recognized and venerated source for career guidance and wisdom. But Canby had little use for formal mentoring. It wasn't her way. Though she certainly learned from superiors, her focus was different.

"I don't know if I've ever sat down with someone and said, 'Help me figure my next step.' I decided what I wanted to do and then figured out who I needed to talk to to get there. That is a lesson you need to know: who can help you move your agenda along? To this day, Mort Downey and I are on at least one committee together. We're back and forth with each other on a pretty regular basis. You just develop relationships over the years and when something comes up you figure out who you know—you hope you can *remember* who you know at this point in life—and call them to help you think about it. I have many enduring friendships from my transportation work, including Sarah Campbell, Jackie Gillan, and Grace Crunican, whom I continue to see and work with. What is so nice is that we seem to keep running into each other through new ventures."

Reflection

Canby tends *not* to look back on her career and achievements. To her, she's "not done yet." But when pressed, she provides great illumination for those starting out.

"I created my own path, but I was never really conscious about what I was doing. I just followed what made sense and kept an eye out for new opportunities. You went to work because you had to feed yourself. You tried to find something that was interesting enough to do, paid the bills, and didn't take up too much of your life.

"I'm a change agent. But change is hard, no matter what. That's life. But it's particularly hard when you're coming in at the top and facing people who are there on a day-to-day basis looking at a career and a pension. There's a whole cadre of people who need to be led. But when you're the head of an agency, *you are the leader*. It's one thing to get projects done, but that's not the same as building a workforce that's effective and efficient and understands what its mission is. Establishing yourself as the leader is really important in terms of being effective."

Advice

It is said that the best way to succeed in life is to act on the advice you give to others. Anne Canby has. That's one reason her counsel is prized. But for young professionals in transportation, her advice is invaluable.

"You start by doing. You learn it. You keep doing it. You build a network. I reached out to someone to get the McCloskey job. Someone reached out to me to do the congressional campaign work. I used the network I developed from the campaign work to get a job at the USDOT. From there on, people reached out to me. I never went to a search firm and asked for help to find a job.

"But listening to people and understanding where they are so that you know where you're starting from is important. You have to understand the ground you're on and then figure out where your opportunities are. You have to size up where you have support and where you don't. One thing that one of the nonprofit leaders I've worked with says, that has always stuck with me, is that you've got to think about what the *other* person's self-interest is and how you're going to satisfy at least some of that as well as your own. Because if it's all you and nothing about them, it's going to be hard to get anything done.

"When I was in New Jersey, a legislator said, 'Pretty good for a woman.' You just shrug your shoulders when someone says something like that. What are you going to do? The guy is old. He doesn't get it. He's never going to get it. If you let that kind of stuff totally get to you, you'd be paralyzed. You don't have time to change everyone's mind. You have to find the people who think you're good, who don't care what your gender or race is and work with them.

"There are many women in large organizations trying to figure out how to rise up. I came in totally from the outside and at the top. So it was totally different for me. Maybe they ought to leave their agency for a while and go do some other aspect, like working on a transportation legislative committee. Get a different perspective on the business, rather than being in the agency all of the time. That might give them a broader perspective. I certainly jumped around. I can't imagine spending 30 years at one place, not that I ever had the chance to do that.

"But everyone should learn how to listen, not just hear, but *listen*. If you really want to get something done, be persistent. You've got to keep pushing. Somewhere there will be an opening. Never give up. Keep a sense of humor. Don't take things personally, if you can avoid it. But I know sometimes that's hard to do."

Some people are born into transportation. Others come to it by design. Though she may have just fallen into it, Anne Canby has made quite a career out of the road less taken.

Chapter 8

MARY JANE O'MEARA

My first day on the job at the Tobin Bridge I come off the elevator and see a sign that says, "Slippery: Wet Floor." And I fall in front of the rec room where the toll collectors eat lunch. None of them come out to help me. I'm laid out on the floor. My shoe is off. And I'm trying to get my dignity back to walk to my office. And I hear these guys going, "I bet that's the new Operations Manager." When I leave that night, the elevator breaks and I'm stuck between floors. They pry the door open with a broken broom handle and there's this 98-pound supervisor standing there—and I'm not a thin person. He says, "Jump!" And I'm thinking, "If I jump I'm going to kill this guy." I told him to turn around because I had a skirt on and I sat down, knelt down, and then jumped. And that was my first day on the bridge.

Mary Jane O'Meara has an indomitable spirit. After beginning her career on an urban revitalization project for a small consulting firm, O'Meara went to work on Massachusetts Congressman Joe Moakley's campaign. Through connections there, O'Meara began consulting at the MBTA despite "not knowing anything about transportation." It was 1983. A year later the MBTA brought her on staff as the Chief Railroad Services Officer. In 1985, she became an Assistant Project Manager. Then she got a call from a friend in WTS asking if she knew anyone who wanted to run the Tobin Bridge for Massport. She didn't. The friend convinced her she should do it.

In 1988, O'Meara became the Operations Manager for the Tobin Bridge. Four years later, she became the Director of the bridge, a post she held for 18 years. In 2010, O'Meara ran the Massachusetts Turnpike Authority (MTA) for six months. Then she returned to Massport, as the MTA Authority and the bridge were folded into the newly created Massachusetts Department of Transportation, an entity that combined many of the separate transportation agencies into one agency. She oversaw the ending of her own job. But her expertise was in demand. She soon joined HNTB Corporation as an Associate Vice President and office leader in their Boston office, where she works today.

O'Meara is a longtime, active member of WTS. She served as Boston Chapter President, and Boston Chapter Board member, WTS International President, and as a WTS International Board member. In 1994, both WTS Boston and WTS International named her Member of the Year. She was also actively involved with the International Bridge, Tunnel, and Turnpike Association (IBTTA), where she served as President, as a board member, and on a host of committees. She has garnered numerous awards for her service to the state of Massachusetts and the transportation industry.

O'Meara possesses an infallible sense of humor and indefatigable geniality. Tough when she needs to be, she is also generally regarded as one of the nicest people in transportation.

This is her story.

Transportation by Mistake

Harking back to a different era, Mary Jane O'Meara was told she could be a nurse, a secretary, a teacher, or a housewife. She had other plans. She began working for Congressman Joe Moakley's campaign when his general manager told her she'd be "great in transportation." She listened.

"I went to work for the MBTA as a consultant. They were extending the commuter rail and needed to do a lot of community meetings. So I was the bridge between the community, the contractor, and the MBTA on all of the project issues during construction. I did that for two years and then I wound up in the Construction Department working on the Orange Line, which at that time was the largest construction project ever done in Massachusetts, and that was really exciting!"

The Right Color, the Right Name

But O'Meara also understood some of the other realities in the MBTA at that time.

"I was told when I got the job that I was 'the right color and that I had the right name,' as the MBTA was very Irish dominated. What they didn't know was that my maiden name was Nicolazzo! I remember telling my husband, 'There are some real issues there with women and women of color.'"

O'Meara worked there for four years. Then the phone rang.

I Don't Have That Kind of Experience

A woman from WTS told O'Meara that Massport had a request. Massport was the authority responsible for the operation the area's three airports, its seaport, and the Tobin Bridge—a considerable revenue producer.

"They were looking for someone to run the Tobin Bridge. And she said, 'You would be good at that job.' And I said, 'How could I be good at that job? I don't have that kind of experience.' Three weeks later, Massport hired me as the Operations Manager of the Tobin Bridge. Two years later, I was the Director. And I worked there for 22 years."

The Bridge of Size

Her entrance to the bridge would become legend. Overcoming slipping and getting stuck in the elevator on her first day, O'Meara soon began to learn the ropes and assert her authority.

"I was in charge of toll collection, the toll collectors, opening and closing the roadways, emergency maintenance, and contracting. But most bridges and toll roads were built or opened in the 1950s. The Army Corps of Engineers built a lot of them and many of the entities kept a military structure. So there was Captain Henry Punch, Lieutenant Diamond, five sergeants who were supervisors, and about 34 toll collectors, most of them from the World War II era. It was like working with my father. And with these guys, you had to earn your stripes. But I think that's the case with anything you do."

And O'Meara had to stand firm to earn her stripes.

Passing the Union Test and Earning Respect

She had a lot to learn. O'Meara had worked with unions at the MBTA. But these were Teamsters (Local 25) and it was much more intense.

"The union was always testing. The supervisors would ask to change the schedule or to do things differently, and I knew I was being tested. So I had to really understand what they were asking. I had to be careful because once you change anything, and you're working under a collective bargaining agreement, then the change becomes permanent. For example, if they wanted a half-hour break instead of a 20-minute break and I say okay, I'm the good guy. But once we go to collective bargaining, they get that half-hour break because I've already allowed it. So I had to be really careful."

Another regular test she faced had to do with weather, and whether or not it was safe for toll collectors to staff their posts.

"I fielded a lot of weather stuff by putting on my jacket, my safety vest, and grabbing my radio. And I would go up and stand in the tollbooth or the roadway to see how bad the weather was. If it was unsafe, like a blizzard, and I thought they were going to get hurt I would pull them out of the tollbooth. I had the authority to do that, and the bridge would go toll free. I would always go up onto the top deck and really check the situation out and then confer with the supervisors on duty to see how they felt because some of these guys had worked there for 40 years. And I would listen very carefully. That's how I earned their respect. I never made a decision that would change the way they worked without sitting down to give everyone an opportunity to debate it with me."

Getting Your Boss's Job

O'Meara earned the Teamsters' respect by respecting them. She would earn Massport's respect and appreciation through her strength of character.

"Joe, the gentleman on the bridge who hired me, was fired four years later for theft. Money had been disappearing out of petty cash. One day an administrative person, Evelyn, came to my office very distressed. The bridge belonged to a number of organizations: the Chelsea Chamber of Commerce, the Chelsea Rotary Club, and the IBTTA. The IBTTA and the Chamber hadn't received our dues checks. I asked Evelyn, 'Did you mail those checks personally?' She said, 'No, I gave them to Joe. He wanted to deliver them.' We both suspected that he had stolen those checks, but we didn't want to believe it. I said, 'Call Accounts Payable and put a trace on both checks.' Well the tracer came back that they were deposited into his personal checking account."

But O'Meara was *not* next in line to be Director.

"Massport Executive Director Al Raine called me and told me that Joe was going to be terminated. I was going to be made Acting Director of the bridge effective immediately. My first thought was, 'What about Russ? Russ was the Assistant Director. I'm only the Operations Manager.'"

O'Meara realized that Raine felt Russ was not a good option. He had a reputation as a hothead and for not treating people well or with respect. So O'Meara became Director of the bridge and one of the few women on Massport's senior leadership team. But that put her in a very difficult position with Russ.

"He was really angry. But Al Raine said, 'Mary Jane, could you try to work with him? We don't want another big issue on the bridge right now.' Al Raine knew the press would pick up on Joe's firing, and he was right. So I did my best. I worked with Russ, but he resented it. One day I said to him, 'I didn't ask to be put in this position. You should take a look in the mirror and figure out why you were bypassed. And if you want to be here, it's up to you to try to work with me.' Well, about six years later he was terminated for theft."

How Do You Defend Nonhuman Urine?

But O'Meara faced even greater challenges.

"We implemented a drug policy, which the union knew about up front. Everyone knew. My people needed to be tested for drugs and alcohol because they all had commercial drivers' licenses and were driving big trucks. So they would get randomly tested. One day I get a call, 'Mary Jane, I've got bad news. One of your guys tested negative on his drug test. It came back as nonhuman urine.' He was the first person ever to test negative. So I sit down with the union. And they start arguing with me that I can't discipline him because, 'Well, it's nonhuman!' And I said, 'I want to know how he got a cat to pee in a cup. If you can tell me that we'll settle this.' Even the union rep started laughing. How do you defend nonhuman urine? The guy was human, right?"

The offender was suspended for 45 days without pay. But O'Meara had not yet seen the end of this situation.

Stories from the Bridge: Walking to Maine

O'Meara has many tales from the bridge. Never knowing quite what to expect, she prepared for everything.

"I always had the two-way radio on in my office. And you don't really notice it until you hear a certain tone in someone's voice, and then it snaps you to attention. So I hear one of our tow trucks guys say, 'There's a woman walking on the bridge and she's carrying a suitcase.' I grab the radio and say, 'Pick her up. Bring her here. Get the state police. No pedestrians on the bridge.' Believe it or not, there is even a law that says no horses on the bridge.

"So they bring her up. And she was not young. She had to be in her eighties. And she had a little teeny suitcase. So I said, 'Where are you going?' And very calmly she said that she was walking to visit her sister in Maine. We later learned that she had escaped from a nursing home in Brookline. How she got to the bridge, I'll never know."

Stories from the Bridge: A Cement Hat

Part of O'Meara's responsibilities included managing contractors on the bridge. But she never thought it would go this far.

"We were re-decking the upper deck, and they were pouring concrete. The contractor was DeMatteo Construction. And the owner, Mr. DeMatteo, papa himself, who was in his seventies, was driving along the bridge in his Mercedes or Lexus with the sunroof open. And his company is pouring concrete, and it goes through his sunroof and covers him. I go out and there's an older gentleman in a suit standing there with concrete dripping off of his head. And I burst out laughing, because all I could picture was this poor man wearing a suit of hardened concrete! Well that was the worst thing I could have done. I tried to apologize, but at the same time it was *his* people that did it to him. But he was not happy. . . ."

Stories from the Bridge: Kill Her

Not all of her stories from the bridge were funny or amusing.

"Once I was threatened by a union person who left my office and said that she was going to get that 'effing bitch and kill her,' meaning me. One of my state troopers heard her and they wouldn't let me walk alone to my car for weeks. But I didn't take it seriously. I had my life threatened like that two or three times by employees that I had to fire."

Sometimes the problem wore a suit.

When Unions Attack, Literally

O'Meara sometimes had to dismiss employees. It was never a pleasant task. But because of the union, it was also always a process.

"After a hearing, they could request a 'two-plus-two,' which meant we would bring a lawyer and they would bring their lawyer. The head of the union worked in Charlestown. From the beginning the man did not like me, and I can get anybody to like me. But at one of the hearings, he jumped up and came at me.

"I think he was going to grab me. He was so mad at me; the veins were popping out of his neck. But my Assistant Director,

Jim, jumped in front and grabbed his arm. And I said, 'Jim, why did you stop him! If he just touched me I was going to own the union! My husband's a lawyer!' Everyone else in the room laughed. But he was furious with me because I wasn't giving in to what he wanted. And it had to do with the guy that failed the drug test with nonhuman urine. I finally said to him, 'John, if you read the policy it calls for his immediate dismissal. We're giving him a break with only a suspension.'"

That wasn't her only run-in with this union representative. She had several. But O'Meara also remembers the last time she saw him.

"He came to my retirement party. And he said, 'You were the toughest manager I dealt with at Massport, but I have to admit you were always fair.'"

Just Until They Find a Permanent Person

In 2009 Massachusetts Governor Deval Patrick signed a transportation reform bill that created the Massachusetts Department of Transportation (MassDOT). Deval wanted O'Meara to serve as Executive Director for the Massachusetts Turnpike Authority during the transition while it and the Tobin Bridge were folded into MassDOT.

"I was supposed to be there for six weeks. I was there close to six months. But it was one of the saddest times in my career. The Massachusetts Turnpike Authority was like Massport, an independent, vibrant, and proud authority. We had a lot in common, and I knew the Turnpike people quite well. I walked in and I see people afraid to make any kind of a decision. I mean, they made an announcement that they were going to lay off more than 400 people. But they didn't do it right away. So people were frozen. It was an agency taken over by the politicians. And because it was the remainder of the Big Dig days, the money and the bonds and all of it were being drained, so no money was being spent on the turnpike. Projects were behind, and maintenance was being skipped. People felt like second-class citizens."

O'Meara recalls talking with then-Massachusetts Transportation Assistant Secretary Jeff Mulan about the entire situation.

"I told him, 'Jeff, this is not a merger. This is a hostile takeover.' And he got very angry with me. It was clear from the outset that everything needed to be merged together, but whatever we put on the table that was not part of the highway department was immediately dismissed. It was discouraging and disheartening. I can remember Jeff saying to me, 'Mary Jane, we're going to be taking the bridge. So we really need to figure out what you're going to be doing.' I said, 'With all due respect, Mr. Secretary, I'm not coming to work over here.'"

Going Against the Governor

Just when she thought things couldn't get tougher, they did. But O'Meara had her limits.

"Bernard Cohen, who was now the Transportation Secretary, asked me to fire Mike Lewis, who was one of the best managers they had working on the Big Dig. And that was it. I said I wouldn't do it. And Bernie Cohen said to me, 'You are refusing an order from the Governor?' I said, 'I was asked to come over here while they are looking for an Executive Director. I am a placeholder. I'm not firing Mike Lewis. I will not fire him.' I knew that if they fired him he would lose his pension. I also knew that if we dissolved his job instead that he could then get a full pension.

"They hounded me for a week. But I really stuck to it. Finally Secretary Cohen said, 'Okay, you can just dissolve his position.' So I called Mike. But Mike already knew because I had told Mike what they were up to. I didn't want the guy to get blindsided, because I just had too much respect for him. I knew the job he had done. So I was able to just eliminate his position, so that he didn't lose his pension. I went against the Governor's office, but I didn't care. You have to stick to your principles, and what they were asking me to do was wrong."

Protecting Her People

O'Meara left the turnpike authority and went to Massport, where she continued to look after her people as the merger and transition continued. It was a very painful time. But her greatest concern was her people.

"Most of the people on the bridge were very senior and were covered by the collective bargaining agreement. They were all taken care of. But I was worried about my administrative staff. At the time Tom Kinton was the Executive Director at Massport. I went to Tom and said, 'They need to have jobs, and they need to be comparable.' He was such a great Executive Director that between him and me and the Human Resources Director, as jobs became available, we found them positions."

O'Meara refers to this time as the toughest part of her career. But she kept up appearances, and for good reason.

"I still had to be upbeat every day. If I went back to work and I was a little bit down about what was going on, my whole staff would fall apart. So I tried to be as upbeat as possible, positive about the new positions that they were probably going to get at Massport."

When One Bridge Closes, Another Door Opens

She worked at Massport for about a year after the bridge transferred to MassDOT. But it wasn't the same.

"I was bored. I was used to running operations! Working on special projects here and there was just not doing it for me. I knew I wasn't quite ready to retire, so I put out some feelers about consulting work and I got a few offers. HNTB made me the best offer. I had worked with them over the years and I really liked the people that worked at that company very much."

Today, O'Meara serves as an Associate Vice President in HNTB's National Toll Group.

The Toll Road to Success

O'Meara never expected to spend most of her career running a bridge. But she believes that no matter what you do, there are certain things integral to success.

"Respect and listening. Listen and don't be afraid to ask questions. Don't ever be afraid to ask for what you want. People may say no, but they will remember that you asked and that you were interested in moving and growing in a new direction. And you don't have to like everybody you work with, but you have to respect each other."

O'Meara also credits much of her success to her family. Married for 31 years, she makes sure that family time is sacrosanct.

"I always carve time out for family. My family is very important to me, from my mother to my sisters to my own children. I make sure we have certain times together. I host Thanksgiving. I host Christmas Eve. I host a big Fourth of July party with all of our family and friends. You have to stay connected to your family because that's your roots. That's who you are. And every Friday night is date night, even if it means buying a pizza and staying home."

There Was Nobody Around When I Started

When O'Meara became a transportation professional, she couldn't help notice that she was often the only woman in the room, with one notable exception.

"WTS has meant so much to me because it's more than just your career and meeting people. It's about friendship. You don't have other professional organizations with members that care that much about the people. If I get a phone call and the caller ID says 'WTS,' they get a call back first. That is so comforting when you are in a career where there aren't that many women that do what you do, like run a toll bridge."

But WTS is not the only organization O'Meara praises. She also considers the IBTTA fundamental to her success. But her introduction to IBTTA was slightly different than WTS.

"The first IBTTA meeting I went to was when I was Operations Manager of the Tobin Bridge. When I got off the elevator at the hotel, I went to the registration desk and two gentlemen looked at me and said, 'Oh, are the spouse cards up already?' They automatically assumed I was a spouse for some man at the conference. I responded simply that I understood there was a hospitality suite right around the corner where they could inquire. When I entered the room I realized why they had made that assumption. The room was filled with nearly 200 men—but the only other woman I saw was a staff person. Later in the evening I met those two gentlemen from the elevator again and they apologized. But there weren't very many women in IBTTA back then. Today it is a much different story."

But IBTTA was a profound learning experience for her. She later became President of IBTTA, giving her international experience and exposure, as well as serving as a role model for women in tolling.

Last Word on the Bridge

O'Meara kept a notebook of her favorite stories from her time on the Tobin Bridge. Some of them are off color. All of them are interesting.

"Clint Eastwood used the Tobin Bridge in the opening scene to his movie *Mystic River*. So one day the door opens and there's Clint Eastwood! And I say the stupidest thing ever because I was so nervous. I held out my hand and said, 'You must be Clint Eastwood.' He looked at me with those twinkly eyes and he goes, 'You must be Mary Jane. . . .' He was very gracious. And I said to my husband that night, 'Greg, I've never thought of cheating on you. I never would *think* of cheating on you, but today Clint Eastwood could have had me.' And he wasn't the only star we had visit us. And we never even talked about the animals we saw on the bridge, or the runner, or some of the *really* strange stuff. But that's another story for another day. . . ."

Chapter 9

LILLIAN BORRONE

The first major trip that I took after I became Port Director was to Europe. None of the people I met with expected a woman to be the Port Director. And there were some people that made it very clear that they didn't think very much of my role. They wondered how I got the job is the best way to put it. But after having interacted with me, where I would ask questions or they would ask questions, and I would be able to answer them, they realized that I was just as professional as they were about our business. After that we all got along pretty well.

Lillian Borrone possesses a rare sophistication. She is as elegant, comfortable, and effective in the boardroom as she is on a container dock. But her transportation career had a humble beginning. She started as a transportation technician in the Washington, DC, Council of Governments. Wanting advancement, she shifted to UMTA's Technical Assistance Group. There she gained national exposure by visiting mass transit systems across the United States.

Next she returned to her native New Jersey and started work at the Port Authority of New York and New Jersey (PANY/NJ) as the Federal Coordinator dealing with federal grants. But she also gained important experience in other areas, including legislative analysis, planning, and facilities. She stayed at the PANY/NJ until 1978, when she returned to the USDOT in the UMTA as an Associate Administrator and then Deputy Administrator. Then in 1981, the PANY/NJ wanted her back.

After meeting her demand for equal pay—a revolutionary act at the time—the PANY/NJ named her Assistant Director for Business and Economic Development in the Aviation Department. She would stay at the PANY/NJ for nearly 20 years, rising to serve as Director of Port Commerce and then Assistant Executive Director. She is credited with transforming the port into one of the busiest in the world. In 2003 she joined the architecture and engineering firm STV as a board member, where she continues to serve today.

For many that would be more than enough of a career, but not for Borrone. As a staff member reporting to Lou Gambaccini, she helped found APTA. She was a member of the Transportation Research Board for more than 30 years (1978–2009), and in 1995 was elected as its first female Chair. In 2001, President George W. Bush appointed her as a member of the US Commission on Ocean Policy, where she served for three years. She was appointed to the US Merchant Marine Academy Board of Advisors in 2002, and served as its Chair from 2005 to 2007. A member of the Eno Center for Transportation since 1992, she was elected Chair in 2005 and continues in that position today.

She holds a bachelor's degree in political science from American University and a master's degree in civil engineering and transportation management from Manhattan College.

This is her story.

Three Credits Shy

Borrone, then Cerza, was about to graduate college. But there was a problem.

"Three credits didn't transfer from an earlier university I attended. So that final semester I had to work full time to pay for my education, housing, and everything else. I went to work for the Washington Council of Governments (WCG)."

It was 1968. And Borrone was tasked with processing data for the planning of the Washington Metro.

"I was working for Trudy Muranyi, who was a great individual to work with and a true role model. Her husband was a staff member at USDOT. I graduated and stayed for another year. But I realized that I couldn't really progress because I didn't have an engineering, planning, or mathematics degree. So I started looking for another role."

She landed a job at USDOT. There she would soon discover her passion for transportation. She would also discover that all things were not equal.

"Sorry, This Is a Male-Only Club"

Borrone was not the only woman in management in her group at USDOT; there was *one* other. Still she describes the work atmosphere as congenial. And then she went to St. Louis.

"It was 1969. And the people I had been working with had planned a major dinner to welcome the UMTA administrator and his senior team who were with us. We all went to dinner. We were on the steps of the building and they said, 'Lillian, we made a horrible mistake. This is a male-only club. You can't dine with us tonight. So what do you want to do?'

"And I said, 'Look, I don't want to disrupt what I know is an important evening. But what I want in return is for someone to take me to see the Anheuser Busch Clydesdale horses.' They all had their dinner and I went to see the Clydesdales. The next morning we all flew back to Washington. They hoped I wasn't too upset.

"Back in the office the next day, my boss had asked the head of the Civil Rights Office to speak with me. He asked me what I wanted to do. I told him I didn't want to make a big fuss, but someone has to make it clear that this is not acceptable. And they did that."

Subsequently, the USDOT set policy that officials were not permitted to attend or conduct business in exclusive clubs.

But the incident had an impact on her.

"I was shocked and disappointed. I was shocked because it never dawned on me that I would be in a situation where I couldn't go somewhere. I was disappointed because I had worked really hard with these St. Louis officials to achieve an agreement, which is what we were ready to seal. And I don't think it dawned on them what they were doing until we got there. But they were very concerned I was going to make a big stink. I didn't, though, because I was afraid I would lose my job. I was 24 years old!"

First Port of Call

Engaged, Borrone returned to the New York City area. Through connections at UMTA, she arranged interviews at the New York Metropolitan Transportation Authority and the PANY/NJ. She chose the PANY/NJ because she felt it offered greater opportunity.

"They're both great organizations, and I would have gladly worked at either. But I became the Federal Coordinator for the Port. I dealt with all of the federal grants for the PATH System (the Port Authority Trans-Hudson line, a rapid transit railroad serving northern New Jersey and lower and midtown Manhattan)."

More importantly, she worked for Rail Director Lou Gambaccini. He and his Deputy Director, Jack Hoban, would both became her mentors. Jack Hoban also provided support for advancement. He had Borrone help write a grant application for Manhattan College to establish a master's program in civil engineering and transportation management. The college won the grant and Jack encouraged her to apply. She did and earned a master's degree in civil engineering and transportation management.

Longing for Operations

Gambaccini believed in Borrone. But he had another belief that presented a conundrum.

"At that time, Lou didn't think women belonged in operations. So he's supporting me in the Port Authority organizational structure. He's pushing me very effectively to be involved in the internal Port Authority Advisory Group, which I chaired. He's encouraging me to do a number of other things that gave me a broad look at the workings of the organization. But while he was doing all of that, he was not expecting me to want to get into operations.

"When an opportunity came up in the Terminals Department, I went for it. I became the Special Assistant to the Director of the

Terminals Department. Jack Rosen, the Director, was another one of my advisors. And we had the understanding that after six months in that role he would rotate me and other managers through the facility operations. And he did. He gave me the first opportunity as a woman in the Port Authority to run a facility, and the first one was the truck terminal."

She took to operations like a natural. After the truck terminal, she ran operations at PANY/NJ bus facilities. She was about to take over the Port Authority's largest bus station, the Port Authority Bus Terminal, when she became the Acting General Manager of Operations. She credits Rosen with providing more than just opportunity.

"Jack challenged all of his staff—not just me—to be creative about something every day. Think about a new idea. Think about a new way of doing something. And I really always try to do that, to link things that are somehow different and see if I can figure out a new way of thinking about something or doing something."

Without question, her relationships with Rosen and Gambaccini were invaluable. But how did they start?

"Once they saw I was committed to doing things well, they started giving me the opportunity to serve on committees and do some things that were a little outside the norm of work. And I began to see Lou's influence around the industry and within the Port Authority. So I put in a little extra. The more I did, the more he was going to use me to do the things that were interesting or different."

But as they often do in transportation, things changed.

Equal Pay at the Port

In 1978, Borrone left the PANY/NJ and returned to UMTA. She spent more than two years at UMTA as Associate Administrator and Deputy Administrator, and two years in the private sector as a lobbyist. Then the Port Authority called. But she had an issue.

"When I left the Port Authority I was in a very high-level position, but I wasn't being paid at the same salary level as others with the same title. I said I would take the role, an assistant directorship in aviation, but I wanted to be paid at the same level."

They agreed. And in 1982, Borrone joined the Aviation Department as the Assistant Director for Business and Economic Development *with equal pay*.

"We were working on the development of the three airports. We were also realizing that there were problems with the Port Authority financial structure. We would have long-term budget projections for investments, but we weren't delivering on those investments. So Aviation Director Bob Aaronson and I were agitating with the Executive Director, Peter Goldmark, and others and looking at other departments and seeing similar things. Finally, Peter Goldmark reviewed the whole structure of the authority and set up a new financial structure, including the creation of a department called Management and Budget."

Then Goldmark called her into his office and asked her to become the new Director of Management and Budget. Though honored, Borrone wanted to stay in Aviation to be positioned to one day become its Director. Strategic thinking won the day.

"I thought to myself, 'If I say no to the Executive Director when he offers me this job, what makes you think he'll ever offer you the other one.' So I said, 'Yes.'"

But Borrone lacked deep finance knowledge.

"My background was not in finance, but I had great a financial staff and internal consulting team. It was a very good team. And I learned a lot very quickly.

After her crash course in finance, she helped revamp the Port's budgeting and long-range capital planning processes. This would soon lead to another unexpected opportunity.

"I Need a Port Director"

Borrone was an effective Management and Budget Director. She even did a stint as acting Chief Financial Officer. Then, one day in 1988, everything changed when PANY/NJ Executive Director Steve Berger approached her.

"He said, 'I need a new Director of Port Commerce. We have a search under way, but we haven't found anybody we like. We'd like you to take this job.' I didn't apply for it. I had never thought about it before. I was still thinking I would go for Aviation. We had just completed a board-staff retreat and it was coming up on Memorial Day Weekend. So I said, 'I really want to talk it over with the current Director of Port Commerce, Jim Kirk (who was leaving for health reasons).'"

Borrone harbored real concerns about gaining acceptance by the International Longshoreman's Association (ILA) and the shipping/carrier community. She was also intimidated by "significant problems" with labor. But she held greater concerns about the port itself.

"We were getting killed. Volume was declining significantly because of the shift in production to Asia; cargo was going to West Coast ports. And we still had the reputation of being corrupt and union/mob controlled, of being the *On the Waterfront* port. And we were a very high cost port."

Finally, Kirk helped her see the light.

"On Memorial Day Monday, he said, 'Lillian, you're making more out of this than is necessary. You can do the job. And if nothing improves, nothing will get blamed on you because it was going down before you got the job.' So my husband and I were in agreement that that made sense."

She took the job, but the job took its toll. Already on "rocky territory," her marriage ended because of the "time, effort, and commitment" it took to succeed in her new role.

Building Consensus on the Waterfront

The challenge was monumental. But Borrone brought something unusual to the table—herself.

"I knew the head of the New York Shipping Association, Tony Tozzoli, but I had not met the new President of the ILA, John Bowers. I felt we needed a campaign to introduce me and to show that we were going to work together. So we did a media campaign in the *Journal of Commerce* and a couple of other publications with the three of us as partners."

The campaign proved to be problematic, as it incorrectly portrayed the ILA as favoring the port over other East Coast ports. But the benefits were stark. Borrone launched a new era of cooperation and profitability at the port. However, the industry—especially the ILA members—had doubts.

"People didn't understand the Port Authority's role. But we published a magazine called *ViaPort*. So I said, 'Why don't we use *ViaPort* to communicate?' To do that, though, we had to get labor to allow us to talk to their people. I figured, well, if I had a relationship with John Bowers and the labor leadership, they would say okay. So I started working that relationship with John. I had lunch with him. I talked about the fact that we were not enemies and that I really believed that we could do some positive things for the port. And he liked it. He was new to his role as well. So he said, 'Yeah, let's try it.' So that's what we did. I didn't understand why we were fighting. We were not enemies. We really had common interests."

This was revolutionary. And it worked. Borrone invited all sides to the table to work through a host of issues and gain understanding of each side's perspective. It was a bold move, particularly for an outsider. But Borrone didn't stop there.

"I was trying to show that we appreciated them, that we recognized that they were working hard, things were changing, and that they were having problems with the changes, too. One of the things that helped us was that we had a common issue, the dioxin issue. Dioxin is a toxic contaminant dispersed by dredging. We had to work together and figure out how to solve the dilemma the feds were hurling at us by restricting the amount of dioxin that would be allowed in sediment disposed in the ocean from dredging activity."

It took Borrone about nine months to feel comfortable at the job. Most importantly, Borrone knew how to apply her strengths and compensate for her weaknesses.

"These weren't all my ideas. They were the accumulation of great ideas from the staff and from people outside who told us what we really needed. I always felt that if you see a good idea someplace and you can adapt it, why not? My strength is that I can see big-picture things in relationship to other things. I also am pretty good at lots of follow up. I can knit things together. I can knit people together to make things happen. So we started by building relationships on the dioxin issue. We built relationships on the channel-deepening issue. We built relationships on the rail intermodal program issues. They were all areas I wanted to make sure we were invested in because I saw that they were going to be critical factors for us."

Taking the Show on the Road

Borrone won over her critics at home. But could she transfer the magic abroad?

"I used to go to Europe and Asia every year to meet with the shippers and carriers and anyone we were doing business with. In the beginning it was all complaints. Toward the middle and the end, it became, 'Here are some new ideas. Here are some good things you're doing. And here is where we still have some issues or problems.'"

But the trip held additional importance. Port Commerce Assistant Director Frank Caggiano believed correctly that production was shifting to Southeast Asia, something very important for the port's economic future.

"We were looking to convince at least one carrier to go through the Suez Canal, and that was a radical notion. We had invested in an origin-destination study, had done modeling, and had figured out what number of vessels it would take at which port of calls to service us in a faster rotation than coming through the Panama Canal. And we convinced Neptune Orient Line to start that service. That was in the early 1990s, and it was really groundbreaking."

It made the Port of New York. But Borrone's prescience did not stop at port relationships and logistics.

Built by Associations

Borrone networks well. And she believes industry associations serve a very important purpose in that regard, particularly for young professionals.

"It's important to be involved, but not only because it gives you visibility. It also gives you the opportunity to meet people in your arena, to learn skills, to influence the industry, and to give you the chance to do things you would not normally do."

But there are other avenues for advancement.

"Every step of the way I've met wonderful people. They've had influence on me. I've had influence on them. We've referred each other for different roles and activities. People look at me and think, 'How do you know all of these people? You know everybody in the world!' Well, I don't know everybody in the world, but I do know a lot of people from the opportunities I've engaged in throughout my career."

Relatively Shy

It would be easy to assume that Borrone is brash. Nothing could be further from the truth. But there is something that brings her out of her shell.

"Passion is very important. You have to really like what you're doing. You would never know from listening to me go on at the mouth, but I'm a relatively shy person. So I had to challenge myself every step of the way. Some of these organizational activities, like WTS, were a way to challenge myself. I'm also pretty optimistic. Maybe I'm overly optimistic. But I always think there's a way you can figure out how to achieve something."

But careers like hers can take their toll.

"People talk about having it all. You can have it all, but you can't have it all at once. You have to make choices. My husband and I weren't fortunate enough, in my first marriage, to have children. But I have stepchildren now, and I'm fortunate in that regard. I also know that having a high-powered career can put a lot of stress on you, and I suffered healthwise for it. But I also realized I could do things to mitigate the stress. And that's helpful. If you have a partner, if you can be open with one another about what your commitments and expectations are for each other and to each other, that's the important thing."

Lessons Earned

People make mistakes, even in successful careers like Borrone's. Borrone views mistakes as learning opportunities.

"Early in my career, Lou Gambaccini made me a Special Assistant. I had a particular model in mind of what the role should be, and I moved too fast to try to achieve that model. So I got rotated back into a Special Assistant's position that was for projects rather than for management. Of course later in my career I would have handled it much differently. I would have taken the time to sit down with everyone and see what they thought, talk with them about what I was thinking, and see how I could take steps to integrate their thinking in a more effective way."

She recalls another learning opportunity about relationships.

"CEO and Chairman Lew Glucksman of Lehman Brothers, a Port Authority board member, asked me a question at a board meeting once and I didn't understand what he was asking. But I answered anyway and my answer wasn't appropriately responsive to the question. That was a mistake. Subsequently I educated myself on the issues, and I tried to learn from that and not provide an answer without understanding the question."

Counsel to Those on the Rise

There are no secrets to success. But there are strategies that only successful professionals can impart.

"Young people should look at the big picture, not just their technical skills. Focus on communication skills, knowledge of the larger world, and how their technical capabilities fit within that larger setting. Next, don't limit yourself. If you want to take a chance on something, consider the risks, but you can take risks as long as you've thought them through. Take risks and look at the bigger picture.

"If you feel like you're stuck or trapped or you're not making the kind of progress you want, think about a shift into a parallel field. Sometimes just moving into discussions in that field are enough, because they can give you a different perspective. Additionally, if you haven't taken advantage of training programs or industry activities where you can show off your skills or enhance your skills, think about those things, too. I just took a course yesterday, and I'm taking one on Monday. You always have to continue to enhance your knowledge."

Port Royalty

When Lillian Borrone took over as Director of Port Commerce, the port had been steadily losing ground to other ports. Today it is one of the busiest ports in the world. And her influence extends well beyond its boundaries. Lillian Borrone is an exemplary professional who has helped change the world of transportation through her own smarts and fortitude.

Chapter 10

ELIZABETH (LIZ) LEVIN

When I started at M&E, women did not accompany men on business trips. I was the first. One of the men said, "I could never go with some-one like you on a business trip." I said, "Why not?" He said, "My wife wouldn't let me go." I just looked at him and thought, "Does that mean I should sit at home? Maybe you should sit home." But most people at the management level were glad to have the talent that I provided, as I could do things that other people couldn't do.

Liz Levin made success look easy. But she achieved success through hard work, determination, and fearlessness. After grad-uating from Wellesley College in 1967, she began her career in the US Department of Housing and Urban Development in New York City. Continuing in housing and urban development, she left New York for the District of Columbia Redevelopment Land Agency. When she married in 1970, she joined the Massachusetts Department of Community Affairs in Boston. Then she turned to the private sector.

In 1972, Levin joined Metcalf & Eddy (M&E) as a planner. She was not an engineer, but she provided expertise that others did not have. Levin climbed the ladder quickly, becoming M&E's

youngest project manager. Subsequently she became the manager of M&E's Environmental Planning Group. But Levin kept busy outside of work as well. She had two children and earned two master's degrees.

Levin stayed at M&E for 13 years. In 1985 she joined former M&E colleague Bill Rizzo in his start-up firm Rizzo Associates. Sharing the firm's philosophy, she helped build a vibrant business, serving as a Senior Vice President, Principal, and on the Rizzo Associates Board of Directors. After the sale of the firm to TetraTech, Levin left and formed Liz Levin & Company, a management consulting company serving transportation, design, and environmental companies. She also joined the Board of Directors of Normandeau Associates.

Levin is an ardent supporter of public service, particularly through professional associations and boards. She has served on the boards of MassDOT and the MBTA. She chaired the Massachusetts Government Appointments Project, the Greater Boston Chamber of Commerce Women's Network, and the Environmental Business Council of New England. Levin also served as WTS International President and Chair of the WTS International Advisory Board.

Levin has been recognized by many organizations for her contributions to transportation and the advancement of women. They include the Golden Shoe Award from WalkBoston, the Pinnacle Award from the Greater Boston Chamber of Commerce, the WTS International Member of the Year Award, and the Phyllis Rappaport Alumnae Achievement Award from Simmons School of Management.

Liz Levin advocated for women in transportation by living her beliefs in her work.

This is her story.

Growing Up Fast

Levin learned life lessons at a very young age.

"When I was six, my dad, an entertainment lawyer, died of leukemia. My mom, also a lawyer, went to work in his Los Angeles law firm. But she had three little children to raise. From that early age I understood that life changes quickly and that you really need to be prepared. It was a time of stay-at-home moms. However, I knew I would be a working mom. I understood how important it was for the family."

The question centered now on what kind of work she would do.

"When I was a senior at Wellesley, I realized that I liked cities and government. I thought of government as a source of good jobs and work that matters."

My Miniskirts Were Too Short

Levin's first three jobs were in housing and urban development.

"I liked working in all of these places because the goal meant something: creating jobs, housing, and transportation for people and communities. Government was a pretty good place for women. There was opportunity for advancement, and there were at least *some* professional women."

Still, she did experience typical issues for the period.

"The Regional Head of the Housing and Urban Development office in New York told me my miniskirts were too short. I questioned him as to why he objected, since most of the other young women also wore skirts just like mine. He told me that I was a professional, and that he found it distracting. So, I made a deal with him. I would stay off of his floor so he didn't have to look. I never went on his floor again."

But in another instance, bias worked in her favor.

"I was looking for a job in Boston. A contact called and said a job was available at the Massachusetts Department of Community Affairs (DCA) in the Sargent Administration. I was hired immediately. I learned later that they had previously fired a Jewish woman, so they acted very quickly to hire another one."

Definitely Not for Me

Of the three government jobs she had, Levin liked DCA best.

"I had a really great leader, Deputy Commissioner Bill Richardson, a military hero. He had a very high-profile project—the Park Plaza Project. It was a mixed-use, mega-development adjacent to the historic Boston Common. Ed Linde and Mort Zuckerman, powerful developers, proposed it. Boston Mayor White supported it, as did the unions. There was intense pressure to approve the project.

The stakes were high. Levin would learn about the darker side of government.

"We showed that the project should be rejected for several reasons, including that the area was not blighted—a legal requirement for urban renewal and weak financial feasibility. Bill convinced the new Commissioner, Miles Mahoney, that the project should be rejected. The Commissioner turned it down with Governor Sargent's support. Subsequently, the developers resubmitted the project with some changes and purportedly with the Governor's okay. Commissioner Mahoney turned it down again and then resigned. The Governor overruled the Commissioner's decision. Later Bill Richardson was squeezed out of his job. Interestingly, the Park Plaza Project was never built."

The experience affected Levin greatly. She faced a crossroads about her future.

"I saw many state workers with their heads down, afraid to make waves in any way for fear of losing their jobs. 'Heads down' was definitely not for me. So I took a job in the private sector with M&E (now part of AECOM)."

It was an important move. Levin would also flourish in the private sector.

The Benefits of Not Being an Engineer

At first, M&E didn't seem like a good fit. Her first boss treated her like an engineer, which she was not. She decided to give it a year. Pretty soon a new supervisor, Richard Ball, changed her experience.

"He gave me the chance to work on really fascinating large planning projects. He recognized that my skills were different from an engineer's and that made me valuable. I liked to work with regulators and technical people. I could figure out the facts of complicated projects and share them in a straightforward manner. I liked writing and speaking, which many engineers did not. I understood newer environmental issues. I also was very direct and honest, so when I interacted with community people they found it refreshing."

Though unconventional in the engineering world, Levin fit in perfectly.

"I was nonthreatening to the guys, except that they found my high energy and enthusiasm very different. But I appeared acceptable as a woman professional, because I did the work well, was married, and was personable. So they were very happy to work with me."

Advancing Through the Ranks

Levin advanced quickly. She was the youngest project manager. But she had a secret to success.

"I had a willingness to do what others did not want to do. So I was extremely helpful. For example, M&E had a large contract with the Boston Water and Sewer Commission for a 10-year wastewater capital improvement program. The contract was over budget. The client wasn't happy about the cost or the work. The engineers didn't want to touch the job. So I was asked to take it over. That was very unusual for a woman who was not an engineer. They asked me because (1) they were desperate, and (2) the client manager was a woman, Libby Blank, and she scared the guys."

Levin didn't blink.

"I still remember my weekly meetings with Libby. I learned to let her vent for 15 minutes, and then we would solve the problem. We cleaned up the mess and I earned a lot of respect in the company. I was assigned more of the problem jobs. Taking those jobs got me a lot of attention. And I got to work with all of the upper-level people in the organization, because they wanted to get those jobs back on track."

Her ability to excel where others dared not tread became a hallmark of her success.

Two Babies and . . .

In addition to work, Levin always intended on having a family.

"When I was at M&E, I had two babies and got two master's degrees. With my first child, I worked up until three days *after* my due date. The people at M&E were very nervous. Finally someone said, 'Would you do us a favor and not come to work?' They had never had a professional woman work through her pregnancy. At the end of my pregnancy I ended up doing crappy little jobs because they didn't want to assign me anything too long-term.

"By the time I had my second child, a law had been passed for paid sick time that covered pregnancy. So I asked them about getting paid for 10 days of sick leave. I put my request in writing, but heard nothing. For me it was an issue of principle rather than the money. After a year, I wrote them a note, 'My child is a year old and that's enough time to decide whether I am eligible under the law for 10 days of sick leave. Please let me know in writing.' The next thing I know I received a check. They never wrote me a letter, but they wrote me a check."

. . . Two Master's Degrees

In addition to having children, Levin pursued her education.

"I received a master's of urban affairs, which gave me credentials as a planner, and a master's of business administration. I wanted the MBA because I knew that understanding both the technical work and the financial end would put me in a pretty powerful place in the organization."

Levin's MBA was unique. She attended an all-women's, feminist business school.

"It was the Simmons School of Management, led by Anne Jardim and Margaret Hennig. This education was wonderfully exciting. We had case studies that actually had women in them! We had mostly women professors, and we had vigorous all-women discussions. It was just so refreshing in contrast to the all-male culture at M&E. I graduated Simmons with highest honors. I was proud of that, because I couldn't dedicate the same kind of time a lot of the women could. I considered Simmons a life-changing experience. It formed the core of my belief and activism for women's leadership."

Working while going to school was not easy. But Levin was shrewd about it.

"I was pretty clever at not calling too much attention when I went to school. My school was usually at night, but there were times when I had classes during the day. So I just left my sweater on my chair and the light on so it looked like I was there! I focused on doing the M&E work well and people really couldn't complain. My mother and my mother-in-law thought I was crazy to go to school at night and work, while having young children, but I knew I could do it."

Leaving Metcalf & Eddy and Joining Rizzo Associates

At 39, Levin had been with M&E for 13 years. She realized it was time to leave.

"I looked at the older white guys leading the company. They were really lovely people, the work was interesting, and I was certainly on track for the upper levels of management, but I knew I didn't want to be there in 10 years. I went to a former boss of mine, Bill Rizzo, for advice. A few years earlier, Bill had started Rizzo Associates, which was an entrepreneurial environmental, transportation, and engineering firm. He asked that I join him."

On paper, Rizzo Associates was not a perfect fit.

"Rizzo Associates was a startup with around 10 people. It did mostly hazardous waste work, which I didn't do. It did mostly private sector work, which I didn't do. But I said yes. In fact, I didn't hesitate. I totally believed in creating a multidisciplinary company with science, planning, and engineering that approached projects in a more holistic way. I *loved* that. I also was eager to create a corporate culture based on strong values. It turned out to be a great choice for me."

Building the Business. Living the Culture.

Growing a business appealed to Levin on many levels.

"We grew our hazardous waste and environmental business, developed a civil engineering group, added senior talent, and built the transportation group from scratch. We also bought a transportation firm and hired a lot of really good people. We took a lot of risks, and we picked ourselves up when we failed. We also became an employee stock ownership company, so that employees could share in the profits. We believed their engagement mattered."

Levin praises Rizzo Associates for many reasons, but she cites one element as a differentiator. "What distinguished us was our great corporate culture. It emphasized integrity, honesty, openness, and treating people fairly with respect, whether they were an employee, a client, a regulator, a community advocate, or a colleague in the industry. We really lived the culture."

It was so open, in fact, the firm did something most firms never do.

"We posted our financials monthly on a bulletin board. Employees and anyone visiting could see our financials. We were open about salary information. We had very family-friendly policies. We had a lot of trust with our clients, regulators, and the public, because we shared both the good and the bad. We became very successful, but we kept our adventurous, entrepreneurial spirit."

Levin served in many capacities at Rizzo, including Senior Vice President, Chief Marketing Officer, Transportation Group Leader, Principal, and on the Rizzo Associates Board of Directors.

Joining with Other Women

While at Rizzo Associates, Levin became active in the broader women's community.

"We couldn't just rely on men for our success. We needed relationships with women. So Robin Ellis, who was at MassPort, and I brought some senior public and private industry women together for a party at my home. We became the Women's Environmental Network. We opened the group up to any woman in the environmental business. We had no officers, no dues, and no agenda. We just threw a party every several months. All we wanted to do was to build relationships and have some fun. And that's exactly what we did, forming many lasting relationships."

But Levin didn't stop there. At the invitation of Ann Hershfang, a member of the Massachusetts Turnpike Board, Levin joined the

WTS Boston chapter, where she found many kindred spirits—so much so that she would later serve as WTS International President from 1998 to 2000.

"Serving WTS was a real gift. I was amazed at the leadership. Often without resources or support, I saw the ladies use their hope, imagination, and persistence to run these outstanding transportation programs. I saw them developing their leadership skills and becoming local and national leaders. Many of the women changed the industry, going from infrastructure builders to community builders, because they cared about community. I saw this collective power of women creating their own opportunities."

WTS became an integral part of Levin's professional and personal life. It was the perfect complement to her work at Rizzo. But things at Rizzo would soon change.

Endings Can Be Difficult

Rizzo Associates was transformative for Levin. But its ending was tough.

"In 1999, Bill announced that he wanted to step down as President. We had a transition plan where the three senior leaders—Sam Park, Rick Moore, and I—would be part of a new leadership team. We also understood that if we couldn't agree, we would sell the business. We ended up in a stalemate over who would be the next President. Sam and Rick both wanted the job. I didn't throw my hat in the ring; we did not need three people vying for President.

"We could not agree. So in May 2000, we sold the business to TetraTech for a substantial price. Sam left. Bill stayed as President. At Bill's request I stayed. In 2001, Bill stepped down. Rick succeeded him and made it clear there would be no role for me. I asked Bill for—and received—a generous severance package."

Next Step

It was time to reassess.

"I took a year off. It was the first time since I started work at 21 that I hadn't been on some kind of a fast track. I used the year for reflection. I decided that my next career step would be something that allowed for more creativity and flexibility, but kept me in touch with the profession and the people I liked so much. After soul searching, I figured out that I really loved to help organizations fulfill their promise. So I started a management consulting firm, Liz Levin & Company, to do just that."

Levin provides services in strategy, organization, and leadership for environmental, transportation, and design clients.

"I work with companies at critical stages in their businesses— repositioning the business, developing new leaders, diversifying markets, and managing succession. I also joined the Board of Directors of Normandeau Associates, a national environmental science firm led by Pam Hall. Both in my consulting practice and in my role on Normandeau's board I feel like an invited guest to a family event who has the good fortune to help at a critical time and make a lasting impact."

MassGAP and Binders Full of Women

Levin found her time after Rizzo Associates to be wonderfully creative and fulfilling.

"A highlight of that period was the Massachusetts Government Appointments Project, or MassGAP. In 2002, the summer before the gubernatorial election, a group of women leaders gathered around my kitchen table. We were tired of doing business with government as it was constituted. The top policy decision makers are usually guys. We envisioned how much more welcoming government would be if there were more women at the top. It would mean better decisions, better access, and a positive impact on our pocketbooks.

"So we founded MassGAP, a coalition of women's groups. Roni Thaler, Executive Director of the Massachusetts Women's Political Caucus (MWPC) served as Executive Director of MassGAP. I served as the Chair. Our project was simple: get commitments from the gubernatorial candidates for a fair share of top positions for women; bring the new administration résumés; and monitor progress."

MassGAP's accomplishments were multifold. But one particular incident would gain national attention.

In 2002 Republican Mitt Romney was elected Massachusetts Governor. Romney designated Lieutenant Governor Kerry Healy as MassGAP liaison.

"We presented résumés of the most qualified women to the Romney Administration in binders. We gave them binders with women's résumés so that they would have no excuse about being unable to find qualified women. Then we monitored progress.

"Healy and the Governor were glad to have MassGAP's résumés. We contributed to many positive results. For example, 42 percent of Romney's early appointments were women, a number of them from MassGAP. We removed the excuse that there weren't enough qualified women and we engaged women statewide in the process."

However, some of its positive effect would be short lived.

"At the end of the Romney Administration the number of women in top positions hadn't really budged from the 30 percent before his administration. In fact, it was slightly lower. It demonstrated the need for constant vigilance."

Levin's efforts would reappear on the national stage.

"During the second presidential debate of 2012, I bolted up in my seat when I heard Mitt Romney say, 'I went to a number of women's groups and said, "Can you help us find folks?" And they brought us whole binders full of women.' I said to my husband, 'That's our project!' I knew the following morning that Mitt Romney and MassGAP had a problem when my grown-up son e-mailed me and said, 'Mom, would you send *me* a binder full of women?'"

The media filled Levin's e-mail box when Romney referenced the project. Though the media focused on the sensational aspects of the project, Levin took solace in the fact that MassGAP brought national attention to the paucity of women in top government positions.

Back to the Roots of Public Service

In November 2009, Governor Deval Patrick appointed Levin to the board of the newly formed MassDOT as well as the MBTA.

"MassDOT was the centerpiece for major transportation reform, for openness, transparency, efficiency, and accountability. MassDOT combined into one transportation agency many separate former agencies. The same board members that served on the MassDOT board also served on the MBTA board. Billions of dollars went through MassDOT and the MBTA annually. So I promised myself that to live up to my oath of serving the Commonwealth, I would live the values of transportation reform and feel comfortable about the matters that I voted on. I also gave up my transportation clients to avoid conflicts."

Levin took her service most seriously. She also loved it.

"It was a fascinating time. I loved that each board member had different talents and perspectives and that we were diverse. We had two women and three men. We were 80 percent women and minorities. Andrew Whittle, a MIT professor, was our sole white male. I liked working with the Secretary of Transportation, Jeff Mullan, and his staff. I liked the people who worked for MassDOT and the MBTA. There was much to do, and tremendous potential."

Though she and most others acted nobly, political realities would take their toll.

Keeping Things above Board

Levin felt most comfortable on the board, and with good reason.

"I knew what the organization needed to do to live its reform values of honesty, openness, and transparency. I was also an advocate for a well-funded and efficient multimodal system that would improve infrastructure for all modes, including walking and biking, and result in better public transportation, roadways, and communities. I understood the importance of sound finances to achieve that."

Levin filled many board leadership roles, including chairing the Compensation and Labor Relations Committee and the General Manager Search Committee (where they recommended in 2012 as one of two final candidates the first African-American woman, Dr. Beverly Scott, for MBTA General Manager). She also served on the Finance and Audit Committee and as Board Secretary. But trouble was brewing.

A Surprise Ending to Board Service

In September 2011, Rich Davey, the General Manager of the MBTA, became Secretary of Transportation. Jon Davis became Acting General Manager of the MBTA.

"The next year was rocky. We had a contentious MBTA fare increase. There were a number of big capital projects. And there were some important commuter rail decisions to be made about a future contract. But it got harder to get information and facts. Secretary Davey was more interested in 'yes' votes than in the deliberative process. When summer 2012 approached, Janice Loux, our most politically astute board member, asked Secretary Davey about proposed legislative changes to the board. The Secretary told us the only significant changes were that the board would be expanded to seven members and that the Secretary would serve as an *ex officio* member. I had no issue about expanding the board. But I thought to myself, 'They developed legislation that affects the board and reform without mentioning the legislation to us or asking for any input!'"

Levin and the board received copies of the legislation *after* it passed.

"In August 2012, Board Chair John Jenkins surprised us all at the end of a meeting by indicating that it was our last board meeting. He told us that under the new legislation there would be new appointments to the board. We would need to reapply for our positions. I realized immediately that I would lose my board seat."

Singled Out

Disappointed, Levin knew why events transpired as they had.

"I received a call from Secretary Davey *one hour before the press announcement of the new board.* He let me know that I was not reappointed. All of my colleagues were reappointed. I was glad for them. But the new board composition was six men and one woman. It was not my idea of a positive, new direction. I was not reappointed because there was no interest in my strong eyes and probing questions. The leadership was particularly nervous about the upcoming procurement of one of the MBTA's largest contracts."

It was a commuter rail contract that was expected to be worth more than $300 million per year for eight or more years.

"The Massachusetts Bay Commuter Rail Company (MBCR), whose representative was Jim O'Leary, was the incumbent company with the existing contract. O'Leary had been an MBTA General Manager. When you deal with someone who used to run the agency that is issuing a contract, it is complicated. It was even more complicated because Secretary Davey had worked for MBCR and for O'Leary as General Manager of the MBCR contract. When Davey joined the state, he disclosed his MBCR relationship and recused himself from all MBCR matters. Evidently, however, the recusal appeared *not* to include recommending which board members would stay on the board when the contract was being considered."

But Levin was mostly concerned about the citizens of the Commonwealth.

"The board understood this commuter rail contract selection would be a watershed decision for reform. The selection process needed to be open, transparent, and fair, and attract robust competition. I thought a place to start was to make sure we all had a good understanding of the current contract performance. So I asked for some basic public, factual, and historic information on the contract. We discussed it briefly in an open Finance and Audit Committee meeting. The information was revealing.

"I asked for an update when the fiscal year 2012 results were available. When FY 2012 ended, I asked again. Finally, I asked that the information be provided for our next Finance and Audit Committee meeting. But the board was officially dissolved in late August, shortly *before* that meeting. The meeting was canceled. Clearly it was not information senior leadership wanted to make available."

The Hardest Part of Leaving MassDOT and the MBTA

For Levin, leaving the board was difficult.

"The hardest part was accepting that we really had not lived our values. And the public and the employees were the losers. From the beginning I proudly carried the message that the board and senior leadership were honest, open, fair, and caring. People may not like every decision, but we were trying our best. When we lost the ability to function on that level, we lost our effectiveness. And that was a real loss for the Commonwealth."

Was it gender bias?

"Not deliberately. However, had just one of the people in the top positions been a woman—the Governor, his Chief of Staff, the Secretary of Transportation, or the Board Chair—the outcome may have been different. First, I don't think I would have been a target. If I were, I would have had far better access, receptivity, and support."

Moving On

"How does one move on? As in the past, I listened to what would move my heart. I concluded that I wanted to spend time with people I care for and work on issues that matter, where I can make a difference. Today I spend more time with my family and friends, particularly my grandchildren. I work with people I like. I'm active on community and transportation issues where I can make a difference. I'm thankful I served the Commonwealth, and that I did move on."

Recipe for Success

After a dynamic, successful career, Levin offers advice.

"We each have our own view of success and our own recipe to get there. In my case family is first—my husband, sons, their families, and my close network of relatives. Working throughout my career was an integral part of keeping the family strong. The paycheck was important, but the work opened up a whole exciting world of experiences. My entire family benefited. For me, advancing women, transportation, and the environment has been important work. In doing that work, I became a leader and an advocate because I needed those skills to succeed. I led from my strengths. I really didn't worry about my many weaknesses. Those strengths include a strong value system, an ability to seize opportunity, serving others, and being persistent. They were my foundation.

"My advice to both women and men is to figure out your own view of success and recipe for it. The more it is yours, the better it will be. If that view is cloudy, determine what's important—both in the workplace and in terms of family. Know your strengths and weaknesses and use your strengths to your advantage. Relish new experiences."

Advancing Women: There Is Work to Do!

Levin worked to advance women. But she recognizes her role as part of a greater movement.

"Since the late 1960s, there certainly has been progress in the advancement of women. However, we just haven't seen the kind of change we had anticipated. Why? I think women from my generation who succeeded were risk takers because they needed to be to survive. We had to keep cracking the glass ceiling. And we broke a lot of glass! We also had to laugh when it hurt. In some ways we took really big risks, but sometimes they weren't so big, because there wasn't much to lose.

"For the next wave of ladies the ceiling has been higher; there are more doors open. But I also think they have been too accepting. Women have been following the guys. They learn and follow the rules made up by the guys, e.g., self-promote, be aggressive, find a sponsor, have a big goal. Some women do get to the top that way, but they are relatively few. They make the changes they can, but are often constrained. They and the women following them in the pipeline often resign themselves to the idea that 'That's just how it is.' Some choose their own business or businesses run by women—often a better choice. Sadly, some just drop out altogether."

Advancing Women: Changing the Soul of Our Organizations

Levin believes devoutly that women have every right to their place at the table. But she thinks that we need to change the table, the meal, and perhaps the place.

"We will not make progress just by working harder and improving ourselves. We've certainly done that. It is not just about more women in top positions and on boards, although that matters enormously. If we want significant progress, we shouldn't just follow the guys and be like them. We need to lead more boldly as change agents. We need to use our gift of women's leadership to change the soul of our organizations.

"For example, we should champion more value-driven organizations where trust, integrity, openness, and transparency guide every decision. We should develop caring organizations where we treat customers, employees, job seekers, colleagues, and vendors as we want to be treated. We treat people in a caring manner in our homes, and we shouldn't accept less in our workplace. Finally, we need to create organizations that welcome new and different ideas. All of these changes are critically important to our future if we're really going to effect more meaningful and permanent change."

Levin believes that collective change starts with the individual.

"Each woman needs to take a piece of the agenda that interests them and engage others. We need to ask for what we know in our hearts is right. We need to lead from whatever seat in the organization we have. There is informal power at all levels. If we wait for fancy titles and formal power, we will always be waiting. It takes more than just women at the top. It takes women at every level moving together to make lasting change. The next decade will be our time, if we seize the opportunity."

That is exactly what Liz Levin has done throughout her career.

Chapter 11

LAVERNE FRANCIS REID

I don't remember exactly the name of the group, but an organization was catering a state aviation luncheon in eastern Tennessee. There were airport managers from throughout the state. I was at the head table and they began to serve lunch. They served everybody except me, and it wasn't because I was the only female. The aeronautical director, a retired Navy officer and Top Gun pilot, was sitting to my right and he was getting very upset. He offered to give me his plate, but I would gently push it right back. And I assured him, "Do you think I'm going to eat the food when I do get it? No." He continued to apologize and he said, "I've seen a lot of things, but this is just too blatant and awful."

A situation like that could have been very discouraging; however, it did not derail me or put me in such a spin that I couldn't function. I like to think that my faith is the foundation that kept and keeps me from being discouraged and enables me to stay centered. The fact that it took place in the mid-1990s—not in the '60s—did surprise me. One would only hope that the country, the agency, and people in general had moved past the racist ideas of the earlier times. By the mid '90s, I had achieved a certain level of success. Then to be confronted with

*such blatant discrimination . . . well . . . it was surprising not only to
me but to my colleague.*

Few people are more resilient than LaVerne Francis Reid. An
African-American woman born in the segregated South of the
1940s, Reid pioneered an uncharted path from the humblest
of beginnings, navigating a series of formidable challenges and
achievements along the way to begin her transportation career
unobtrusively. A recruiter from the FAA approached her when
she was a bank teller. She joined the FAA in Alaska as a realty
clerk in May 1969.

In 1973 Reid passed the air traffic controller exam, becoming
one of the first female African-American air traffic controllers.
While excelling professionally, Reid endured great struggle in
her personal life, including ending an abusive marriage and the
tragic death of her two children. Reid persevered and emerged on
the other side determined to "be an agent of change, rather than
a victim of change." After completing her BS in business administration at the University of Alaska—a quest that she pursued
diligently for 11 years at five institutions—Reid earned an MS in
public administration from the University of Southern California
in June 1980.

In 1981, she left her position with the FAA to return to Alaska,
joining the US Department of Interior's Minerals Management
Service. In 1989, Reid rejoined the FAA in human resources and
then transitioned to become an Airports program analyst, the
position she wanted originally. She advanced within the FAA,
holding many different positions and posting to many different
locations throughout the country. She served in the FAA until
2011, when she retired as the Airports Division Manager for the
New England Region.

Reid participated in several professional organizations during
her career. In 1970, she joined the Business and Professional
Women's Foundation (BPW), an international organization that
supports women through research, scholarships and advocacy,
and helped form the BPW North to the Future chapter in Alaska.
Reid also became BPW's first African-American national President.

In addition, she served on the WTS International Advisory and Foundation Boards and as Chair of the WTS 2011Transportation You DC Summit Steering Committee. In 1989, President George H. W. Bush appointed her to the US Small Business Administration Council.

LaVerne Reid crafted an exceptional transportation career despite great professional and personal hardship.

This is her story.

Separate, but Unequal

LaVerne Reid began her formal education in a segregated elementary school in Texas. An above-average student, Reid did not attend an integrated school until high school. But integration would not be the only fateful event that year.

"I entered San Angelo Central High School in 1963, and it was a major culture shock in so many ways. It was also the same year John F. Kennedy was assassinated *in Texas*. The John F. Kennedy speech where he says, 'Ask not what your country can do for you, but what you can do for your country,' had really resonated with me. So his assassination affected me deeply, and his words have been in my mind throughout my career in federal service."

In 1964, Reid was chosen as a semifinalist in the National Merit Scholarship Program for Outstanding Negro Students, a considerable honor. She received many university scholarship offers. But something would soon interfere with her educational plans.

"I met a young man, Andrew Collins, in my senior year. He was in the Air Force and eight years older than me. We got married two months after my graduation. In 1965, my first son, Andrew Collins, Jr., was born. I was still committed to being a wife, a mother, *and* a career person. But my parents were not happy that I married and started a family so early. They wanted us all to get an education. My father said that if I got married he would not pay for my college education, but he did say said that, 'If you ever graduate, I will be at your graduation.' That was our deal."

Resolute, Reid enrolled at Angelo State Junior College in 1966.

A Very Indirect Route to Transportation

Reid had completed just one semester at Angelo State when her husband was sent to Vietnam. In the interim, Reid's parents had moved from San Angelo to Lubbock. Reid joined them. Her mother babysat while Reid started classes at Texas Tech University, where she completed two semesters.

"I wanted to be an accountant. But I switched my focus to management because I wanted to be around people. In any case, my desire was to have a business degree."

Her husband returned from Vietnam and was reassigned to Lackland Air Force Base in San Antonio. Reid commuted 70 miles each way to college in San Marcos, because it was the least expensive school in the area. Two semesters later, she would relocate again.

"In the summer of '68, Andrew was reassigned to Elmendorf Air Force Base in Anchorage, Alaska. We drove through Canada on the Alcan Highway. We camped out all the way there in a 9-by-9 tent with our 2–year-old. It was an adventure. It was also the first time I had ever been out of Texas."

It would prove to be an important move. Alaska would become her home. And Reid got her first job in Anchorage as a credit union teller earning $400 a month. She would have that job for less than a year.

"A recruiter from the FAA asked me if I would ever consider working for the federal government. He brought me some brochures and asked if I would take some tests, which I did. The first test was for air traffic control. I took it, but didn't have enough work experience for them to rate me. So they encouraged me to update it every three to six months with my education and work experience. I was also encouraged to take another test, called the Junior Federal Assistance Exam. It required less education and provided me an opportunity to become a GS-3, a clerk. A man named Larry Snell hired me for that position."

Mr. Snell would become a very important mentor for Reid.

Gaining Independence

Reid began her federal service career in 1969, as a realty clerk in the FAA's Logistics Division of the Real Estate and Utilities Branch. In 1970, Congress passed the National Environmental Policy Act, establishing a national policy for environmental protection. This would have a huge impact on largely undeveloped Alaska—and Reid's office.

"That office really helped me to develop personally and professionally. Larry encouraged me to continue to take courses at night school. I took classes in real estate and procurement law, classes that helped me on the job and to get my degree. Doris Mintz, who had been in the military and worked for the government, also was a wonderful mentor. So was Wink Avery, who was on the school board. He talked to me about the importance of getting involved in community activities. They all taught me about life skills."

These mentors were critically important, as the biggest challenges Reid faced had little to do with the work itself.

"What was most difficult were my own limitations, my own limited life experiences. I moved from my father's house to a husband's house. I was very dependent on my husband. But I went from dependency to independence, and it was out of necessity that I found independence. The economy of Alaska required two people to work, so I knew I had to work. And I always wanted to work. My education drive was still that chatter in my head of my parents saying, 'Education is the key to move on.' But I also had encouragement in this office, which made a big difference."

Reid responded well. But one particular event stood out.

"Doris Mintz invited me to attend a meeting and become active in the BPW. That would become very important for me. That same year, 1970, I was also notified that I then had enough work experience for the Civil Service to rate my scores for the first time, and that I had received a rating of 97 for my air traffic control exam. Because I was in the 97th percentile, I could go from a GS-3 to a GS-7! I was very excited about that and immediately said, 'Yes, I want to do this!'"

Reid passed several tough panel interviews. Then, she took a required physical and found out some interesting information.

"I was pregnant with my second son. Big decision time: Do I go into air traffic control training in Oklahoma City or not? Eleanor Williams was another major mentor in my life, and she became a lifelong friend. She was the first African-American air traffic controller in the nation. She was in Anchorage and had been a single mother when she was trained. She talked about how stressful it was—the washout rate in air traffic was pretty high for everyone, particularly women. So I decided to wait. I talked with the Civil Service Commission and they said they would suspend my rating if I updated my experience and education."

That's what she did. In September 1970, she gave birth to her second son, Kevin Michael Collins. But her air traffic control career plan would change.

"I went back to work for about three or four months. But I had problems finding childcare, so I resigned from the FAA to stay home with my sons. But in December, Richard Nixon signed into law the Alaskan Natives Claim Settlement Act. That had a major impact on the real estate office where I worked. So between 1971 and 1973, I went back to work with the FAA part-time, because my younger sister would come up from Texas and babysit. I worked as a clerk in the public affairs office and in the civil rights office."

She would not be there long.

Earning a Degree

Things changed again in Alaska. Those changes would affect Reid's career path again, significantly.

"In 1973, the discovery of oil in Prudhoe Bay caused a spike in exploration activity. That created a quick and strong demand for air traffic controllers. After about nine months of training, I became an air traffic controller at the Air Traffic EnRoute Control Center in Anchorage."

A year later, Reid earned her first college diploma, an Associate of Arts degree in political science from Anchorage Community College. But she was having a problem obtaining her bachelor's degree, as several credits did not transfer from Texas. Determined, Reid sought help.

"Larry Snell had copies of my transcripts because it was part of my FAA application. He gave me some advice: 'There are some courses you could take where you could get your degree and also help with your development in this office.' He encouraged me to take real estate law and procurement law, those types of courses. They did apply toward getting my degree and helped me grow professionally."

Four years later, Reid earned her bachelor's degree in business administration from the University of Alaska. It should have been a golden time. But life would soon test Reid's mettle in the most extreme ways.

Life Out of Balance

Today it seems almost archaic. But back in the 1970s, traditional values saw women staying at home.

"Looking back, I understand why Andrew felt threatened. I might have gone off to college and he wouldn't be part of my life. Then with the air traffic control job and additional education, it seemed like insecurity seeped through him. Unfortunately, the best way he saw to deal with that was through emotional abuse and eventually physical abuse. I recognized immediately what was happening, because at BPW we had programs advocating against domestic violence. Part of me knew that it would not stop."

It did not. One night, a sharp blow to Reid's eye necessitated a hospital visit.

"I was adamant that this could not happen again. The attending physician was very supportive, urging that I made sure Andrew was immediately removed from our home and that I get a protective order for the future. He also said that if I didn't take care of it, he would."

Reid knew the violent event marked the end of her 10-year marriage. But her greatest concern was for her two young boys.

"I tried to protect them. They never knew I wore bandages because of their father. But they knew something was going on. When their father moved out to the barracks, they wanted to know why. I explained it by saying, 'We both love you very much and this is about the differences that your father and I are having.' But once we were separated, Andrew did not include them in his life. He would promise to pick them up and take them places, but it didn't happen. That was very hurtful to them and me."

There were also professional consequences to the abuse.

"Every year air traffic controllers must pass a physical. Part of the physical involved an eye exam. I could not pass my eye exam because of the injury caused by the domestic violence. So I had a choice: take a federal medical disability or to go into another position within the FAA."

Reid took a position returning to Larry Snell's FAA real estate office. He noticed a difference in her immediately.

"Larry said, 'You left here very, very shy, but you're coming back more self-assured and confident. You're calling me Larry. You always called me Mr. Snell before.'"

Reid attributed the difference to her intense personal and professional experience.

"Air traffic control tested my mettle. It was primarily a male environment. And this was before there were sexual harassment laws. There were occasional hands-on things that happened. There were also photos, comments—it was pretty bad. But for me it was always zero tolerance with that stuff. Once I had to slap someone and then tell him, 'Now you explain that to your wife when you get home!' But that was just the environment then. And as Eleanor always said, 'Never let them see you sweat. Never cry. Stand up to it and take nothing.'"

That advice steeled her for work. But nothing could prepare her for what would come next in life.

An Unspeakable Tragedy

Reid filed for divorce in January 1976. Six months later, she took an appraisal course in Dallas. She made the trip from Anchorage with her two boys, leaving them with her parents in Lubbock. One of Reid's brothers planned to fly the children to Alaska from Detroit. After finishing the course, Reid planned to return to Alaska and finalize the divorce.

"While my parents were driving my sons to my brother in Detroit, they were involved in an automobile accident in Oklahoma and my sons were killed . . . that was a major turning point. Two weeks after burying my kids in Lubbock, I went back to the real estate office in Alaska. I submerged myself in community activities and school and finalized my degree in December 1977, the same year my divorce was finalized."

Reid coped as best she could. But insult was added to injury.

"I pursued a wrongful death suit in 1978 on my children's behalf. It was filed in Oklahoma City. The attorneys prepping for the suit ran some statistics about children's death in order to see how much to penalize the trucking firm that hit the car. For children that age, they project forward to see what their earning potential would have been in life. But when race was injected into it, the projected difference they came up with in earning potential for African-American children was about 10 percent of what it was for white children. So for every $100 a white person was expected to earn, a black person was expected to earn $10. That was the value they assigned to my children.

"Just this past summer the investigator for the accident called me when I was in Alaska. He said he had to talk to me. He was in his late 80s. He wanted me to know that he had lost his son since then. He said, 'I knew that the results of that research were terribly unfair. It was terribly prejudicial and it was strictly based on race.' He wanted to clear his conscience."

Reid's grief was only compounded by the case.

The New Normal

Now an FAA staff appraiser, Reid immersed herself in her career and self-improvement. She was selected to participate in an FAA public manager training program, one of only 12 FAA employees in the nation to receive the honor. She journeyed to the University of Southern California in Los Angeles.

"I didn't do anything but go to the library and study. It was really therapeutic, but also telling about how I dealt with my grief. I felt driven, too, because I had talked to my sons about one day going to graduate school. I was fulfilling not only my own dream, but also my commitment to them."

She completed the training and took extra courses to earn a master's degree in public administration. Then, in the summer of 1980, Reid accepted a job as an international aviation analyst, a high-level FAA position in Washington, DC.

"That November, Ronald Reagan was elected President and many things changed. I was involved in technical assistance to third-world countries, and that activity slowed to a crawl. So I moved to a program analyst position; I was purchasing aircraft for the aircraft program division. But because things were slower, my grief started to overwhelm me. I needed to exit my career at FAA headquarters and return to a supportive environment—which for me was Anchorage—and try to re-find my way and attend to my unresolved grief. I had been going full steam ahead for six years, really trying to outrun the grief, but it had come to a point that I had to deal with it."

Reid sought counseling in Anchorage.

North in Alaska

Because of a hiring freeze at the FAA, Reid landed a part-time job with the Department of Interior's Minerals Management Service (MMS), the federal agency responsible for offshore oil and gas leasing. For seven years, Reid accumulated a wide range of experience in various positions with the Department of Interior, including program analyst in the Leasing and Environment Office, regulatory petroleum analyst, and paralegal with Offshore Oil and Gas Leasing, Field Operations.

"For most of that time, I was working 24 hours a week. I started my own small business specializing in real estate appraising and financing. I also was heavily involved in community activities. Then I received a gubernatorial appointment as Commissioner of the State of Alaska Real Estate Commission. I chaired the Education Committee and I also received a mayoral appointment to the Anchorage Aviation and Airport Advisory Board. That move was to keep my aviation experience on my résumé current."

In 1984, Reid also began a six-year commitment to serve on a national level in BPW, first as treasurer and later as the first African-American national president. In 1987, the *Anchorage Times* featured Reid in a story about BPW. That press garnered more than just professional notice.

"It was in the 'Faces of Alaska' section; it was kind of a life profile. A man named Robert Reid read it in August. In September, he asked me to lunch and I said yes. We dated and in January he asked me to marry him. I said, 'Here's my calendar for the next two years. I don't know when we'll have time to get married. I don't really have time for dating!' And he said, 'Oh yeah? Here's a date, March. We'll do it in March.' And in March, 1988, we were married."

Finding Her Way Back into Aviation

Reid continued to expand her professional experience and training outside of transportation, including learning to be an administrative law judge. But as she broadened her experience, her husband's work changed.

"Bob was selected as a customer service manager for Alaska Airlines and moved to Seattle. So I commuted. In July of '88, I went to the BPW convention in Albuquerque and met President Bush and Elizabeth Dole. I kept in touch with people in the Bush administration and was appointed President of the National Advisory Council of the Small Business Administration, where I served for three years."

This was in addition to her role on MMS. In 1989, Reid took a leave from MMS and joined her husband in Seattle. Within a couple of months, she returned to the FAA, Northwest Mountain Region.

"I conducted an informational interview about being a program analyst in the Airports Division, because program analysts were responsible for real estate matters relating to airport expansion and I had real estate experience. But I had more airside experience, and this was landside, so it seemed like a natural progression. Initially, they had no openings, so I went into the resource management/human resource office. In July 1990, they had an opening for a program analyst, and I took it. That was a major turning point for me. For the next 20-plus years, I was in airports—a place that fascinated me. I felt I could grow and contribute."

And did she ever. In 1992, Reid moved to Oklahoma City, where she managed training programs. She also held several temporary duty assignments throughout the United States, including in Atlanta and Washington, DC. In April, 1995, Reid was selected as Manager, Memphis Airports District Office, where she experienced the less-than-subtle discrimination at the luncheon she described earlier. She continued to advance at the FAA, despite occasionally experiencing harassment and ill treatment. Reid took her last assignment as the Boston-based Federal Manager of Airports for the New England Region. She retired from the FAA in January 2011.

Casting a Wide Network

Reid attributes her success to many things. But one element stands out, her involvement with BPW.

"I was elected Treasurer in 1984. I became the first African-American President in 1989. I met my husband because of BPW. I met President Bush and Elizabeth Dole through BPW. But in addition to networking, BPW was also about mentoring. My motto is, 'Lift while you climb.' Every time you have a mentor you should have a protégé, regardless of where you are in your career. That's one of the reasons I went into BPW. I just felt that with all of my life experiences that I had an obligation to help other women address the barriers they faced.

"For example, when I divorced, I had problems getting credit in my own name. My car insurance was canceled, because they said, 'You're a divorcee. You're too emotional so you are a high risk. We don't want to insure you.' Through BPW, I had opportunities to advocate for the removal of these kinds of artificial barriers and to provide guidance and mentoring to women experiencing these kinds of difficulties."

Reid also joined the WTS International Advisory Board in 2009 and its Foundation Board in 2010.

Keeping It *in* the Cuff

Reid excelled at networking through BPW. But that was in no way her only strategy for advancement.

"One of the things I would do is informational interviewing. I would identify positions I was interested in and interview the manager or some of the people who were holding positions I was interested in to find out what their plans were for the next couple of years. Then I kept *cuff records* (simple notes in a file) on things that were happening related to that field. Then I would do a self-assessment of the type of skills I had. What do they need? What might they need in the future? And I would try to target them to make sure I was prepared if the position became available. Even when you're in the position you want, you might have an opportunity to gain experience that not only helps you in your current position, but also helps you in the next position you're aiming at. So I encourage people to do that type of evaluation."

But Reid also believes strongly in giving back as part of any networking strategy.

"I believe in what I like to call servant leadership. Provide opportunities for people to do their best work. Help them experience their best days and hours of their lives at work. In other words, lift as you rise. I have always shared the networks and connections I've made, so it was always more about service than networking. With good networking, you always take on different roles at different times: sponsor, advocate, mentor, and coach for people inside and outside of organizations."

A Look Back

Reid likes to say that, "Service is the price I pay for the space I occupy on Earth." Without question, she has given selflessly through her service as a transportation professional. She has paid her dues. But she wouldn't have it any other way.

"My journey has encompassed many mountaintop moments, several unsettling valleys, and everything in between. But through it all, my faith in God has kept me grounded and allowed me to continue to find and fulfill my life purpose—service to my community through volunteerism, service to God by demonstrating my faith daily, and service to my country—with more than 41 years of federal service. These two guiding principles in my life, faith and service, give me resilience when things happen and the strength, perseverance, and ability to adjust and adapt."

Chapter 12

MARY PETERS

The next day I told him, "I can't do my job if I can't be involved in meetings like this. And you really can't exclude me. If we want to work together successfully, I have to be a part of that." So he said, "Well little lady, we thought the language might get a little rough over there. . . ." And I said, "Look, I was raised by a Marine Corps Gunnery Sergeant. I could turn your ears blue if I decided to do that. I won't do that, but don't exclude me from a meeting like that again." And he didn't.

Mary Peters turns obstacles into opportunities. An Arizonan through and through, Peters began her transportation career as an entry-level secretary at the Arizona Department of Transportation (ADOT) in 1985. She soon advanced from being a secretary to Contracts Administrator to Deputy Director for Administration to Deputy Director of ADOT. In 1998, then-Governor Jane Hull appointed her as Director of the agency, a job she says she would have been "happy to retire in." But she didn't retire.

President George W. Bush called Peters to Washington, DC, in 2001, to become the first woman to lead the FHWA, which she did until 2005. She then returned to Arizona and became the National Director for Transportation Policy at HDR, Inc., a global architecture and engineering firm. Only 11 months later, the phone rang again. President Bush had another request. This time he wanted Peters to join his cabinet. She did.

On October 17, 2006, Mary Peters became the fifteenth US Secretary of Transportation and only the second woman to ever head the department. She set out to tackle serious issues during her tenure. Peters looks on her time in Washington most fondly, with nothing but "the greatest respect for George Bush." Evidently the feeling is mutual. At her swearing-in ceremony President Bush noted that, "Mary is a dedicated public servant, an experienced leader, and one of our Nation's most innovative thinkers on transportation issues." Today, Peters is president and founder of the Mary E. Peters Consulting Group, LLC. She also serves on the Board of Directors of HDR, Inc.

Peters has amassed numerous awards throughout her career. But there are two she regularly cites. *Arizona Business Journal* recognized her as the Most Influential Person in Arizona Transportation in 1998. And WTS International named her the 2004 Woman of the Year. She is also a proud Harley Davidson–riding grandmother dressed in red leather.

This is her story.

From Secretary to Madame Secretary

Though Peters gained her first professional transportation experience with ADOT, it was not her first exposure to transportation as a profession.

"It was almost prophetic that I got into transportation. Right out of high school, I did an internship out at Luke Air Force Base right outside of Phoenix. And guess what, it was with the 4510th Transportation Squadron."

Even before that Peters discovered the importance of transportation through her father, a seminal figure in her life.

"He was a *zanjero* [one in charge of water distribution]. They were responsible for a pretty good swath of the canal-and-ditch-irrigation system here in Arizona. When there was flooding, he was gone 24 hours a day trying to deal with that. Many times the flooding resulted in road closures. We didn't have a good flood control system back then. So that was my introduction with the transportation system, trying to get to school when the roads flooded out. It really made me think, 'There's got to be a better way to do this than everything just shutting down when there was a flood.'"

Married early, Peters and her then-husband moved several times, including a brief stint in Indiana, where she served as a negotiator that dealt with a butchers union. But she made things happen when she returned to Arizona.

"I was hired as a secretary in the office that let the contracts to hire engineers and architects. It was an entry-level position in ADOT in early 1985, when they were planning for a major transportation initiative that was put on the ballot in November of that year. Basically, they were going to build a regional freeway system using a local-option tax, Prop 300, a half-cent sales tax. I got in on the ground floor of that, and that's what really got my feet wet in terms of transportation.

"But the woman running the office at the time, Virginia Powell, was very interested in work I had done in Indiana with the United Food and Commercial Workers or meat cutters. And she said, 'I figure that if you can negotiate contracts with people who carry knives to work, then I think you can negotiate contracts with consultants.'"

Powell knew she had more than just a secretary in Peters. Steadily given more responsibility, Peters rose through the ranks to Contract Administrator. Then Powell retired. And Vern Doyle replaced her.

"Vern was a very good mentor and friend, and he pushed me out there. And I never worked harder in my life than I did when I worked for Vern. He gave me an opportunity to prove my capabilities. That really made the transition to leading the contracting office much more palatable to other people who might have looked at it differently in the past. Before he retired, Vern actually went over to the state engineers and told them, 'Look, she had to go through a competitive process here. And Mary is qualified to do this. Don't just summarily turn her down.'"

They did not. And Peters excelled at the work for a number of reasons. But one particular reason stood out for her.

"When a new person came into the office, I would drive them around the Valley of the Sun and show them the projects we were working on. I would tell them, 'We're not just hiring engineers and architects to design this system; we're helping build this system throughout the state. And the contracts that you let are building transportation improvements for the citizens of this state.' I would always keep that in mind. That's what we're here to do. We're not here just to write contracts and authorize payments."

Peters continued to advance. Under Governor Fife Symington, she became the Executive Assistant (essentially Chief of Staff), and Deputy Director of the Department. But all was not always well within ADOT.

Doing What's Right When People Do Wrong

Peters and ADOT pioneered public-private partnerships, among other firsts. But some people within ADOT were striking out in different, less noble ways. And as ADOT Deputy Director she had to handle it.

"Someone took a state credit card, which was to be used only for travel expenses related to his job, and took out a bunch of money, gambled, and lost it. He might have gotten away with it, too, except that he didn't pay the bill! I felt that this was unforgivable. Even though he was a civil service employee, I fired him. Of course I talked to ADOT Director Larry Bonine before I did that, but I fired him. He appealed through the State Personnel Board and later he was going to be reinstated. So we negotiated a settlement, because I didn't want him back in the agency and I didn't want that kind of exposure for the agency. I knew it was a gamble, that he might be reinstated when I fired him, but I felt it was that important to not have that go unpunished and to set the right example."

Unfortunately, the credit card scammer was not the only outlier.

"Later in a very public event I fired the head of the Motor Vehicle Division and one of his deputies, because they had, as a favor to one of the members of the legislature, taken a drunk-driving conviction off of a woman's record. In Arizona if you get a second impaired-driving conviction within a 10-month period your license is automatically revoked. The woman knew someone at the statehouse and they had the state employee expunge the record of one of her drunk-driving convictions. A whistleblower told the Attorney General's office. So I fired both the lead person and his deputy. They were more served-at-the-pleasure positions, so we didn't go through the whole Personnel Board thing. And I would tell people when I went to the FHWA, 'I will be your biggest supporter, but don't do something like that. Don't do something that compromises the integrity of this office or the public's trust. Because if you do I will come down quite hard on you about that.'"

Peters faced yet another very difficult situation in Arizona when she found herself placed between auditors and the Governor.

"One of the largest trucking companies in the state, actually in the nation, was working here out of Arizona. At the time we had a by-the-mile tax, where commercial vehicles paid a fee per miles driven in the state, as well as the fuel tax. It was controversial. The trucking companies didn't like it. And we employed a legion of auditors to monitor it. Some auditors felt the trucking companies misrepresented pretty materially the number of miles their trucks were driving and therefore were underpaying substantially. But they were also big political contributors. And they had supported Governor Fife Symington quite strongly.

"So the Governor called me and said he wanted me to *personally* look into this. He never told me to do anything wrong. But he said that he wanted me to tell him whether or not the trucking companies were being treated fairly. It was a long process and much more complex than I thought it would be going in.

"After about four months, the worst discrepancies were not nearly to the extent that the auditors had felt they were. So we were ultimately able to negotiate a settlement. But I had gotten calls from the Governor on a fairly regular basis. And I had to walk a pretty fine line between doing what was right and being fair. I felt like I was walking a tightrope. I didn't want to disappoint the Governor and tell him these guys were crooks, but I also didn't want to tell my staff that I wasn't supporting what they were doing. Ultimately, it was a good settlement. But it was a pretty tough thing."

On September 4, 1997, the federal government indicted Governor Fife Symington on an unrelated matter (his conviction was later overturned). But as a result, Arizona Secretary of State Jane Hull became governor, and Governor Hull appointed Peters as ADOT Director.

A National Call

Peters thoroughly enjoyed running ADOT. But in the spring of 2001, she received a call from USDOT Secretary Norman Mineta. In Washington, he offered her the position of Administrator of the FHWA. Though prepared, Peters had some reservations.

"I called Governor Hull. And she said, 'Well, think about it. At the end of the day, Mary, it's a great opportunity, but do what's best for your family.' As a family we ultimately decided that I would take the position. And I worked in that position as Highway Administrator from the time that I was confirmed, which was right after 9/11 [2001], to the summer of 2005."

Peters used her time there well, offering unique expertise.

"It was an exciting time. It was a good opportunity to work with Norm and Michael Jackson, then–Deputy Secretary of Transportation, and people like that, and to get to know how Washington works. Because you think you know how Washington works until you get there, but it's not like the civics books tell you it is. It's not like that at all.

"Norm Mineta really liked that I came out of a state DOT and had been on the receiving end of federal programs. So I looked to figure out how to make the federal programs easier for states to work with. Environmental streamlining was a big issue, too. Another thing that appealed to me was that the surface transportation bill was coming up. The last one had been passed in 1998. So in the 2003–2004 year we worked very hard to get the next iteration of the bill. But I learned how hard people work at FHWA and all of the federal agencies. They try to do the best they can with some of the directions they get from Congress and from other places as well.

"We ultimately had 12 extensions of the 1998 law in 23 months before the new law. I was very frustrated that it took that long to get it done. We'd almost get there and then they'd kick the can down the road again. I'm afraid we're experiencing some of that right now."

Putting Family First

While Peters fought the good fight in Washington, a more personal crisis was unfolding back in Arizona.

"During the summer of 2005, more like 2004 into 2005, one of my daughters had unfortunately developed a bad drug habit. That was a tough time for our family. We were trying to get her back on the right track, but when they're over 18, I've got to tell you, it's not easy. But we ultimately decided as a family that it was time for me to come home."

Still fighting for the transportation bill, Peters spoke with Secretary Mineta and devised a plan. She would leave when the bill passed Congress. Despite several attempts, passage was elusive.

"I talked to Norm and told him I had to leave. 'If they don't get the bill done before the August break, I need to take a leave of absence and then come back in September and try to work on it some more, but I need to get a date for when I'll be headed home.' And he was so good about it. Norm was just tremendous. He said, 'Let's just plan for you to go at the end of this month, July. And if the bill is not done, well, you gave it your best shot'. So I did do that. I left and I came home in the summer of 2005."

The bill actually passed Congress on Peters' last day in office. Peters returned to her family and Arizona. She also became the National Director for Transportation Policy for HDR Engineering.

Interviewed by the Leader of the Free World

Peters relished being home and tending to her family. Time passed. Then the phone rang again.

"During the summer of 2006, Norm told me he was resigning. A short time later I got calls from the White House, asking if I would consider coming back to serve as USDOT Secretary. There were other really good candidates out there, and I told them about some of those candidates. It dissuaded them at first, but they came back and asked if I would come and talk to them. And I did. Then I was asked to meet with President George W. Bush. That's not one you turn down real easily. So I met with the President.

"My dad used to tell me that sometimes I didn't know enough to be afraid when I needed to be afraid. This was one of those instances where I didn't have the fear that I should have had. It was evident to me that this was the leader of the free world and we were talking about a position where I would report directly to him. And he really interviewed me. We sat at his desk in the Oval Office. We talked about a lot of things.

"And I said to him, 'If you just want someone who will warm the chair and just keep things going for the next couple of years, I don't know if I really want to do that. But if you want to try to tackle some of the big problems that we're experiencing in America—congestion on our highways and our airways, the systemic, chronic lack of funding and some of those things—then I'm interested.' And he was game. He said that he had more than a fourth of his time left in office and that he wanted to use it the best way he could to serve the American people."

Peters worked tirelessly on a range of issues. She left Washington at the end of the Bush Administration in 2009, particularly proud of her efforts to relieve transportation congestion through innovative and expedited programs. Today, she continues to advance issues like these through her own firm, Mary E. Peters Consulting Group, LLC, where she provides expertise on the planning, funding, development, and operation of transportation, water, and energy infrastructure.

Her Place at the Table

Peters credits many mentors throughout her life, but one stands out from the very beginning.

"My father told me, 'Do not put limits on yourself. You can do whatever you want to do.' And he gave me the courage to try many things. He used to compare life to a merry-go-round, saying that you have to grab a ring every time you go around, because you never know which one is going to be the gold ring. I translated that to mean that if you get an opportunity to do something that may be a stretch for you, don't be afraid to do it. Even when I've failed that has served me very well and given me opportunities I never would have had if I hadn't tried."

Peters also believes that to advance you've got to gain greater perspective.

"Don't look only at the job you're doing. Also look at what the organization is doing as a whole and ask yourself, 'How can I contribute to the overall goals of this organization?' Really look at the organization as a whole and be excited about that."

However, Peters also understands that is not always an easy task.

"When I first got to Washington, I thought, 'Very soon people are going to find out that I am not as smart and capable as they are and I have no business being in this position, so I had better work really hard and solve things.' But I found out that they're people just like you and me. No one anointed them with all of the wisdom they need to be a cabinet member or a White House staffer. They are people doing the best they can every day, and I could play in that world. I have a great deal of regret that I didn't get an advanced degree or go to a big name university, that I got my education pretty much after I was married and had a family. You see, I didn't take the usual route of getting there, so I thought I wasn't qualified or capable of sitting at the table with these folks. But I eventually came to feel that that was okay. We're all just people. At the end of the day we all just put our pants or pantyhose on one leg at a time."

No Woman Is an Island

An eternal optimist, Peters believes that transportation offers challenging, fulfilling careers, particularly for women. But women should know that they need not make the journey alone.

"Nationally there were some women in transportation. Jane Garvey was the Deputy Administrator at FHWA at the time I headed ADOT. There were a few more. But Jane and I used to joke that these were the only meetings we ever went to where we didn't have to stand in line for the ladies room."

Help was also available on a grander scale.

"When I was at ADOT and when I was in Washington, WTS had a network of folks I could go to and vent and just ask a lot of questions. Some of the people had preceded me as women directors of DOTs, like Anne Canby, Grace Crunican, people like that, who had been where I was and had done what I was doing. And I could talk to them.

"WTS has always provided a tremendous network of women peers that I had an opportunity to work with over time. But WTS also shows young women that there are exciting, wonderful careers in transportation. You can get into this field and be successful and solve problems that are important to where you live and the nation as a whole. Bringing up the next generation of transportation women is probably the most important thing about WTS."

Doing It All

Peters believes in herself. Harking back to her Marine Corps father, she learned to succeed through discipline, determination, and risk taking.

"It was difficult. It really was. I really worked hard to finish my degree when my youngest went into first grade. And I started my degree when we lived in Indiana and didn't really finish until we came out here to Arizona. So I was finishing my degree as my responsibilities at ADOT were increasing. I don't think I slept a lot back then. I would go home and get the kids dinner and put them to bed. And after they were asleep I would do homework, and I'd use the weekends for homework. Sometimes you look back and think I should have spent more time with the kids or this or that. And I certainly have some of those regrets as well."

But Peters is sanguine.

"I tell women that I have the privilege to mentor today: 'You can do it all. You just can't do it all at once. You have to decide what's most important and make choices.' That's how you balance it out. My husband became more a part of helping run things at home, out of necessity, but that's okay. He learned how to pick the kids up and take them here or there. But there will always be hardships. At one point, my mother passed away. My mother-in-law and father-in-law both passed away around the same time. There were some tough issues that we dealt with as a family. But you just keep going."

Paying It Forward

Mary Peters has had an extraordinary career. But she has also had help. And she never forgets those who lent a hand when she needed it most.

"My father was definitely a mentor. But he died when I was 23. I didn't have him through a lot of my adult life. His wife, my step-mother, Rose Ruth, was just as important. She was tremendous. When I was trying to go to school and work at the same time, she would take money out of *her* household budget and spend it on *my* education. I'm thinking that I've got three kids growing up and I should just focus on them and fund their education. And she said no, that I should think of my education as an investment, and she was right. I remember one time she gave me a check for $1,000 and I thought that was all of the money in the world! That was a big, big thing. And I said to her, 'I will pay you back.' And she said, 'No don't pay me back. Pay it forward. Take the opportunity to do it for someone else.'"

Mary Peters continues to pay it forward today.

DR. BEVERLY SCOTT

I'm not stupid. I knew something was up when our team at Houston METRO said, "Oh, Bev! We're going to have a public hearing this evening in Hiram Clarke, and we thought it would just be a great idea if you would be the public hearing officer." They wanted a black face at the meeting in Hiram Clarke, a predominantly African-American middle-class suburb where the authority planned to locate a bus garage. They failed to say that we purchased the land with local money and provided minimal legal notice or community outreach. Now, we were ready to submit a federal grant application for construction. So I'm up there, and the room is packed—standing room only. I can still see it now. To put it mildly, the community is "hot," but we're making it through. Then, our aging white male head of the Authority's design and construction/transit system development department gets up. And, he said the words, "YOU PEOPLE." Jesus Christ, I wanted to strangle him! Those words floated in the air, and the fuse blew. The community went off! They were outraged and incensed by our insensitivity. Candidly, I was quite proud of them, and our agency learned an invaluable lesson. So, did I. That meeting went to almost one o'clock in the morning. And I lie to you not, by the end of the meeting I knew every individual's name.

Dr. Beverly Scott does not fear change. She drives it. So when she won a coveted Carnegie Houston Foundation Fellowship in 1977, she transitioned easily from academia to Houston's Office of Public Transportation and the transportation industry. Then in 1979, the newly created Houston METRO named her their first Director of Affirmative Action, and later promoted her to Assistant General Manager of Administration. She spent seven years in Houston before journeying north to serve in various executive capacities with the New York City Transit Authority (NYCTA) between 1985 and 1990, including being the first woman appointed Vice President of Surface Transit—with responsibility for bus service in the five boroughs and Staten Island Rail. She next crossed the Hudson River to become the Assistant Executive Director of Administration for NJT. Then she left transportation for a time.

Scott joined the National Forum for Black Public Administrators (NFBPA), a nonprofit with more than 2,600 members, as its Executive Director. But transportation lured her back. Two years later in 1994, she became WMATA's Deputy General Manager for Administration. In 1996, Scott took the reins as General Manager of the Rhode Island Public Transit Authority (RIPTA), a statewide public transit system.

She headed west in 2002, bringing her expertise to the Sacramento Regional Transit District as General Manager and Chief Executive Officer. Firmly established as a national transportation leader, in 2007 Scott became the first female Chief Executive Officer and General Manager of the Metropolitan Atlanta Rapid Transit Authority (MARTA). She thought this would be her last assignment before retirement. She thought again. In 2012, Scott joined MassDOT/MBTA as General Manager of the "T" and Rail & Transit Administrator for the Commonwealth. She recently announced her retirement after 35-plus years in the public transportation industry.

Scott has received numerous awards for leadership and service from organizations that include the White House (Transportation Innovator of Change), the US Department of Transportation, the Transportation Research Board, National Academies of Science (Sharon Banks Humanitarian Service Award), APTA (past

Chairperson), the American Society of Public Administrators, WTS International, and COMTO. In 2011, President Obama appointed her to the National Infrastructure Advisory Council, and in 2012 she became its Vice Chair.

She also serves on several national boards, including the WTS International Board, Rail-Volution (past Chair), the Transportation Learning Center, and Americans for Transit.

In addition, Scott holds a doctorate in political science from Howard University and a bachelor of arts in political science from Fisk University.

This is her story.

Transportation Finds You

Call it luck. Call it divine intervention. Call it what you like, but Beverly Scott's foray into transportation was anything but planned.

"I was minding my own business as an assistant professor in government and public affairs at Tennessee State University when I was selected for a Carnegie Foundation fellowship to learn about city government. When they asked what city department I wanted—this is late 1976—and I swear to God one of my main concerns was that I didn't want to be in a 'relations' area because most women and people of color were in relations areas back then. So I told them I wanted to be in transportation or sanitation because they were 'nontraditional' areas for people like me, and I knew we'd always be moving people and trash."

Landing in the Houston's Office of Public Transportation, Scott worked with a dynamic group of young women and men who were "smart smart, book smart, and theory smart." More important, she discovered her passion.

"Transportation picked me; I didn't really pick it. The reason I've stayed in it all of these years is because of the difference we make, the genuinely profound impact we have on people and communities."

The lessons were many. From the politics of referenda to the grassroots of consensus building, Houston was Scott's transportation crucible. But little could prepare her for what would happen at one particular community meeting.

Putting a [Black] Face on the Agency

Houston METRO planned on building a bus maintenance facility in Hiram Clark. On the day of the meeting, a Houston METRO official asked Scott to represent the authority. She agreed.

"When you lived in the Hiram Clarke community back in the day, you had really made it. This was first generation, Ozzie and Harriet black suburbia. And I knew of Hiram Clark Baptist Church; it was one of the early mega churches where the minister has a couple-thousand person congregation. So I get to the church in the early evening, and the street and parking lot are full of cars! But it still hasn't quite hit dodo here. I go into the church and guess what the program was! It was us! *We* were the menu! And it hit me, 'Fool — you are the hearing officer!'"

A white male METRO colleague tested Scott's mettle even further, when he addressed the crowd as "you people." But then Scott witnessed the community coalesce.

"They were on it. They put us through our paces, doing the noise study, testing for vehicle emissions—the whole nine yards. When it was finally built, much later than initially planned, it was gorgeous. One of the mitigations was, literally, that we had yellow clinging jasmine as part of the landscaping. I was very proud of that community. You wish you didn't have to have these teachable moments, but the authority learned from that. It was a good lesson. It was Environmental Justice 101."

Define Your Own Timing

During Scott's seven years at METRO, she experienced six different General Managers, Executive Directors, Presidents—acting, interim, and permanent. She felt the organization needed stability. But the leader who arrived was not who or what she had in mind.

"He was a very decisive person, had a solid record of accomplishment, and I give him tremendous credit for being a transit manager who appreciated the importance of image and marketing at a time when few transit managers did. But we didn't get along *at all*. There wasn't open warfare, but I felt like I could see emblazoned on him a condescending attitude that said, 'I know, little girl, exactly where you should be. You're going to be the assistant general manager of all of the *negro* and *women* things.' I had spent the better part of seven years developing a very diverse professional portfolio. And, that wasn't my game plan. I also knew that as a newly appointed President, he wasn't going anywhere soon."

She made the personal decision to leave—no drama, no buyouts, no media.

Toughing Out Tough Times

Scott did not have a plan. She followed her purpose and passion. Never one to sit idle, she joined the Harris County Minority Contractor's Association as its Executive Director and gained approval for Houston's first minority and women's business participation goals. Texas Governor Mark White appointed her to head a state commission establishing the first minority and women's business enterprise program (M/WBE) for the state. In her spare time she worked as a volunteer on a campaign to elect the first African-American Harris County Commissioner. It was a lot of tremendously fulfilling work, but very little of it was paid. And, she was a single mom with a child to feed. Would she recommend her strategy for others?

"No! I would have developed a better exit strategy. The best time to get a job is when you have one. There are things I did when I was younger that I wouldn't do in quite the same way today. You can be more strategic about how you want to make your exit. You don't have to bite yourself, like I did. And there were probably very few people around me who knew what I was going through, that were aware that I could have used some help."

But help was on its way in a very familiar guise.

Transportation Finds You . . . Again

The phone rang. NYCTA Senior Vice President Jim Corbin wanted Scott to come north to help NYCTA President David Gunn. Intrigued, Scott agreed to meet.

"Now I had never met David before. But I go into this man's office and he's in his stocking feet and there's a map of the NYC subway system on the wall. And he says in reference to the map, 'We're going to take it back line by line. And when they mess 'em up, meaning the railcars, we're going to clean 'em up!' Now you're talking about 6,000 rail cars! And he's got this light in his eyes. Eventually I go into Jim's office and he says, 'What do you think?' I laughed and said, 'You know what? I'm going to do it. I think the damn fool is going to do it!'"

Scott went to New York as head of their civil rights and affirmative action program in the wake of a major scandal. The situation was intense.

"New York was a mess. They had the big Donovan-Schiavone case, where eight men and two companies were accused of scheming to defraud the NYCTA of millions on a subway construction project, and where the civil rights, the certification program, had been a sham."

But Scott had Gunn's unqualified support in cleaning it up. Scott relates the most telling example. NYCTA was about to spend billions of dollars on new railcars. But there was a catch.

"Most of the time folks think civil rights issues are just lip service. They wouldn't possibly hold up a multibillion-dollar deal because the civil rights provisions were not taken care of. But I'm serious as a heart attack. David came down to my office, unannounced, and plopped himself in the room with the contractors sitting there and said, 'The bottom line is this. This whole thing in terms of civil rights provisions is serious. She is either going to tell me that it's okay to approve this deal or if she doesn't give me an approval then *you don't have this deal.*' Then he left. But it was clear. For you to get these billions of dollars, you better make sure that these civil rights obligations are taken care of. Gunn is just a tremendous person. I am extremely proud to claim him as the most influential mentor in my transit career. To put it simply, I'd go to hell and back for him."

A few years later, Gunn poked his head into Scott's office again.

"'Bev, how would you like to be the Vice President of Surface, meaning all of the bus service in the five boroughs plus Staten Island Rail?' Would I like to be the Vice President of Surface? Absolutely! Bill Saunders, the Vice President of Surface, was retiring after 30-some years—a total gem. David set it up so that I shadowed Bill for about four or five months. Now for many of the Surface team, I could have been considered an interloper. Any one of them could have looked at me and said, 'That's *my* job, not *hers*.' But that didn't happen because of the way David and Bill handled it."

Scott made the "big breakthrough" into operations in the biggest transit setting in the nation. Everything was right in her world. And then . . .

"Word comes down that the chairman of the Metropolitan Transportation Authority is leaving. And David is going to leave with him. Lord have mercy, Jesus! I'm living in Park Slope, Brooklyn, and the news announces that the leading candidate for General Manager of New York City Transit is the same guy from Texas that I swore to God I would never work for again. I could have just cried in my coffee. . . ."

She also started planning her exit. She told her mom, who thought her daughter was crazy "to leave that good job."

The Value of Networking

Scott prepared to leave NYCTA when Gunn did. She didn't have another position lined up. But once again the phone rang. It was Tom Downs, President of the Triborough Bridge and Tunnel Authority (TBTA).

"Tom says, 'Have you ever thought about doing anything with bridges and tunnels?' I said, 'Well, no.' One thing led to another, and I joined Triborough as the Senior Vice President of Operations and Support."

Thank God I Took the Job

"I am not there for even a good month when Tom gets appointed as the Commissioner of Transportation for New Jersey. The guy who took over, Mike Ascher, was smart, brilliant, and a wonderful person. He and I had worked very well together for several years at NYCTA, where he had been Chief Engineer. We were a good complement. He wasn't very comfortable with the people side of the business, and the TBTA had major labor concerns back in those days. Then I happened to get a call from Shirley DeLibero, who was heading up New Jersey Transit. She asked, why am I over there with bridges and tunnels? She and I met for dinner, and the major transition she was undertaking in New Jersey was very exciting. It also gave me a first-time opportunity to work with a female transit CEO.

"But Mike didn't want me to go. He said, 'Beverly! Don't leave. You're my heir apparent. I'm going to retire in 18 months, two years at most. You'll be the next President!' He stayed for 20 more years. Thank God I took the job in New Jersey."

Taking It to the Next Level

After helping DeLibero reorganize New Jersey Transit, Scott left transportation again and served as the Executive Director for the National Forum for Black Public Administrators. But once more, transportation pulled her back in. Larry Reuter, the General Manager of WMATA, invited her to join WMATA as Deputy General Manager for Administration. But soon after she joined, it happened *again*. Larry went to New York to head NYCTA, leaving Scott in a precarious political situation with an overly ambitious colleague. Scott took action.

"I picked up *Passenger Transport*—that's the honest-to-God truth—and there was a position for a General Manager in Rhode Island. I didn't know Rhode Island. I didn't know anybody *in* Rhode Island. But I said to myself, 'Beverly, you've been some kind of assistant to, deputy of, etc. When are you going to have the keys yourself?' I was General Manager in Rhode Island for six years—and it was a wonderful, wonderful experience."

X Marks the Taxing Spot

After Rhode Island, Scott was named General Manager and Chief Executive Officer for the Sacramento Regional Transit District. She led the district successfully for five years, raising her national profile as an effective transit leader. That's when Atlanta happened. In 2007, Scott became the first female Chief Executive Officer and General Manager of MARTA. If Houston was Scott's crucible, Atlanta was her battle.

"Atlanta has a lot of great things, but it's one of the most divisive cities on the issue of regional transit. MARTA was literally born out of old southern style race politics and civil rights. It unfortunately manifests itself in old local acronyms like 'MARTA — Moving African Americans Rapidly Through Atlanta,' as well as some of the most arcane legislative provisions. For example, you can only spend 50 percent of your pennies for operating and 50 percent for capital. You can't find legislatively mandated restrictive provisions like these in any other transit system in the country—or Georgia either! *Why?* No way on God's green earth they were going to let black folks (and labor unions) wind up having control of all that money without restrictions."

As a result, funding was a perennial issue. But one particular period presented a uniquely difficult challenge. MARTA is funded largely by a 1 percent sales tax. As the system expanded and aged, tax revenue rarely supplied enough funding. Combine that shortfall with the continued restrictive allocation provisions and the major 2008 national recession, and MARTA was in a perfect storm for a deficit.

"We had a loss of $2 billion over a 10-year period. We were down by about $120 million in one year. Even with no salary increases, furloughs, layoffs, major fare hikes, and service cuts, we could not close the gap without cutting into lifeline services. MARTA serves a highly transit-dependent population. All too often, these are voiceless people who don't have the time or the means to run to a bunch of public hearings. So I needed to make a point that this wasn't a game. We could potentially lose as much as 30 percent of our service!

"Without using any taxpayer dollars, one night volunteers—with a lot of help from community activists (including union workers on their own time) and MARTA retirees—painted big X's in red paint on a third of our buses and trains to show what would be eliminated with the service cuts. When they all pulled out the next morning they had these big red X's on them. And people got it. Each red X meant that that bus or train could be cut. This was the wake up, a-ha moment."

Scott made her point. MARTA received $25 million in funding from the Atlanta Regional Commission to avoid the cuts, and some interim relaxation of the funding restrictions. She continued to fight for the system, expecting to retire at the end of her tenure. Before that could happen, she got another call.

Boston Strong

In 2012, Scott became the Chief Executive Officer/General Manager of the debt-ridden MBTA. Scott took a pay cut to join Governor Deval Patrick's transportation team. No one could have guessed what would follow.

"My first day was December 17. The Boston Marathon bombing was the following April. But what most folks outside of Boston don't know is that in between we had Winter Storm Nemo, where total snowfall reached nearly 25 inches, and Hurricane Sandy right before I got there.

"There is nothing like adversity to let you know whether or not your DNA is compatible on your team. Either you fit together or you don't. The Nemo trial run, if you will, was good for me, as someone who was new, who didn't grow up in the system. They didn't know me. So Nemo was actually very helpful for me to gel with our team leading into the Marathon bombing."

Scott was not new to major crises. She had worked through hurricanes in Houston, the first World Trade Center bombing (she was actually in the complex at the time), major snow events in Washington, DC, and tornadoes in Atlanta. She knew instantly what to do and how to do it. Still, even with a tough exterior, events take their toll.

"We had an officer that was struck down, a young man in his late 20s. He has a beautiful family. I just finished coming from visiting his grandmother, Miss Barbara; she's 80-something years old. I just bonded with them so much. It's amazing that he's alive. He was shot and had it not been for the emergency responders, he wouldn't be alive. He just about lost all of his blood. I can't explain how much of an impact the marathon will have on me forever."

Snowmageddon

As these stories went to press, Scott closed this chapter of her transit career in the wake of the most extreme winter snow storms recorded in the Commonwealth of Massachusetts over a month—a record-breaking 110.3 inches coupled with temperatures persistently below freezing.

In characteristic Scott fashion, she did it her way.

Life in the Balance

Transportation careers require commitment. As a result, balancing life outside of transportation can be challenging.

"You can't necessarily have it all at one time, but you can be intentional about what drives or motivates you. I've never run after the dollar or the dime. Who in the world would ever want to have just a job? I've been pretty fortunate to not have jobs, but to have missions, experiences, and exposure, and more times than not be part of teams that were genuinely focused on giving their best effort to serve people and communities. If I could give young people any gift, I'd give them the gift of resilience. Life is not a spectator sport. Do not let something take you out. Scrapping might not be how it is in the storybooks, but if you get knocked down two times—get up three. Absolutely nothing and no one can take you out unless *you* let it happen."

She also believes that no one has to make the journey alone.

"I will tell you something that I say to younger people, but I didn't always do it myself. Make sure you get balance. Figure out whatever works for you and your family, because there are moments in life you can't go back and play again. My second husband passed about four years ago. He was very different than me, very much an artist. Whenever people came by the house, he would laugh and tell them the minute they walked in the door, 'Look, we're not talking about that transit sh_t in here! You guys do that all the time. If you're here, we're going to enjoy, eat, and laugh.' It didn't matter who they were. And I thank him for that. I thank him so much for all of those wonderful memories. But I do play in my head the times when I could have left earlier and done more with him."

Scott also received some sage advice from a different family source.

"I was talking with my son about how people handle it when things don't go their way. It breaks my heart when I hear about young kids that commit suicide or do whatever. My son agreed. He told me how he handles things when they don't go his way. He said, 'That's not the script we wrote, but it's the play I'm in.' That was one of his more profound moments, but it's the truth. We can't choose the cards we're dealt. You get what you get. And if that's the deck you've got, play it."

Resilience. Pride. Advice.

Scott hopes that her invaluable experience can benefit future generations of transportation professionals.

"Have faith in yourself. Know that it's okay to make a mistake. Understand that you'll make mistakes! You'll do better next time. Get yourself up. Dust yourself off. There is nothing that's going to happen where you can't stop and say, 'Alright, it wasn't exactly the way I wanted it to be, but do I have to wind up crumbling?' No. But I'm a scrapper. I make it happen. So resilience is just in me. The other thing is to have pride in your work.

"I take personal pride in wanting things to be done well and right. Leaders need to have a vision. You've got to set expectations as to what's acceptable from yourself and others. And be clear about them. Be very centered in terms of your values. And be prepared to walk the talk. You cannot be sitting up there and running your mouth, talking about you believing in this, that, or the other. People see from your actions who you really are.

"That's my story and I'm sticking to it."

And that is exactly what Dr. Beverly Scott does every day—as she follows her purpose and her passion.

Chapter 14

RINA CUTLER

When I walked in the room there were about 15 guys around this table and I think the youngest was 70. The chairman of the Philadelphia Italian Market Business Association was at the end of the table. He was a little man and he stood up at and slammed his hand on the table and said to me, "Yoo goht a lawt of bawls fer a brawd!"

I, having spent some time in the North End in Boston, which was very similar in spirit and attitude to South Philly, stood up and pounded my hand on the table and said, "You can't park on the sidewalk!" Ultimately they could and did park on the sidewalk. It was a war I knew I could not win, and I made a very conscious choice that it was not even worth fighting. That maturity to figure out what's important and what will matter a year from now is a highly won skillset . . . and I believe that's how I learned to speak Philadelphian.

Rina Cutler plans to pen an autobiography titled *You Can't Make This Shit Up* once she retires. But all of her tales—both off-color and those ready for prime time—reveal a razor-sharp wit and intelligence that helped her navigate the transportation industry adroitly. Cutler began her career when Boston Mayor Ray Flynn plucked her from a community schools program and appointed her Deputy Commissioner in the transportation department. This was Cutler's first role as a change agent. It would not be her last. And people noticed her work.

Then–San Francisco Mayor Art Agnos lured Cutler west to create San Francisco's new Department of Parking and Traffic. After a tumultuous tenure, Cutler returned to Boston, this time as Transportation Commissioner. Next she served as Executive Director of the Philadelphia Parking Authority, where her charge was to turn the authority around. She did. Cutler then joined the Pennsylvania Department of Transportation (PennDOT) as Deputy Secretary for Administration for five years before returning to Philadelphia and a new mayor, Michael Nutter, where she served as Deputy Mayor for Transportation and Utilities for the City of Philadelphia. As these stories went to press, Cutler had just accepted the position of Senior Director for Major Station Planning and Development at Amtrak.

Numerous organizations have recognized Cutler for her achievements. WTS International named her Woman of the Year. In 2011, *American City and County* magazine presented her with its highly coveted Public Works Leader of the Year trophy. And COMTO identified her as one of their Women Who Move the Nation in 2012. Rina Cutler blazed an unusual and entertaining trail in transportation.

This is her story.

Becoming a Change Agent 101

No one was more surprised than Rina Cutler when Boston Mayor Raymond Flynn transferred her to the transportation department. "My only experience in transportation was getting my car booted, but I didn't think that was a criterion for being in transportation." Turns out, she had other talents as well.

"What Mayor Flynn said, which I did not really believe, was that I was one of the best managers he had and that if he put me in a hospital I could run a hospital and that if he put me on a train I could learn to run a train. He had identified a set of skills that *I* had not yet identified. His charge to me was basically, 'These folks don't know that they're in the people business and that everything they do has an impact on people's lives. That's what I need you to go over and do.'"

Although young and inexperienced, Cutler rose to the challenge.

"I was good at managing people. I was good at managing conflict. And I was good at somehow convincing people to think about things in a slightly different way. I ultimately got the support of all the managers in the agency, many who had been there a very long time. They taught me everything I knew about the business at that point. It could have gone very badly. They could have been resentful and not willing to be helpful or to think about any changes."

But Cutler's approach made them both comfortable and accountable.

"I basically came in admitting that I knew very little about what they did, but that I was trying to make it easier for them to do their job, rather than my telling them, 'This is how you should do your job.' It was an evolutionary process, I assure you. Not everyone welcomed me with open arms, but enough of them did and I was able to win them over."

Her success soon became a model that garnered attention.

Fighting the Good, Unfair Fight by the Bay

In 1999, San Francisco floated a ballot question (Proposition E) to create a new city department, the Department of Parking and Traffic (DPT). In looking for a model and a leader, they found Boston and Cutler.

"I had been really excited to go, because I'm a huge baseball person and the World Series was being played out there. I had left City Hall and stepped off the glass elevator in my hotel when the Loma Prieta earthquake hit. I remember thinking, 'This is a sign from God.' What I didn't realize was that it was a sign from God that said, 'Don't come!' I translated it the other way. . . . "

Mayor Agnos tasked Cutler with creating the DPT, an amalgam of disparate transportation elements from 10 other city agencies.

"Traffic enforcement came over from the police department; residential parking came over from the treasurer's office; planning came over from the planning department; and traffic engineering came over from public works. In some ways that's how they got me, because I knew that nobody in my life was likely to ever say, 'Construct a new city agency the way you think it ought to run.'"

But all was not good in the new world.

"I didn't know anybody in San Francisco. I already didn't like earthquakes. I had no idea how I was going to pull this off. So I actually had to fight through a good deal of fear to decide to hold my nose and just jump off the bridge. And in many ways, the decision to do so totally changed my career path forever. It was *not* my most successful endeavor. It was one turf battle after another. And no one was happy."

It was a thankless job. But some of her efforts took thanklessness to a new level.

"I would occasionally look at the parking officers' work sheets. That gave me a pretty good breakdown of their productivity. I remember looking at one sheet and the parking officer had written a lot of tickets. Generally that meant no one was ever going to look at her work. But when I analyzed *when* her tickets were written, I realized that she didn't do any work for the last two hours of her shift. Then I looked at other people's worksheets. It was pretty clear that people weren't working their entire shifts. When I declared they needed to, that's when the *real* war broke out. That made me very unpopular. The union had a very strong presence in San Francisco. They decided I was Attila the Hun. They fought constantly and not always fairly with me. It was very hard."

It didn't get any easier. And the attacks were relentless and public. But Cutler stood steadfast.

"I have a tendency to get more stubborn in those circumstances. I talked about it in staff meetings, so that folks knew I was completely conscious of it happening, but I didn't want it to deter us from moving forward. I, and we, should do our best to ignore it where we could and address it where we needed to, but it shouldn't really distract us from our overall goal of trying to start up a new city agency. That was hard enough!"

Then fate stepped in. Mayor Agnos lost his reelection bid to his Police Commissioner, Frank Jordan.

"When Frank became the mayor-elect, I had a pretty good sense that we weren't going to be a good pair. I've now worked for seven mayors and a governor. And I have developed and refined the ability to figure out who the elected officials are that I can work with. I'm quirky. I don't do well being micromanaged. I'm much better if you tell me what your vision is and how you define success. Then give me guidance along the way if I'm straying too far from what you want or if I'm causing too much controversy.

"If you're a mayor who wants people that are smart and capable, that's a good fit for me. If you're a mayor who wants your department heads and commissioners to not disagree and to stay out of the newspapers, that's not a good fit for me. That's not because I seek out the newspapers, but I have a tendency to end up in them. After I accepted the San Francisco job, I have been told that Agnos called back to my former mayor in Boston and asked what he should expect from me. Ray Flynn said, 'Get used to sentences that start with, "With all due respect . . ." and "Mayor, I respectfully disagree. . . ." Those are the sentences you're going to hear more than anything else.'"

Cutler resigned from the City of San Francisco. But her timing was impeccable.

Returning Home and Anger Management

In Boston, then–Transportation Commissioner Rick Dimino had left for the private sector. So Mayor Flynn had an opening. Cutler was made Transportation Commissioner. And she was thrilled to return.

"I did not truly understand how the job in San Francisco had affected me. I wasn't experienced enough to understand that all big cities were not alike. And I think San Francisco taught me mostly what I *didn't* know. But I knew I was on a career path and I was going to stay in the transportation business. That was probably the most valuable lesson of my career."

Still, something was amiss.

"I was very much in this mindset that I had to just fight about everything, because I had just spent the last two years fighting about everything. At one point, someone pulled me aside and said, 'You don't have to fight anymore. You are the boss. You have the support of your agency. You have the support of your mayor. You need to think about what your style of management is going to be.' For me, that was earth-shattering."

So, Cutler reframed her outlook. She also refined her philosophy for public sector success.

"So much of government is based on relationships. And it behooves people to do what I think I've done very successfully, to figure out who in government I need to be successful and then make them my professional friends. They're not always the commissioners or the department heads—most often they're not. They're the folks that have been in there a long time, who know how to work the personnel system and the finance system and the purchasing system and the political system. San Francisco wasn't as successful for me as Boston was because I was not totally conscious of who could do that in San Francisco."

Knowledge Transfer and Early Dismissal

Cutler believes that working in the public sector is not for the faint of heart. But she also believes passionately in ensuring an agency's long-term success.

"There are three things you need to transfer knowledge. First, I tend, unless sworn to secrecy, to share information with my staff. Sharing that information allows them to know what they need to know to be successful. Second, I bring them with me into meetings to give them access to the people they're going to need to know. Third, you lead by example. How you want your staff to behave is how you behave. It doesn't matter what I tell them. They're going to respond to what they see and hear."

Cutler invests heavily in her people. As a result, Cutler chooses them very carefully. But sometimes it doesn't work out.

"I have made one or two really bad hiring decisions in my career, but only one or two. I have a pretty good sense of what I need and what I'm looking for and where I have control over it.

If it doesn't work, I'm okay having it not work. But there are good and bad ways to handle that. My first inclination is to figure out if I can move somebody to a place where their skillset matches a job description better than the job I hired them for. That doesn't always work out, though.

"Not too long ago I had told someone it wasn't working out. I gave them three months to find another job. The first reaction is usually something like, 'I don't understand. I think I'm doing a good job. I'd like another chance.' And I have to explain about all of the previous conversations we'd had on the subject. They have to know along the way that there are expectations they're not meeting or problems that need to be addressed. So at the point that happens, I assure you there have been many meetings about it. I try not to fire people on the spot unless they do something that actually breaks the law, at which point I'm more than happy to fire them on the spot. But most people aren't in that category."

On the Whole, I'd Rather Be in Philadelphia

If anything is constant, it's change. As Cutler settled in, Mayor Flynn accepted an ambassadorship to the Vatican. Then Cutler received a call from Philadelphia Mayor Ed Rendell and his chief of staff David Cohen. They wanted "significant changes" to Philadelphia's parking operations and they wanted Cutler to make them. Mayor Rendell asked Cutler what she knew about Philadelphia. Cutler explained that she knew only four things about the city.

"Cheesesteaks, which I'm really looking forward to tasting. The Liberty Bell, which I'm really looking forward to seeing. And the other two are a little on the negative side. And Rendell laughed and said, 'What are they?' And I said, 'Well real baseball is played on grass and you all don't play baseball on grass. So that's going to be a real issue for me.' He laughed and said, 'I'll build you a new stadium!' Which of course did happen, even though it wasn't for me, he did take credit for promising me that and delivering it. And I told him the other thing is, 'The previous mayor blew up a neighborhood.' MOVE was one of the things I knew about Philadelphia."

Cutler refers to an event where Philadelphia Police dropped an incendiary device on a house in an attempt to end an armed standoff with the radical group MOVE. As a result, 11 people died and 60 homes were destroyed.

"I frankly could not wrap my brain around the fact that a mayor could drop a bomb on a neighborhood and then get reelected. I remember sitting in Ray Flynn's office with a lot of staff and watching it on TV and thinking to myself, 'That mayor is toast!' But silly me, he got reelected overwhelmingly. So I knew the politics were going to be pretty unusual. Boston in its own way has pretty tough politics, but I will say that compared to Philadelphia they truly are a day at the beach."

Cutler took the job.

What Rendell Knew, and Politics and People in the City of Brotherly Love

Upon her arrival, Cutler set to work. She soon realized that Mayor Rendell didn't exactly reveal the entire scope of the issues she faced.

"When I went to San Francisco, I don't think Art Agnos knew what I was in for. But in Philadelphia, they knew what I was in for and did *not* tell me. About two months in I called the Mayor and said, 'I can't believe that you let me walk into this. Why didn't you tell me what I should expect here?' He laughed and said, 'Well if I told you, Rina, you wouldn't have come.' But it was the start of a great relationship with Rendell, which I have to this day. And it was the beginning of what has been 20 years in Pennsylvania. They still think I'm a carpetbagger, but they're nicer about it. It's funny. When I go back to Boston, they now think I talk funny. When I come back to Philadelphia, they still think I talk funny."

But it wasn't her accent that got her in trouble in South Philadelphia. It was parking.

"They have this funny habit of parking on the sidewalk. But they park on the sidewalk even when there is no car parked in the street in front of the sidewalk where they're parked, because they don't want to get blocked in. I, of course, have a pretty strong sense that people should not be parking on the sidewalk. So I sent my parking enforcement officers down to ticket the cars. And that started a little bit of a hullaballoo.

"The Mayor called me and said, 'What the *hell* are you doing?' And I said, 'My job, sir?' And he said, 'Well, now you need to go to this community meeting and talk to these people. Don't you understand history and legacy?' And I said, 'What about the pedestrians? What about people in wheelchairs who can't get around the cars?' Knowing I was asking a rhetorical question, the Mayor's reply was both simple and sarcastic, 'Semantics, Rina.'"

The South Philly parking problem did not go her way. But Cutler's tough second skin was to be tested in a more serious way.

"I had pulled together my first senior staff meeting and walked through expectations—rewarding merit, etc. At one point, one of the people raised their hands and said, 'You know, Ms. Cutler, you're new in town. So I feel obligated to tell you that everyone around this table has a political sponsor. And that's how jobs and cars and offices are distributed. So your whole theory about merit and performance standards . . . well, you're new, and I'm trying to protect you here.'

"I thought about that for a minute and then I looked him straight in the eye and said, 'So everyone here has a sponsor.' And everyone said, 'Yep.' Then I said, 'Well my sponsor is the Mayor. See if you can top that.' There was dead silence in the room. Then I said, 'I only have one more thing to say about this topic. At some point, one of you is going to do something really stupid. And I'm going to fire you. I believe that when the Mayor is faced with the choice of firing you or my quitting, *you will be fired*. And we are about to test out my theory.' Then I walked out of the room."

A few months later, Cutler's prediction came true.

"One of them did something stupid enough that I knew I had enough ammunition to fire them. And when I fired them they told me that they'd be back because their sponsor would never go for that. Sure enough, within a very short time I got a phone call from the Mayor's chief of staff asking what was going on. I explained it and he said, 'Fair enough.' And that was it. That was all I needed. It only had to happen once. And that sent a message through my organization."

Cutler fixed the parking authority. Then once again, Cutler's mayor was term-limited and she changed addresses again, moving to the state capitol, Harrisburg.

There's a New Deputy in Town

Cutler resisted moving to Harrisburg when she was named PennDOT Deputy Secretary for Administration. And it wasn't just because of its distance from Philadelphia.

"I just had a different perspective in many ways than they were used to. And I very much came in as Governor Ed Rendell's person. That was kind of interesting because I was *not* the Secretary; I was the Deputy Secretary. Al Biehler was the Secretary. Al is a very good man—we still stay in touch—but I think it says something about the glass ceiling. Even as recently as a decade or so ago, I had a Governor that did *not* appoint me, for whatever reason, as the Secretary of Transportation, but put me in the second spot. And we've just now appointed a woman Secretary of Transportation in Pennsylvania."

True to form, Cutler pressed on, effecting change in the state.

"I had not really spent time in the rest of the state outside of Philadelphia and the five counties around Philadelphia and the Pittsburgh area. So I made a very conscious decision that I would get to every one of the 67 counties in the state. It took several years, but I did it. And in many of those counties when I showed up—we had a maintenance operation in every county—they were shocked!

"They were shocked that someone would visit from the central office. They were shocked it was a woman—they didn't know what to make of me, frankly. And they were surprised that somebody would go out of their way to get their input on how operations were going. In any transportation agency, operations and maintenance are where you live and die. But it was the first time many of them had seen a Deputy Secretary ever! But I felt like I needed to make that commitment, and I was glad I did that."

After a five-year stint at PennDOT, Cutler returned to Philadelphia and new Mayor Michael Nutter, where she served until joining Amtrak in 2015.

Paying It Forward

Boston Mayor Flynn changed Cutler's life when he made her a Deputy Commissioner in transportation. Since then, she returns the favor to others.

"Mayor Flynn clearly recognized something in me that I had not recognized in myself. So I am very conscious to try and recognize that in the people who work for me and with me. It's not always clear who is going to be successful and who isn't, because they're just developing their skillsets or they're not yet secure enough. I have a job now that I couldn't have done 20 years ago. I have skillsets that didn't exist 20 years ago! So learning to identify leaders or future leaders is something I'm very conscious of and try to be helpful with."

Rina-isms and Being Voted Off the Island

Cutler is ultimately a positive pragmatist. And she has an inimitable way of expressing that philosophy.

"My friends call them Rina-isms. They are sayings that I've adopted along the way that I think are really important. For example, 'If you're not at the table, you're on the menu.' 'Sometimes you're the windshield and sometimes you're the bug.' That's for people who work for elected officials who may not like you the day after they hire you."

With her philosophy, Cutler defines herself as a change agent. And in that regard, she believes two elements are integral to her success.

"I tend to take an evolution-not-revolution perspective when I'm trying to do change. Because otherwise I'm just trying to push a rock up a hill and it keeps running me over. So I started as a young transportation professional preaching and thinking revolution (I did grow up in the 1960s). But I actually have learned that it's about evolution and that you have to go slow enough to manage the change, and fast enough that you get some momentum.

"The best advice I give myself on a regular basis is that *you* are term limited. You may be more term limited than the elected person you're working for. If you're willing to be voted off the island—and I am willing to be voted off the island—I am totally comfortable that I can find another job. So you have to do your job your way. The first time it happened to me, in San Francisco, I didn't know what that meant. But knowing I was going to be voted off the island I took the first step and resigned. That taught me two things. One, I was not going to stay in jobs that made me unhappy. And two, I was willing to hold my breath and jump off of the cliff if I needed to."

The Work-Life Balance Beam

Many struggle with the work-life balance issue. But Cutler did not, at first.

"I didn't have balance at all in San Francisco. But my family was so far away that it never occurred to me that I needed to balance it. When I was first starting out in Boston, I didn't have it because I was dancing as fast as I could and that required me to work at my craft. So I could completely skew my work-life balance.

"When I came to Philadelphia and started to make friends and a life here, I was pretty conscious that I operated with a type A personality and needed to be able to decompress and lower my stress level. So I taught myself that I could work hard *and* play hard. Now I make my staff take their vacation time. It always freaks them out. But I get more out of them if I make them take their vacation time."

But balance isn't the only work-life balance issue people face.

"I'm not sure I thought much either way about having children. As a young adult, I certainly expected that I would go to college, get married, and have children. It just didn't happen that way and I don't know that I was conscious of it much. When I started to move around the country, it was pretty clear to me that if I had a husband and children at home it would have been a lot harder to just decide, yes, I'm moving to Pennsylvania, yes I'm moving to California, yes I'm moving to wherever the next adventure brings me. So I think unconsciously I had already made the choice. And so once I became conscious of it, the choice to not have children was an easy one for me."

Her Dream Job as Commissioner

"I'm hoping they're going to call me to become the next baseball commissioner. But at the moment it doesn't look good for me. It's down to two people and neither of them is me. That's my dream job. . . ."

Chapter 15

JANE CHMIELINSKI

The MBTA Director of Construction—the late Peter McNulty—and I ended up working for 19 hours straight on a problem. And he was incredulous that we could solve it. I said, "You look so surprised." He said, "To be honest, you always look like you're just fooling around here." And I said, "I am really not challenged by this job. This isn't what I really want to do." And his eyes turned black. I never saw him so serious. He level-set his gaze, and he said, "You better learn to love the job you have to get the job you love." I walked out of my cubicle that night, and I never went back there the same person. And I never worked anywhere where that didn't ring in my ears. I decided I would always be the bright spot. And I credit that moment with propelling me on to do so many of the things that I did.

From the vantage of her father's East Boston car repair shop, Jane Chmielinski learned about politics and life. Through her father's political connections, she secured a job with the Massachusetts Highway Department and then at the Massachusetts Bay Transportation Authority. She did not love the MBTA at first. But after her late-night epiphany, she grew to love her work there. Then things changed again, and she saw her future in the private sector.

She joined Frederic R. Harris (FRH), in 1993 because of its "entrepreneurial nature." She made a good choice. By 1999, she was the Deputy Unit Manager in Boston.

In 2000, FRH merged with DMJM to form DMJM Harris, all legacy companies of the *Fortune 500* parent company AECOM. Chmielinski rose precipitously and moved to New York, where she became the DMJM Harris Chief Operating Officer, then President. In 2008, when AECOM united into one entity, Chmielinski became the Group Chief Executive for Corporate Development, an office that spanned AECOM's global operating groups. She became AECOM Chief Operating Officer, as well as President of the AECOM Americas Group. She also served as a member of AECOM's Executive Committee at the enterprise level. She retired in April 2015 after 37 years in the infrastructure space.

Chmielinski believes strongly in corporate social responsibility and championed a number of initiatives at AECOM. She is also actively involved in several professional associations including WTS and currently serves on the Board of Directors of the New York Chapter of the Women's Forum and the Beverly Willis Architecture Foundation. Over the years, she served on the Board of Directors of the March of Dimes, as well as the Norman Mineta School of Transportation in San Jose, CA, and the National Academy of Construction.

Jane Chmielinski rose from humble beginnings to some of the highest corporate heights in the infrastructure industry. And she did it with humor, effectiveness, and compassion.

This is her story.

Politics 101: An Italian-American Takes an African-American through East Boston

Jane Chmielinski grew up in Winthrop, MA, but her early education was spent in her father's East Boston garage.

"My dad was very active in politics. He was Massachusetts Governor John Volpe's campaign manager. He had been George Lodge's campaign manager when Lodge ran against Ted Kennedy. And if you give me an address in East Boston, I could probably still tell you what ward and precinct you were in. I saw at an early age that politics was a path to power. My dad owned a garage, but it seemed his greatest passion was politics. Every politician came through there. And when Senator Ed Brooke was in *Look* magazine, he was in a photo with my dad, because it was about an Italian-American taking an African-American candidate through East Boston—a big deal at the time. That one act was a terrific lesson in standing up for your beliefs. And if you want to speak, speak up!"

Getting Started in the Combat Zone

Through her father's influence, Chmielinski got a job. But this was not your typical patronage employment.

"My first public sector job was at the Massachusetts Highway Department. My job title was something like Junior Right-of-Way Agent."

Her job title sounded innocuous; the job was not. It had to do with eminent domain, the process where a government entity expropriates private property for public use and provides compensation.

"We went out to people's houses and interviewed them—and you're taking their home! I think the men actually enjoyed shunting the young ones to do this, to see how we handled it."

But in 1978, her work took her to a unique part of the city, Boston's infamous Combat Zone, an area known at that time for its strip clubs and brothels.

"We were asked to interview the prostitutes, because we were taking the buildings where they plied their trade. They wanted to be considered a business, but the federal government didn't recognize prostitution as a business. So we were relocating them as a home. I remember one of the women got really mad and swore at me. The guy I was with yelled at her, 'Don't you swear in front of a lady!' Then she started really yelling at me, and I said, 'No, no, no. It's really fine!' But I thought she was going to kill me. The overriding thought I had was that she was being judged and measured on the 'lady scale,' just like me! It taught me not to judge others so quickly."

After a workforce reduction, Chmielinski lost her job. Once again through connections, she got a job at the MBTA.

Here's Your Corsage and Your Sash

Her start at the MBTA was less than auspicious.

"The big American Public Transportation Association (APTA) conference was coming to town. The MBTA was a sponsor. One of the executives asked me and fifteen other women around my age *if we would be hostesses!* He asked us if we would take care of the spouses of the attendees. And we asked, 'What do you mean take care of them?' And he said, 'Someone may need a hair dressing appointment. . . .' So we wore corsages and sashes, and we took care of the spouses. The thing that was so bizarre was that there were other women back at the MBTA that were jealous!"

Chmielinski accepted the inequity at the time, but it left a lasting impression.

Powerful Women Changing Things

Her time at the MBTA provided complex and indelible lessons, but there were few female role models in the industry. She would find those elsewhere.

"Coming from East Boston you had some real spitfires and characters like Anna Defonzo, Philippa Pizzi, and Alice Christopher. Those women shaped Logan Airport by protesting its expansion. These were mothers who took their baby carriages and stood in front of bulldozers to prevent a runway from being built. So I got to see that powerful women can make a change. It was fascinating that a small group of really smart women could change the course of transportation. Luckily over the years we got to make major impacts through different tools and tactics, but it was the beginning of the sea change of things to come."

That fascination would not end there. And those were by no means the only spitfires in Chmielinski's life.

"My mother, aunts, and my sister definitely fell into the powerful women category. They all taught me life lessons that no MBA could ever teach. When you say, 'You need to see it to be it,' well, I had ringside seats."

Do You Mind Taking Notes?

Back at the MBTA, things continued apace. Though treated differently because of her gender, Chmielinski valued and cherished her time there.

"Sometimes I might have only been a potted plant in the room. But I got to learn how things really got done, and it isn't terribly different in the private or public sectors. And I know if I started out in the private sector, I would have not been allowed in those rooms for a long time.

"I also learned a valuable, early lesson: being the scribe could be pretty good. The meeting was pretty much described as *I* saw it. Too many women get all bent out of shape if somebody says, 'Do you mind taking notes?' But there was a certain power in it if you used it right. Don't make a career out of it, but if you took the notes, you told the story. That also helped me learn another important lesson: pick your battles. That's especially important when you're starting out."

Seeing opportunity where others did not would become a valuable skill in her career.

A Fabulous Time in Massachusetts Transportation

There was another reason she prized her time at the MBTA. It was a golden age in Boston transportation.

"There were requests for proposals (RFPs) going out left and right and the T (MBTA) had some of the most innovative and fantastic projects in transportation in the Americas. But one thing that really stood out was that we were not on good footing relative to environmental permits. Environmental was very important, because it could stop a project cold and cause tremendous fines. But doing environmental work in the agencies at that time made you somewhat of the skunk at the garden party. But I was lucky to have wonderful people like Massport Environmental Director Robin Ellis and Massachusetts Turnpike Authority Manager of

Environmental Engineering Doug Cotton. We all became very good friends. And when people started to realize how important environmental management was to good project governance, we started to have a bond with operations and construction alike."

Her environmental work here would prove crucial later in her career.

"I'm Surprised You and Mary Jane Get Along"

Her MBTA job was serious. At that time, though, Chmielinski could not say the same thing about herself.

"When you walk back the cat and you think about it, you're in your 20s and you're developing your thought processes. I can't lie. I honestly thought I was there for a good time, not a long time."

She would change her attitude after her interaction with Peter McNulty clued her into the need for an adjustment. But the gender bias would last longer. And it sometimes took strange forms.

"I remember men saying to me, 'I am so surprised you and Mary Jane O'Meara get along.' And I would say, 'Why? Did she say something about me?' And they would respond, 'No. Women just don't work well together.' And I would think, 'We get along fine.' In fact, I can't think of a woman that I've ever *not* been able to work with because she was a woman. It might have been some other character flaw that either I had or she had or we just didn't gel. And Mary Jane and I laughed about it so hard, because they asked us so many times. 'My god, I can't believe you get along so well.' It was the most shocking thing to them. But I have to say, Mary Jane and I still get along very well all these years later!"

She did not blame the MBTA. She felt those attitudes were simply the prevailing societal norms. Still, it hurt. But that wasn't the only revelation she would have about organizational roles.

"As I started to get a little bit higher in the ranks, one phenomenal thing that I recognized is that everybody loves you when you're mid-level management. And the day you become their boss, it's interesting how you're not as wonderful and hard working and great."

She would soon put that theory to the test.

The Private Sector

In 1991, William Weld became governor of Massachusetts. Chmielinski was about to be named MBTA Deputy General Manager of Environment. Things seemed to be going well.

"But then some of the folks I enjoyed working with left the MBTA. And once you start to work some place where you no longer feel like a major contributor, you really shouldn't take a paycheck from them. Then, my longtime friend Joe Aiello, who was running major programs for the MBTA, left and that was the last straw for me. I knew it was time for me to make a change."

But where would she go?

"Joe Aiello called and said, 'Why don't you come over to Frederic R. Harris?' I had never thought of doing that, of going to the private sector. But I knew Ira Levy, a senior vice president running the Boston operations. He can be a little bombastic, but he is also a very clever consultant that helped us solve incredibly complex problems. Then Joe said something very interesting, 'You could go to one of the more established firms, but I don't think you'll go as far as fast, because this is a very entrepreneurial firm that has a vision. They're still kind of a sleeping dog, but they are going to come on strong.'

"I heard more about the company and realized what a scrappy group of people it was. They bought the company back from Ashland Technology and created an Employee Stock Ownership Plan. And I'm saying to myself, 'These people mortgaged their homes to get money to invest in this company. That's a commitment.'"

Joe intervened on her behalf. He recommended to Ira Levy that he hire Chmielinski to start a transportation planning department. Ira accepted the recommendation. Given her lack of negotiating experience, Chmielinski accepted the offer outright, but learned a profound lesson, one she coaches women on today.

"When I coach women about their compensation, I advise them not to go to the mat about a 2.4% versus a 1.4% raise, if you deserve a material raise. Fight for it and have a game plan should you not get what you want. As for bonuses, they're always appreciated, but never a guarantee. Bonuses also usually become your 'fun money,' and are used for short to mid-term life enhancements. What to really fight for are long-term incentives—they are what build wealth and can provide lifetime financial security. Too many women do not even know their companies' policies and what the road map is to achieve eligibility for long-term incentives!"

Chmielinski faced a transition. Fortunately, she landed in a good place for her.

"I was lucky that Frederic R. Harris didn't have a meaningful transportation planning presence in Boston. And right when I got there, we started going after significant transportation jobs. We already had a job with the Federal Railroad Administration in a joint venture with our sister company DMJM, and I was immediately put on that job as the Project Director. I also learned the god-awful fact about 100% billability. That was probably the biggest change, but the transition went great. I had the chance to build a department. I had a lot of support from senior leadership in Boston, and people like Ira, Joe, and so many other colleagues and upper management on both coasts that were very helpful. The biggest lesson was to learn how to transfer the skills from the public sector to the private sector—and to put the firm's success above any personal power base. I considered this vital to a smooth and successful transition."

Learn she would.

Getting on the Radar Screen

"In addition to running the department, I ended up running the EIS (environmental impact statement) and planning for *Tren Urbano*, a big transit job in Puerto Rico. I went to Puerto Rico for a three-month assignment and ended up living there five years. I was one of the first women in the company that had done that kind of big move. And I think that put me on the radar screen. Another life lesson, take chances and stretch assignments."

Things would continue to advance. Soon, Chmielinski would be asked to relocate again.

"You Really Should Get Your Name Off This Report"

Chmielinski went to Puerto Rico. But John Dionisio, DMJM Harris CEO, came to Puerto Rico to visit the *Tren Urbano* project. This would be her third meeting with him and it would prove to be important.

"He did a town hall and he talked about something called *loss margin*. I didn't understand all of it, so afterwards I went up to him, because I was too shy to ask in front of everyone. And I said, 'I'm on the loss margin report, but I don't even know why I'm there.' Then John gave me a wonderful piece of advice.

"He said, 'Three of the projects that you are shown as an officer in charge of have loss margin. When I was on the loss margin report, my then-president and CEO said to me, 'If you ever want to move ahead in this company, you should really get your name off this report.' And, you know, Mrs. Marmo might not have had beautiful daughters, but she had relatively smart ones. And I dug into the projects. I found out why we had a loss margin problem and corrected it. And from that point on—and that would have been in 1996—I've never been on the loss margin report again."

Getting on the Track

Chmielinski was on deck to become the Unit Manager in Boston, an important job in the Frederic R. Harris structure. She was also working on transportation pursuits in the New York office, working more with John Dionisio and Fred Werner. Then Dionisio asked her to come to New York to be his Chief of Staff.

"I hated the title. If it were government, that's different. But I didn't want to be a glorified secretary. However, I loved the fact that I would now be in the corporate office and learning the business of the business. So I cut a deal and I said, 'John, let me keep my job in Boston as Deputy Unit Manager, and I will figure out how to do both jobs.' The job was important to me because understanding the business of the business was the hole in my experience. I knew how to make money on a project. I knew how to make money in an operation. I knew how to win work. I knew how to manage people. And I knew how to deal with clients. But I didn't know what happened after we handed over the money from the Boston operation. And that's what I wanted to learn."

Dionisio agreed. And the timing was important. Soon the firm would win the Second Avenue Subway megaproject. But first they had to complete the proposal.

"I got the brilliant idea of looking at the RFP. And I noticed something: a position on the project that they absolutely needed, but didn't have listed. The position was for somebody to liaison between the team doing the engineering (us) and the team doing the EIS (Vollmer). So I said, 'I guarantee you they will get an EIS record of decision on something totally different than what we're designing, and it'll cause mayhem.' Everybody said, 'We can't insert a position they don't want!' We put it in anyway. We didn't have anybody to do it, so everybody kept saying well, 'We'll put your name in.' So they put my name in. When it came time to do the interview, only five people were allowed to go. I was one of the five. And we won the job."

She always recounts what a fantastic win Second Avenue Subway was and that working on that project was a challenge, as well as an honor.

Chmielinski became Executive Vice President and was in line to become the COO of DMJM Harris. In 2006, DMJM Harris/AECOM reorganized and she became President of DMJM Harris.

A Doctorate in Managing Anxiety

AECOM grew exponentially. And Chmielinski served a key role in guiding and managing that expansion. It was not easy work, but a true character builder.

"It's kind of like rewiring your house with the electricity still on. You're trying to bring everything together while still developing strategic plans, hitting financial plan, delivering projects, and delighting clients. It's quite a time in any firm. But we just could not keep going to market with 27 authorized company names. So I left being President at DMJM Harris to go to AECOM corporate to integrate 27 companies. When John asked me to come to AECOM to do this, my first thought was, 'Are you crazy?' But I accepted the position, even though it felt a bit like a lateral move, at best. However, I saw the potential in the position. Plus I knew I would learn a lot."

She rose to the challenge.

"It took two years to bring together the global operation. But it was very challenging trying to get 45,000 people to rally around one brand when we had all been very used to our own brands and cultures. So I got a doctorate in managing anxiety, from really learning how to listen to people to understanding that sometimes the words that people were using were just code for what was really bugging them. You know you laugh about it in hindsight, but some of the seemingly little things that matter to staff and teams are the really important seminal issues. But through that experience I made so many wonderful friends and met so many terrific professionals in the company, so that when I did go on to COO there was no operation that was foreign to me."

But in dealing with integrations of this size, the challenges are not only internal. And they were about to double. In 2014, AECOM acquired URS, also a *Fortune 500* company roughly equal in size to AECOM. That integration is well underway and is poised once again to change the trajectory of AECOM.

The CEO of Jane

She has held many different corporate ranks, but one title is immutable.

"I never aspired to be a CEO or COO at a company or within the industry, but I always knew I was the CEO of Jane. From as long as I can remember, I always had my own board of directors. They were people that I valued. They were my sounding boards, trusted advisors, and my true-north leaders, and they changed depending on what phase of life I was in, but I have always had that. There are key moments in my life where I can point to people or a person who gave me phenomenal advice, people that were there for me personally and professionally."

And she maintains that position today.

Self Worth and Net Worth

Chmielinski ascended the corporate ladder quickly, assuming many different roles. But there was one constant she held onto throughout the journey.

"Without leaving the company, I had to reinvent myself about eight different times. Each time I ascended a little bit closer to the top, I kept saying, 'Oh man! Am I feeling like Icarus!' It was daunting. I was always the only woman or one of very few women. There wasn't a lot of room for error. And the stakes got higher and higher. But in all of this, I had to make a conscious decision and work at it every single day to say, 'Don't let my net worth and my self-worth cross, because if I do one day I will be crushed.'"

Away from Home for Fifteen Years

Work-life balance is tough. On first glance, it seems that Chmielinski stretched the concept to its limit. But maybe not.

"I would never say it was a sacrifice because I did it absolutely willingly—but remember I was away from home for fifteen years. I went home on weekends. But I was so lucky to have family and friends that supported me. I could not have done this if they had said, 'Sorry, you need to be here.' I give them a lot of credit."

She also offers some advice for time spent with family.

"Make every minute count. When you're with your family, be in that moment. If you have to use your BlackBerry, hide! But don't sit there on your BlackBerry in front of everybody. Be in the moment. I went to a lunch in Boston about 100 years ago for communications and PR firms and Leslie Stahl was the speaker. And she said the best thing about work-life balance that I ever heard. She said, 'Everybody has a lot of balls up in the air. Just know which one of those balls is made of crystal, because when they fall and break, you can't fix those. The rest will bounce. So the trick is to figure out which are the crystal balls that you're carrying.' That, for me, has always been part of my work-life balance."

Using My Power for Good

Providing an essential service for the public good is one of the virtues of working in transportation. But Chmielinski always felt the need to do more.

"Sometimes I think, 'Did I actually contribute to anything, or did I just look like some psycho running around?' But I have to say I loved AECOM. I loved what we did. I loved the people, the projects. I even embraced our insanity and our mistakes. But the thing that I'll look back on in my career that makes me the happiest is being able to say, 'Whatever power I had, real or perceived, I tried to use that platform to help others in and outside AECOM or our industry.' That was the greatest satisfaction."

She helped many people on an individual level. But she also launched grander initiatives.

"I was passionate about getting the company to invest in things many companies never would have thought about investing in at the time. We started a diversity inclusion program pretty early on in the game. Five years ago, we started to really take our corporate social responsibility seriously and in a new direction, something that a lot of our competitors weren't even thinking about. We're not regulated to do it. We did it because that's the kind of company it is. So whatever it felt like I sacrificed, I got so much more back."

A Velvet Hammer and Other Tools

Women can have a tougher time in a male-dominated industry. But Chmielinski believes tools can help level the playing field.

"If you have something to say, speak up. Sometimes, especially with younger women, it's hard getting them to understand that you can deliver a hard message. You can be a velvet hammer. But if you have to have one of those tough conversations, step back. Practice it in front of a mirror. But the worst thing for women is that you get accused of being emotional. You have to subvert that. I have not always been successful, but I keep trying. I've actually had a coach that has helped me learn to speak more slowly and drop my voice. But the real big thing is that you've got to find what you really love to do. Take some time to do that. Invest some time in yourself to say, 'What will make it really soar for me?' Because if you're not happy at this, none of it is worth it."

Saying Goodbye

Chmielinski started working at AECOM in 1993. Saying goodbye has proved most difficult.

"Everywhere I go, I look and I say, 'That's our project. I remember that project. We did that.' It's the projects. It's the people. It's the experiences, too. You know, I will be a puddle the day I don't carry an AECOM card. But I think I have to leverage everything I've done here and use it somewhere else. What really makes me happy is that I will not be leaving infrastructure. There will be something in my future that I will do that impacts infrastructure and that I love.

"My mom and dad always taught me that you learn, you earn, you return. So I am at the 'return' stage of my life and looking to start a foundation that focuses on providing help to women in the 35 to 45 year old age group that need help in getting stalled careers moving. It would provide both mentorship and sponsorship. And if things go well, it could even provide financial support to advance career goals."

A Moment of Reflection

Outspoken, bold, effective, and compassionate, Jane Chmielinski has led an enviable professional life. So, how does she see herself and what does she recommend for young people entering the transportation industry?

"I'd like to think that people think of me as a very hard worker, someone who is collaborative. I came out of a planning background. We're external thinkers and I've actually found that to be a good trait to have. Be collaborative. Don't be afraid to be inclusive. Also I think one of the traits for being successful is that you need to suck it up and recognize the difference between failure and feedback."

Chapter 16

GRACE CRUNICAN

My first official paycheck was in high school at the Portland Zoo. The guys who drove the trucks and delivered the supplies got $2.10 per hour. I was paid $1.80 an hour as a canteen worker. The jobs for driving the trucks went only to the guys, because they lifted the CO_2 tanks on and off the trucks. One morning a truck driver didn't show up for work and had the truck keys with him. I helped the General Manager carry these tanks up the hill—and they're heavy. I asked, "Do I get the driver's pay during these two hours?" He said, "No, women can't hold that job! It involves too much lifting, and the state has laws in place. I can't pay you that wage." This was while I was carrying the tanks up the hill! That small incident was the beginning of my strong belief in equal pay for equal work.

Grace Crunican's interest in transportation began with an internship in the Portland Mayor's office, where she worked on transportation projects. In 1979, the Presidential Management Intern Program brought her to the US Department of Transportation in Washington, DC, after she earned her MBA from Willamette University. She started working for the Assistant Secretary for Policy and then for the Assistant Secretary for Budget. She rotated to the Washington Metropolitan Area Transportation Authority, and went over to the political side and worked on the US Senate Appropriations Subcommittee, where she stayed for two years.

In 1983, Crunican returned to Oregon to help a friend and state legislator run for Congress. Afterward she joined the City of Portland Transportation Office to serve as Capital Project Manager and ended as Deputy Director. She then became Executive Director of the Surface Transportation Policy Project (STPP) back in Washington.

Crunican ran the STPP for a year and a half, before switching to the Federal Transit Administration (FTA) as Deputy Administrator. While at FTA she filled out papers for the adoption of two children. During the adoption process, a friend contacted her asking if she was interested in applying to be the Director of the Oregon Department of Transportation (ODOT).

She was and she did. After being with ODOT for five years, Crunican served as Director of Transportation for the Seattle Department of Transportation (SDOT) for eight years. After a new Mayor took office, Crunican resigned and was consulting when she received a phone call, this time from a headhunter representing San Francisco's Bay Area Rapid Transit (BART). BART hired Crunican as General Manager; she runs BART today.

Crunican has served on several boards such as APTA and WTS International, and currently serves on the board of the Mineta Transportation Institute and Railvolution.

This is her story.

A Foot in the Transportation Door

Just after high school, Crunican landed an internship in Portland Mayor Neil Goldschmidt's office. This was her entry into transportation.

"They were working on a transit mall in downtown Portland and needed an intern to take citizen complaints on the project and other community issues. It was great to see the inner workings of what was a very dynamic Mayor's office. I got to observe how he interacted with people and how his staff worked. They went on to do amazing things. The Mayor went on to be US Secretary of Transportation and Governor of Oregon. I was exposed at a young age to a bright group of people, but I was also exposed to issues like affordable housing, parking policy, transit policy, and street design.

"I also had the opportunity to work 'night coffees' in the neighborhoods. These were community meetings in someone's home where Mayor Goldschmidt would talk with 20 or 30 neighbors. And someone would say, 'There's a stop sign down at such and such a place,' or 'the street dips over here,' or whatever. He would say to me, 'Make a note.' I'm not sure he knew my name, but I took notes, found the responsible departments, and then followed up with them."

It was an important first experience for Crunican, one that would help shape both her undergraduate and graduate education.

Inside the Beltway

A federal civil service reform created the Presidential Management Intern Program (PMI). Designed to bring post-graduate degreed people to Washington, the PMI program sought to inject the government with bright young talent fresh out of graduate schools. After completing her MBA, Crunican was selected.

"When we got to Washington they rotated us around. I ended up going to USDOT. I started with the Assistant Secretary for Policy. Then I rotated over to the Assistant Secretary for Budget, Mort Downey. Both Anne Canby and Sarah Campbell were in his office. They *knew* the Washington side of transportation. They *knew* the Hill. And Mort is the smartest guy you will ever meet in terms of legislative content, policy, and money related to transportation. This team was a great find so early in my career."

She did not waste the opportunity.

"As a PMI I rotated to the Washington Metropolitan Area Transit Authority. I did an allocation study on service, subsidies, and revenues between the District, Virginia, and Maryland—each jurisdiction subsidizes the system. The final rotation was on the advice of Walt Boehner. He said, 'You've got to work for Congress to understand the bigger picture.' So he secured a slot for me on the US Senate Appropriations Committee. They needed help and they wanted to look lean, so they were happy to get a PMI from USDOT. I got great experience and was there for six months when they said, 'Why don't you come work for us permanently?' I did and worked there for a couple of years."

Crunican continued to broaden her experience.

"I had handled the Urban Mass Transportation Authority, Federal Highways, the Saint Lawrence Seaway, the Panama Canal, and the Federal Railway Administration accounts. It was great to learn their budgets, programs, and funding sources. I was also able to learn a little about how the Senate works and watch outgoing Senate Majority Leader Byrd and incoming Senate Majority Leader Baker work together. Staff members were able to sit on the Senate floor in the staff seats and watch the transition of power. We staffed the hearings and markups, and I tried to absorb as much as I could at 24."

It was an unparalleled education.

You Can Go Home

Crunican enjoyed working for Congress. But something wasn't right.

"I wasn't a Republican and it felt a little dishonest not making that known. So I left this great job and went back to Oregon to help state legislator Peter Courtney work on a state sales tax. The sales tax didn't pass and he lost his Congressional race, but today he's the Oregon Senate President and has been a friend for many years. It was fascinating to learn the state's tax structure.

"After looking for work for about six months, Vic Rhodes asked if I'd come to work for the City of Portland, raising money for transportation as the Capital Projects Manager. I said yes. I needed a job. With the city, I helped put together money packages and worked with other jurisdictions around the state to create something called the Road Finance Committee (RFC). The RFC had two people each from the county, city, and state at the staff level. Then we replicated it at the policy level. We worked to get the Oregon gas tax increased significantly. Each year the gas tax was raised about two cents during the time all of these entities were working together."

Crunican thrived in the position. When new Commissioner Earl Blumenauer—now a Congressman—was elected, he eventually promoted her to Deputy Director.

"This whole time was a good run. We got a lot of money into transportation by pulling the cities, counties, and state together. The same thing happened at the regional level on the transit side. The whole process really reinforced the power of coalition building and networking."

In January 1992, the Director of the Surface Transportation Policy Partnership, Sarah Campbell, called Crunican.

"She said, 'Is there any chance you would be interested in coming back to Washington to help run this program?' It was a very innovative nonprofit. They were implementing the ISTEA and all of its changes. It was a chance to work with another group of very creative people, consisting of architects, planners, engineers, historic preservationists, and bicyclists."

Though excited about the opportunity, Crunican wasn't ready to leave Portland. She also wasn't ready to leave her family again. But the opportunity was too great to pass up. She made her decision.

A Last Cross-Country Drive

Crunican's parents were advancing in age. She was hesitant to break the news that she'd be leaving again. But she had an idea.

"My mom was particularly bothered by my leaving. She said, 'I know this is a good career move, but . . . ' I said, 'Mom, why don't you drive cross-country with me?' And we had a great week and a half together. Within six months of our trip she died of an aneurysm. She was 68 years old. She was the most influential person in shaping who I was. She was born in 1924 and worked her whole life. She only took three months off to have me, and two months off for each of my brothers, and that was it. She was a real role model for me. She had been an executive, a mom, a wife, a community volunteer—she did it all."

Crunican was rocked by the loss. But there was a job to be done.

The Surface Transportation Policy Partnership

Fortunately for Crunican, it was a great job.

"We set up eight learning sessions around the country. We brought in 500 or 600 people from a wide cross section in each state. We brought in community activists, professional organizations, cities, and the state DOTs. We put together a *Partner State Program* to find four states that were fairly progressive and four states that were less progressive. We had some interactive games to help people realize that ISTEA funds could be flexible. This wasn't one of those very stiff and uptight conferences. This was enlivened by the diversity of the participants. We walked through the changes to ISTEA and also tried to develop coalitions that replicated the national coalition. I knew the states were more than leery of the advocacy, but the smart ones knew it was an opening to reduce the tension."

For Crunican, the benefits of the work went well beyond transportation.

"It was really empowering. There were lots of women and people of color who were participating. It was going very well. Then, the new Clinton Administration was elected. They were filling posts in their administration and we tried to get some of our members into the administration. At some point, Mort asked me to join. He was the USDOT Deputy Secretary. I talked to Sarah and the team and they said, 'We want to get somebody in the administration. . . .'"

Serving Its Purpose

Crunican had not been looking to join the Administration, but when asked she committed to making the most of it.

"FTA allowed me to build skills for my later operational work. There was a very wise man there named Bob McManus. Bob had been there for a long time. He was the lead bureaucrat. He was a good guy to work with, especially in the beginning, because he understood how things were done. The new team was full of new ideas, but he knew the rules and what could be realistically done. He also knew Mort, so he was very helpful in guiding the new Administrator and his Deputy, who were probably pushing too hard and too fast for the bureaucracy.

"Gordon Linton was the Administrator and I was the Deputy. He was from Philadelphia and I was from Oregon. It was a good balance. My job was to work with the regions. We also had some policy shifts to initiate. We were trying to enliven the employees in the process and get some product out the door. McManus came up with the idea to get a bundle of full-funding grant agreements together and obligate federal dollars. Since 1996 was an election year, it was a good year to get the money out the door. Getting billions of federal dollars matched by local funds was a big deal. It meant a lot of great transit projects would take root."

Crunican helped start some landmark transit projects throughout the country, including what became the Silver Line in Boston and the first light rail line in Salt Lake City. With these accomplishments in hand, Crunican turned to another important arena.

Figuring Out the Whole Marriage and Adoption Thing

Whether it was her work or her home life, Crunican applied her hallmark determination and thoroughness. It was time to focus on her home life.

"I turned 40 in 1995. I wasn't married and I hadn't had kids. If I took you back to Oregon, when I was being raised, that was always on the agenda: get married and have kids. I wasn't great at dating, for sure, but I knew I was good with kids. So when I was at FTA I began an artificial insemination program. It didn't work, so I spoke with a board member of an adoption agency on December 26, 1995. I filled out the forms and waited."

Of course, her professional life didn't stop because of her focus on her home life.

"While I was in the process of adoption, I was contacted by Ted Spence, an Oregon transportation institution, who asked if I was interested in applying for the job of Director of the Oregon Department of Transportation (ODOT). I considered it and thought it would be better to raise kids in Oregon, so that they would know their family. It also would allow me to slow down the career, so that I could raise the kids while working."

Crunican interviewed for the position. In May 1996, she was named ODOT Director.

"I started running ODOT in May and the adoption people called me in September. I had two weeks to get to Russia and adopt the kids before the Russian system was going to shut down because of a change in policy. So I went to Russia and adopted them, nine months to the day after I had met with the adoption agency."

It Takes a Village

A project manager by trade, Crunican set to work.

"I'm single. I had a house in DC to sell. I had to oversee the moving of all of my things to Oregon. I had to close on a house in Salem and set it up for the kids—I had nothing for the kids when the call came. It was amazing. As I was adopting these kids, helping hands came from all over the place. Within two weeks, one friend—Sarah Power, from Montana—agreed to fly with me to Russia, and another friend, Carmen Hunt, helped sell the DC house and oversaw the packers. Another set of friends unpacked things in the Salem house and still others brought in a crib, bed, and the clothes needed for the kids. They even decorated the kids' room with a colorful border. It was unbelievable."

With everything in place for her children and after having been gone for two weeks to retrieve the kids from Russia, Crunican returned to the job.

Turning the Perception of ODOT Around

In addition to parenthood, Crunican faced a considerable challenge at ODOT.

"My first task at ODOT was to get to know the employees and let them know I wasn't there to destroy the agency. But we had two big problems when I started. The first problem was that the DMV had a computer system upgrade that was $134 million over budget. The other critical problem was the extremely negative *perception* that the agency couldn't get things done—couldn't build a highway project. We had to turn things around. To do that, I worked with the staff, the transportation commission, and the governor's office. It was clear to me that we also had to build an external constituency at the same time."

But Crunican faced some nagging foes.

"The Chair of the Transportation Committee at the time had the trucking interests coaching her to a large degree. The trucking association wanted to keep their weight-mile fees down, so they worked to further the misperception that the department wasn't very effective. When we would testify on the budget, they would have these little anecdotes prepared and would use them against the department. Things like, 'Why did you buy these expensive cars with leather seats?' The answer was simple; we bought them from the state purchase list. They were cars from a dealership that hadn't sold. We didn't know that they would have leather seats. But you would make a presentation about road construction and you would get a question about buying five cars with leather seats. This happened over and over. The committee was run more like a call-in talk show than a government hearing. So we developed a notebook with a list of their routine questions/criticisms. By doing that, we could then flip through and say, 'On December 15th we sent you a letter explaining this. I'd like to provide it for the committee.' It was a polite way of saying, 'Asked and answered.'"

Crunican continued her focus on building up the public's confidence in the department.

"We created a new conservative constituency. I went around the state and met with local Rotary, Kiwanis, and city councils to introduce myself and listen to what people had to say about ODOT. We gathered business cards of all of these people that were really down on ODOT and then created what we called the Efficiency Committee. We also educated the committee on the 42 federal and state regulations we had to follow to construct any project. I gave each Efficiency Committee member a letter that said, 'This member of the Efficiency Committee is allowed entry inside any ODOT shop or building.' They could walk into any maintenance facility in Oregon just by showing this letter. I think the committee members expected they would just pop in somewhere and see people sitting around playing cards or doing nothing.

"The committee members came back and said, 'This is the fourth station I've stopped at and the guy or gal was working hard.' So they became great advocates for the department. I left ODOT before we got a gas tax passed, but ultimately the department's reputation changed. That kind of transparency is a risk. But we took the risk and it worked."

Seattle Substance and Politics

Crunican left ODOT in 2001. After consulting for less than a year, she received yet another important phone call.

"Newly elected Seattle Mayor Greg Nickels had some large projects he wanted built. The job sounded great. My hesitation was not the work, but the impact the move might have on the kids. Transition is especially hard on adopted kids. Ultimately I spoke with the counselor to understand what they would need to make the transition a positive experience. In the end, it was a great move for everyone.

"The difference between ODOT and the Seattle job was significant. In Seattle there was a Mayor who was all about the substance and a Deputy Mayor, Tim Ceis, who was all about the politics. So you had to keep them both fed. But the two of them worked very well together. They provided amazing leadership.

"The Deputy knew his job was to help deliver a specific set of projects, policies, and programs, and if you were delivering, he backed you up. We pushed the envelope further in Seattle than anyplace else, but that was because when the Mayor said, 'I want you to do this list of things,' he cut you loose and supported you. The viaduct alone would have been enough for an eight-year term, but we set the stage for the Alaskan Way Viaduct to come down and open up the city's waterfront. We built the Mercer Corridor Project and the Spokane Street Viaduct widening. We built the first modern streetcar line in the city and we bought King Street Station and began its renovation. We changed many policies, and made way for bicycles and transit throughout the city. We sponsored women in key construction posts who hadn't been given opportunities in the past."

Crunican enjoyed tremendous success. But unusual weather would prove to be a watershed event.

Snow Job

It snows occasionally in Seattle, usually for three or four days and it's gone. But one particular snowstorm in 2008 became known as Snowpocalypse—it had lasted 16 days.

"It was just before the Mayor's third reelection race and during the final decision-making on the Alaskan Way Viaduct. We had snow plans that were designed for handling major storms. We trained for snow, but again this snowstorm lasted 16 days. Basically, three things went wrong.

"First, I had recently appointed a new head of maintenance, who I later found still had some rough edges and did not have the support of a select number of employees. They wanted to sabotage him, and they were so disgruntled that they would go out with the snowplows and raise them 2 to 3 inches *above* the snow, leaving roads covered with packed snow. Unfortunately, I didn't know they were doing this until it was too late.

"Second, we were trying to reduce our use of salt for environmental reasons. We were converting to calcium magnesium acetate (CMA). We didn't get a solid base of CMA down at the outset, so ice built up over the 16 days because it never got above freezing for that entire time.

"Third, it appeared to me that the Seattle newspaper wanted a new mayor. They hadn't supported Mayor Nickels's position on many of the transportation projects that we were doing. Their reporter teamed up with some of our disgruntled employees to create all sorts of strange tangents and out-of-context exaggerations, ignoring many facts covered by the rest of the media."

In spite of many accomplishments, a year later a new mayor was elected. Crunican resigned feeling bad about Mayor Nickels not getting a third term, but great about the progress made and the team she worked with for eight remarkable years.

BART

After consulting for about a year, a headhunter representing Bay Area Rapid Transit called Crunican, wanting to know if she was interested in becoming General Manager. She was. BART hired her on an eight-to-one vote.

"I've been at BART about three years. And in those three years we have come up with about $3 billion in financing for replacing our entire rail fleet. We've allowed bikes on BART. We've organized the Asset Management System so the investments will be well prioritized. We've increased fares and parking charges to pay for part of the systems replacement. We are also beginning to modernize some of the management systems and are preparing to request a bigger investment to replace our aging infrastructure. We made national news with our labor dispute two years ago. The labor force had had four years with no raises when we came into that contract and were attempting to replace lost raises four years back and four years forward. We were determined to control costs and reinvest in the aging BART system. We also asked BART employees to begin to make a contribution to their pension and health care costs. We had two strikes over our current contract but employees now contribute to their pension and health care. We lost two workers who were killed while inspecting track during the strike.

"The labor contract was resolved. The big issue ahead of us is rebuilding the trust between the unions and management. It has been eroding for many years. We have a highly capable work force. They are smart, highly skilled, and very hard working—labor and management. I have a great deal of respect for our team and the tough challenges that lie before us."

When Something Personal Happens

Crunican had been Director of SDOT for two years when she discovered a lump in her breast. It was cancer. She dealt with it head on.

"I hate to be cold about this, but I managed it like a transportation project. There was a surgeon, an oncologist, and a radiologist. They were meeting on a regular basis. It looked like project management to me, and I had a great deal of confidence in my team. And that took away all of the emotional aspects of it for me.

"They laid it all out for me. So I said to them, 'If I do the surgery, the chemo, and the radiation, I have a 92–94 percent chance of survivability, right?' They said, 'Yes.' So I said, 'Fine. Do your thing.' I asked questions and followed their instructions, because they were the experts, just like you do in transportation project management."

But there was another aspect to it.

"I didn't tell the kids, because Sarah was at a very difficult age. She was 12 and in sixth grade and was having a hard time. So I went through several months of chemo and at some stage they told me that my hair was about to fall out. Just before that, I sat the kids down and explained to them, 'Mom is taking some medicine and the medicine is going to make my hair fall out.' And my daughter said, 'You're not going to come to school with no hair, are you?' I put a scarf on and said, 'I could do this or a wig or . . . ' Then I threw a bra on my head as an option, dangling over my ears, and she was mortified. So she selected the wig and said, 'Okay, but don't stay long at school.' That was my daughter's reaction. My son, who was younger, said, 'Okay, now can I go out and play?'"

Of All the Jobs . . .

Crunican succeeded at some of the tougher transportation jobs in the nation. But one job stands out as the most challenging.

"The toughest job and the most rewarding one I've had was raising kids. Sarah and Andrew have been through their own trials, and being a single mom was a wild ride for all of us, but I have to say that my life would be nothing without the kids. I'm so proud of both of them. We all share a healthy sense of humor and only made it through the ups and downs with the support of many, many friends and family members. I feel privileged to have been able to experience parenthood."

Success

On the topic of success, Crunican cites a key ingredient for her.

"Success comes through working in teams. I don't think any individual does anything on his or her own, at least that's true for me. Teamwork means it's not about you; it's about getting the best out of every team member."

Chapter 17

NURIA FERNANDEZ

I thought things would be easier in the public sector. I really did. I thought people were used to working with individuals of different races and ethnicities, whereas in the private sector it's not as diverse. But my experience in the private sector was different. It was much easier in the private sector to have a seat at the table. In the public sector there was this barrier to being a black woman at the top. It was just not something that was embraced as much as it should have been, given the diversity of the people that work in the public transportation industry.

Nuria Fernandez is a versatile woman. Born in Panama of Jamaican descent, Fernandez is a civil engineer with an MBA who speaks Spanish, English, and Portuguese. She began her transportation career as an engineer with the Panama Canal Company in 1982. She then moved to Chicago and joined the city's Department of Public Works in 1983. In 1987 she transitioned to aviation, working on the first major development program for O'Hare International Airport. Success there led to her joining the Chicago Transit Authority (CTA) to address a challenging project backlog. She addressed that backlog, furthered her reputation, and rose to CTA Senior Vice President of Design and Construction.

In 1993, Fernandez moved to Washington, DC, to join the US Department of Transportation. But she only stayed for a year before moving to WMATA, again as a Senior Vice President of Design and Construction. In 1997, USDOT Secretary Rodney Slater and FTA Administrator Gordon Linton convinced Fernandez to rejoin USDOT as the FTA Deputy Administrator. She later became FTA Acting Administrator until she left for the private sector in 2001.

Fernandez became a Senior Vice President for Business Development with Earth Tech. There for five years, she then returned to Chicago as the Commissioner of the Department of Aviation in 2006. It was an ill-fated move. After two years, she resigned and took time off to care for her ailing parents. In the fall of 2008, she returned to the private sector, this time as a Senior Vice President with CH2M Hill. But the public sector would soon call again. In 2011, New York Governor Andrew Cuomo named her Chief Operating Officer of the Metropolitan Transportation Authority in New York City. Then in 2013 she obtained the top spot as General Manager/CEO of California's Santa Clara Valley Transportation Authority, a position she holds today.

Fernandez believes strongly in education. She holds a BS in civil engineering from Bradley University and an MBA in finance and administration from Roosevelt University. She is also a long-time member of WTS International and has been named both Member of the Year (1999) and Woman of the Year (1997). Numerous other organizations have bestowed awards on Fernandez for her accomplishments in transportation.

This is her story.

I Did Not Get the Job, Which Led to a Transportation Career

Growing up in Panama, Fernandez's family and her neighborhood shaped her singular outlook on life.

"My formative years were all about a sense of exploration and discovery, spending time outdoors working on experiments. I was drawn by science-related things and had a great affinity for mathematics. But I also had a creative side. I wanted to be an architect. Back in the 1970s, though, there were too many architects, and my dad suggested that I consider engineering."

After high school, Fernandez earned a civil engineering degree in the United States, at Bradley University.

"We had a very small group of women that graduated in my civil engineering class and we each applied for openings with private companies in the area. I did not get the job I wanted so my friend and mentor, Sharon McBride, suggested I look into the public sector. However, I went back home to Panama instead, and returned to the United States a year later and landed a job with the Chicago Department of Public Works (DPW) working on transportation projects. And that was the beginning of my 30-plus year fascination with transportation."

That fascination continues today.

Make Yourself Indispensable

Fernandez was welcomed at the DPW, where one person was particularly instructive.

"An engineer from Iran, Esmail Raisian, told me, 'As a black, Latina woman in this field, you need to make yourself indispensable.' He was an immigrant who had struggled, but he recognized that my struggle was going to be much deeper. I took what he said to mean, 'Build significant depth in an area within your field to be called upon as an expert, but learn just enough about a lot of different things to be credible. Don't just stay in your box.'"

Fernandez still follows that advice.

Always Leave the Place Better than You Found It

It was 1987. While at the DPW, Fernandez joined the project team on the first major development program for O'Hare International Airport. There were five years left on the program, and she completed her part in three.

"Then Clark Burrus, Chairman of the CTA, approached my boss and said, 'I'm looking for someone that can help us. We received $1 million from the state for capital projects and the organization's backlog is such that if we do not obligate that $1 million we are going to lose it.' My boss told him, 'Nuria can make it happen.' I got hired away by the CTA.

"I was told, 'It's going to take you at least two years to get this program organized and the Engineering and Construction Division back on track. You also need to add the time it will take to get these projects bid-ready, that is, complete the assessments and cost estimates to move them into the procurement pipeline and then award the contracts.'"

Fernandez put together a team of planners, grant analysts, and engineers and got the capital program under way in a year, committing all of the backlogged funding. She also learned an interesting fact about her coworkers.

"Many of them were very concerned about their jobs. There was no commitment from the state government to provide funding for a new capital program once these projects were under construction. The future of the capital program was a big question mark, and they were stringing things out. As one of the managers later confided, the word was out 'there is a new sheriff in town and we better get to work!'"

Having completed everything she was assigned, Fernandez had to figure out what was next for her and her coworkers.

"I received a commitment to do a systemwide assessment of CTA's infrastructure to catalog the condition of the physical assets and build a baseline of projects and costs for the five-year capital program. This had never been done before. To this day the organization is in a much better place because of that. Of course nobody remembers how it all started, but that's not important to me. What is important is to always leave a place better than you found it."

If Not Now—When?

Fernandez knew how to get the job done. But she was always willing to be mentored on other elements and avenues that would help her to be successful in the transportation industry.

"A few years earlier, a mentor shared his advice for success: 'Get an MBA and a law degree. I'm sorry, but this is just the plain truth for women. The job market in this field is male-dominated, competitive, and unforgiving. The more credentialed you are, the more opportunities will be available to you. And then there will be no question why your supervisor is offering you the promotion.'"

Fernandez took this advice to heart.

"At the time, I had just gone back to work after giving birth to our second child and I decided that I was getting an MBA and that I would do it in two years. I was not going to stretch it out. I remember saying to my husband at the time, 'If not now—when?'"

"Those two years were a blur of juggling family, work, and study. I knew it would take physical and mental stamina and then it would be over. I was sacrificing precious time with my young family, but I decided that I would make it up to my girls later. And I have. Unfortunately, the marriage did not survive."

Making a Federal Case

While working at CTA, Fernandez received a call from a WTS member, Louise Stoll, whom she didn't know at the time. However, she would get to know her well.

"Louise was a Senior Vice President at O'Brien-Kreitzberg & Associates. And we just hit it off. A couple years later she called me to share her good news: President Clinton had just nominated her to be the Assistant Secretary for Budget and Programs for the US Department of Transportation. She asked if I would be interested in coming to Washington, DC, to work with her in the Office of the Secretary of Transportation. That was the beginning of a lifelong friendship and an amazing journey. One that took me from just managing projects to the larger theater of national transportation policy and funding."

Fernandez would stay at USDOT for only a year. It was an extremely important introduction, and she would return.

Making Connections

Fernandez benefited greatly from working with Stoll, particularly in terms of access.

"We always went up to Capitol Hill with the USDOT modal administrators for their budget hearings. On this particular day, WMATA General Manager Larry Reuter was testifying on WMATA's budget. I met Larry during the break and we had a brief conversation about capital programs, projects, and funding.

Shortly thereafter, he reached out and said, 'Nuria, I have a multibillion-dollar construction program and I really need someone who not only has the technical background, but someone who understands the bigger picture of budgeting, community engagement, and working with multiple governments.'"

After some deep thought and discussion with Stoll, Fernandez agreed to join WMATA as the Senior Vice President of Design and Construction. She stayed for three years. Then, in 1997, newly appointed USDOT Secretary Rodney Slater and FTA Administrator Gordon Linton persuaded Fernandez to rejoin the USDOT as the FTA Deputy Administrator.

"Now I was responsible for all 10 regions of the FTA and the regional offices and administrators. I was also responsible for formulating and building the mass transit component of the transportation authorization bill. So I worked with my team on what later became known as TEA-21, the Transportation Equity Act for the 21st Century. That was my claim to fame."

Getting to Know You . . . and You . . . and You

Serving as Deputy Administrator proved most valuable to Fernandez.

"I reviewed all applications for New Starts funding from transit agencies throughout the country wanting to expand their existing rail systems, as well as build new rail lines. It was a pretty powerful position. I met a lot of people. And everyone was groveling for funding. That is how I got to know the people behind the projects and built such a strong network in this industry. Because of that, so many people know who I am. Of course I don't know them all, but they remember me from their project groundbreaking, ribbon cutting, or from seeing my name on their funding commitment letter. My network just kept getting larger."

After working at FTA for four years, Fernandez knew that another chapter was coming to an end when the new administration of George Bush was ready to take office. "We lost our lease and it was time to move on."

More than She Bargained for at O'Hare

Fernandez joined Earth Tech as a Senior Vice President for Business Development. She was with Earth Tech for a little more than five years when the public sector drew her back again.

"I was asked to head up O'Hare and Midway Airports. At the time O'Hare was the busiest airport in the world and they had a multibillion-dollar modernization program. I wanted to go back to Chicago as well. Unfortunately, it was one of those job opportunities that, on its face, appeared to be very attractive, but once I got into it, it was much more complicated."

The complications had little to do with the actual work.

"Politically, there were personality issues and differences of opinion that made for a very difficult work environment. But I took the high road, never compromised my integrity, and worked with a team of professionals to do the job as I knew it had to be done."

Fernandez continued to fight to do the job and bring about the changes necessary to improve the organization. But personality conflicts got in the way of progress and ultimately she was asked to tender her resignation, which she did.

Something that Really Mattered

Timing in life is everything. The timing of her resignation proved to be fortuitous.

"The week before I resigned, my mom had been diagnosed with Alzheimer's. I took three months just to spend time with her and my dad and help get all of their affairs in order, because I knew it was going to be a very difficult road ahead."

Fernandez temporarily moved in with her parents in Washington, DC. While there, the phone rang.

"In the first month that I was out of a job, I received an offer to work for CH2M Hill, as their Senior Vice President for Business Development on major programs. I accepted, but told them that I could not start until after Labor Day, and they were very good about that. I took the time off to care for my parents, and I am so glad I did. I would have been extremely sad if I hadn't, especially now that I've lost them both."

Well Why Not, That Will Be Good

Fernandez returned to Chicago and CH2M Hill. The phone rang again.

"In the fall of 2011, New York Governor Andrew Cuomo's Chief of Staff asked me to join his administration. He put it very plainly, 'I think there's a terrific opportunity for you here.'"

In transportation, the New York Metropolitan Transportation Authority (MTA) is the holy grail. It's the largest transportation system in the country, and the third largest in the world. But for Fernandez it was not an easy decision.

"The private sector had been really good to me. It opened up tremendous opportunities, financially and professionally. I traveled to different parts of the world, lived in different countries, and worked on different projects, which was terrific. But everyone in the industry wants to work at the MTA. So I said, 'Well why not, that will be good.'"

The Top Spot in the Valley

Representatives from California's Santa Clara Valley Transportation Authority (VTA) approached Fernandez a couple years later.

"'We would like you to consider being the CEO of VTA.'

"I had planned on staying at the MTA for several more years but I also wanted to retire from the industry at the top of my game. The VTA Board was offering me the opportunity to run a transit system."

Fernandez accepted the job. She continues to lead VTA today.

Diversity in the Workplace

Fernandez credits several women leaders with leveling the playing field.

"Diane Creel led Earth Tech. Working for Diane was easy. She really allowed women—and she had a lot of women in leadership positions—the opportunity to build their groups, spread their wings, bring ideas, and challenge the status quo. She gave us the opportunity to present, justify, and then take risks. If we failed, she allowed us to get up, dust off, and start over. Working for her was one of the highlights of my professional career.

"When Jacque Hinman invited me to join CH2M Hill, she was an Executive Vice President. Engineering firms are a reflection of the infrastructure industry, that is, very male dominated. Jacque was one of two females in executive leadership. Nancy Tuor was the other. In an environment where it can be very difficult for women to be at the table and have their voices heard when so many more male voices could drown them out, Jacque was absolutely brilliant at pulling us up and leveling the field—and now she is the woman at the top of CH2M Hill!"

Success Has to Be Prepared

Fernandez sees her overall professional experience as unique, but her advice is universal.

"Four years of college could never give me the lifetime of experience that my peers had gained in understanding how to navigate the political and professional environment. I had a language barrier and cultural differences, but I was very anxious to learn. I had a number of individuals that kept reminding me to build a depth of experience in areas that were portable that would position me as a differentiator when it came to upward mobility and opportunity. And I did that.

"I took my time. Even though my career looks like it happened in a meteor flash, there were always people around me who said, 'Oh, it's *my* turn now.' I notice it even today. I have aspiring professionals that have approached me to be their mentor. They want things to happen in a microwave nanosecond. But success has to be prepared. You have to get the advanced degree. You also have to step up and do things that nobody else wants to do. That's why I've been successful. When I made it happen, people thought, 'Oh that seemed easy. I want it now, too.' But it wasn't easy. I prepared for it."

Don't Wait for a Bad Situation to Get Better; Trust Your Instincts

Fernandez also schools young professionals on how to manage difficult situations.

"I strongly rely on my moral compass. If something is not right, I don't justify it. I call it out. It is who I am and how I was raised. I stand firmly by the choices I made throughout my career, even the ones that resulted in my drawing the short end of the stick!"

I Did a Lot of Juggling

When it comes to work-life balance, Fernandez believes it should be more of a practical construct than a theoretical one.

"I come from a generation where we talked about just making it through each day, and if we happened to do something fun in the intervening hours that was great. That was the balance we hoped for. It's interesting to talk about it now with young people. They question whether they can have it all. Should they raise kids and then come back and claim a rung on their professional life? Where will that put them on the organizational ladder? I was a single mother for the majority of my daughters' formative years, so I became a master juggler. I redefined the balancing act to fit my reality—no one else's. I didn't sit back and say, 'My, what a whole lot of things I have to do today.' I just went ahead and did them. I didn't belabor it. I didn't make it an issue. I just did it.

"I also did a lot of traveling for work. During the summertime, the girls would come along and they loved it. To them it was all an adventure. Particularly if we were going to a WTS event or an APTA conference. They grew up in WTS, really. If I happened to have family or friends that lived in the city where I was attending a meeting or conference, they helped out. If not, I just brought them with me and they had to sit through my presentation. Then we would go out and do something fun. It's important to live the reality that's best for you. I really couldn't prescribe how individuals should deal with work-life balance. All I can say is that life is unpredictable. Do the most with those you like being with in the time that you have."

Fernandez continues to live by that philosophy today.

SUSAN MARTINOVICH, PE

People kept telling me, "You have nice legs." So I learned that it was okay to use them as an asset. I wear dresses. I wear skirts. I dress like a woman and do not try to be like a man. I had other friends say, "You don't look like other engineers." But because of that I was often underestimated. Then when I started talking—when I actually started producing and doing the work—that changed people's perception of me.

Susan Martinovich, PE, is a woman who loved math and who became an engineer when these were still far from conventional expectations for a woman. And in a time when people change jobs routinely, she stayed with the Nevada Department of Transportation (NDOT) for nearly three decades. Susan started at NDOT as a summer intern while enrolled at the University of Nevada, Reno. Upon graduation in 1984, she joined NDOT as a rotation engineer. There were no other women applicants for the position.

She rose through the ranks quickly. First she became a project manager in the Design Division. Then she moved to the Bridge Division, where she was one of only two women. Then she moved back to the Design Division as one of its leaders. Each move meant a rise in rank. Always volunteering to take on the toughest projects, she soon became Assistant Director of Engineering, again leap-frogging over others. She continued to work hard, delivering on complex projects. In 2003, she became NDOT Deputy Director. Three years later, Nevada Governor Gibbons appointed her NDOT Director—the first woman appointed to this post, and a position she would hold for nearly six years.

In 2012, after 28 years of service with NDOT, Martinovich joined CH2M Hill as the Director of the Transportation Business Group's North American Highway/Bridge business, where she serves today.

Throughout her career, Martinovich has been actively involved in many national transportation organizations. In 2011, she became the first female President of AASHTO. She serves on the American Road and Transportation Builders Association (ARTBA) Board and the Committee on Planning and Design. In 2013, ARTBA bestowed on her its Ethel S. Birchland Lifetime Achievement Award. She also serves in several capacities for the Transportation Research Board, and was a member of its Executive Board. And she is a longtime member of WTS, currently serving on the WTS International Board of Directors.

Susan Martinovich forged a career in transportation that opened up important roles for women. She embraced challenging situations, and was resolute in her expectations of herself and others.

This is her story.

I Was Much Happier Doing Math

Unlike many female transportation professionals, Susan Martinovich's entry into transportation was pretty straightforward.

"I was much happier doing math than other things. I received a couple of scholarships for the university and I went into civil engineering. Nevada DOT had a summer intern program. So I worked summers for NDOT and then after I graduated I applied and got into the department as a rotation engineer."

She was also the only woman applicant for the position. She saw that as an advantage.

"You need to be visible. If you are visible, then people recognize you. There is even advantage in just having someone know your name. It's a connection. I really always tried to be visible. Because I was a woman in an area where there weren't a lot of women—and because I had good grades—I got noticed."

Martinovich used her visibility to her advantage. But that visibility also brought greater responsibility.

They Don't Know What You Don't Say

Martinovich describes herself as a self-conscious, geeky engineer—an introvert. Becoming visible presented some challenges.

"I had to force myself to do presentations. I would watch the agency directors or some of the department leaders do presentations and they would just be so smooth, and I thought, 'How can I be smooth?' I finally realized that my superpower was my *passion*. Of course, you have to know your subject, but after that realization I felt, 'I can do this. Just be brave.' Somebody told me once, 'They don't know what you don't say.' I'm the expert. I can say whatever I want. As long as I believe it, it's all okay."

She would soon test her belief. NDOT wanted to widen Tropicana Road—the most heavily used road in the state—at Las Vegas Boulevard in Las Vegas, which was growing by leaps and bounds. As Project Manager, Martinovich had to do a project presentation to VIP stakeholders. It was her first big presentation.

"I remember being hesitant and thinking, 'Am I wearing the right thing? Do I have spinach in my teeth?' I was stumbling, and then I remembered, 'They don't know what you're not saying. Say what you have to say with confidence. They can disagree with you, but show them that you can lead this.' And I did that."

Martinovich won them over with her presentation. She advanced the project and her career.

The Bridge Girls

Martinovich was one of two women in the Bridge Division. They were known as "the bridge girls."

"It was okay. Because as long as you did your job, the stereotyping disappeared. So I worked my way up. The Bridge Division was great because there was an automatic progression to a *Level Three*. The entry-level ranking for most people was a *One*. People worked their whole careers to become a *Three*. There were some later opportunities for promotion, but I didn't get them because I didn't have any supervisory experience. I thought, 'I've got to get that experience.' So after six years in the Bridge Division, I took a transfer.

"Doing that pushed me out of my comfort zone. People become your family. You see people at work more than you see people at home. If you transfer into another division, that raises a lot of eyebrows. But I took the transfer and then I had to prove myself in the Roadway Design Division, too. But I became a *Four!*"

Advancement wasn't as simple as she makes it sound. That's because Martinovich did something few others in the department did.

"You Make Us Look Bad"

NDOT had many projects. Martinovich saw that roster as an opportunity.

"We would sit in these rooms and say, 'Who wants to do this project? Who wants to do that project?' Nobody would volunteer. So I would say, 'I'll take it.' One of the guys next to me said, 'Would you quit raising your hand! You make us look bad!' But doing that gave me the opportunity to work on really big, very visible projects. And that goes back to what I said before about the importance of being visible."

Visibility paid off.

"Here I am, a *Four*. I was leading only a section of the Design Division. But because of those projects, I got into the front office and I would be the one talking to the Director. These were major freeway projects at the time, projects in Las Vegas and projects in northern Nevada. But we had one project that was kind of a turning point."

Boss to My Old Bosses

Driving to Las Vegas from Los Angeles was extremely popular. As a result, the route often became overcrowded.

"People would come up to Las Vegas from Los Angeles via the I-15 corridor. Then they would all leave on Sunday afternoon and the I-15 would become a parking lot. We wanted to fix that. So NDOT actually gave money to Caltrans—the California DOT—and oversaw the redesign of a key interchange in Barstow, CA. We did that because the California process to retain a consultant was too long and cumbersome and the Nevada process was quicker. I got to be Project Manager. I remember flying with the NDOT Director and the Federal Highway Administrator to California to meet with the Caltrans district people. And I kept thinking, 'Wow, I get to do this!'"

This project gave Martinovich tremendous exposure.

"I became very visible to the front office. Then when a new Director came in, who was very hard to work with, the whole front office decided to leave. That left a vacancy for the Assistant Director of Engineering. I applied and got it. I jumped over a lot of other people who didn't apply. Now I was a boss to a lot of my old bosses."

It could have been difficult. But Martinovich won people over.

"People in the department were comfortable with me because I went into it with the attitude of 'I need your help. We are all a team on this.' They also knew my work ethic. But it still comes back to this: I was always willing to do what others weren't, and I believe that made the difference. I have never said, 'That's not my job.' I didn't like hearing it and so I could never say it. And that is how I approached things. But I also tried to balance things because I had two little kids and I was married. So the thought process was, 'How can I do this and not be working all of time?'"

He Doesn't Know What I'm Thinking

A recurring theme, speaking up became central to Martinovich's approach. In 2003, the NDOT Director tasked Martinovich with the lead on an important project, the Spaghetti Bowl, the nickname given to a freeway interchange near downtown Las Vegas.

"He comes in and he's yelling at everybody. I knew that pretty soon it would dissipate. But it bothered me, because I had everything going well on the project. So I went in to the Deputy Director, and said, 'I will do this job, but you need to keep the Director away from me.' The Deputy just looks at me and doesn't say anything. So I walk out.

"A couple of days later, I get a page. I call my assistant and she says, 'The Director is leaving.' I go back to the office and I saw the Deputy and I said, 'I told you to take care of it, but you didn't have to do it that way!' Then the Deputy was appointed Director. So I thought, 'I want to be the new Deputy.' But it dawned on me that he doesn't know what I'm thinking. He doesn't know I want it. So I walked into his office and said, 'I want to be your Deputy.' And he just looks at me. So again I'm thinking, 'Do I have spinach in my teeth? Am I speaking English even?' Then he goes, 'Oh, okay. All right.'"

Two days later he formally invited Martinovich to serve as NDOT Deputy Director. She accepted.

"Do You Really Want That Job?"

Martinovich served successfully for three years. Then a new Governor, Jim Gibbons, was elected. His reputation preceded him.

"Governor Gibbons had a history of being difficult to work for. The Director was in his 50s and he had just had twins. He was offered a great opportunity to take a job where he got paid the same, but was only supervising three people instead of running an agency. So he said he was going to leave and recommend me as Director. So I tell my dad. My dad had worked for NDOT for 30 years. And he says, 'Do you really want that job?' I said, 'You know I do.'"

Her father understood that it was a very difficult job. He was trying to protect her. But Martinovich also knew that no one would just hand her the job.

"So I started doing a lot of the stuff that I really don't like doing, like cold calling people and saying hello to political people who were in the Governor's circle. I told them, 'I really want to be the Director.' That was hard for me, but I thought, 'I need to let people know what I want, that I'm interested, and let them have a chance to get to know me.'"

Her Efforts Worked

"We were celebrating our Christmas party at the Carson City Cigar Bar. It's Christmas. It's Friday. We're drinking martinis and I get a call. And the person goes, 'This is Governor Gibbons. Would you like to be my DOT director?' And I said, 'Well, hey, Jim.' I called him by his first name! Of course, I should've said, 'Oh thank you very much, Governor!' And I'm thinking, 'Okay, I think I have the job. . . .'"

She did have the job. And even though she had been with NDOT her entire career, being Director would present some unique challenges.

And This Person Starts Chasing Me

Having to fire people was one of the most difficult tasks Martinovich faced as Director, and she always handled firings herself. But nothing could prepare her for one particular employee.

"I took firings very seriously, because you are affecting people's lives. Of course there is always one person who is a real problem."

The individual was a pilot. In her opinion, and based on supporting information, he had put lives in jeopardy. After consulting with Human Resources and technical experts, Martinovich fired the pilot. The fired individual took NDOT to court multiple times.

"One day people gave me a ride to my car. I'm getting into my car and someone starts chasing after me. And it's just panic. So I get into my car and I start pulling away. Well he grabs onto my back door and the door starts to open. Then all of a sudden he's pounding on my car door and yelling, 'You ran over my foot! You ran over my foot!' Well my heart's pounding and I just drive away.

"I thought, 'Oh my God. I need to tell somebody.' So I drive to a police station, file a report and call the Governor's office, and explain what happened. Once I started thinking about it, I realized this individual just wanted to give me a subpoena for one of the court hearings. Then I told the Governor, 'The guy says I ran over his foot.' But I didn't know if I did! I call my lawyers. I provide a police report. It turns out that the police knew about him. He was the guy who had been putting up huge banners across the street from the state capital and in front of the Attorney General's office that said, 'The AG is corrupt. The Governor is corrupt.' And after this incident, I got my own banner, 'Susan Martinovich is corrupt. She runs from the police and is corrupt.' I was in good company. At the end of the day, the court upheld this gentleman's right to protest. But then he started stalking me. So I had to get a restraining order against him. So that wasn't fun."

Unfortunately, repercussions from this event remain.

"If you Google my name the incident is all over the Internet. They even accuse me of drunk driving. It is terrible. I've had blogs about how my hair looks, what I was wearing, etc. I just don't read them. I can't read them, because they make me so upset. They are either so critical personally or they are totally not true. And that is the part that's been frustrating about being in the public light; that is the dark side of public prominence."

Martinovich ran NDOT under Governor Gibbons for four years. He was not reelected. Governor Brian Sandoval assumed office in 2011 and reappointed Martinovich. Then she retired in 2012.

"I liked and respected Governor Sandoval, but I was ready and it was on my own terms, which was a great, great way to do it."

Starting Over in the Private Sector

Martinovich left the public sector after nearly 30 years of service. It was no small change to join the private sector.

"I left a job that I knew how to do inside out, upside down, and backwards. People would call me and ask, 'Do you remember this memo?' And I would know where to find it. I knew who to call and what reports were due. Then I went to a job where I really didn't even know how to use the Xerox machine. I had to turn in my own timesheet! Before, I had people who did that for me and now I was on my own."

Martinovich joined CH2M Hill in 2012, and serves as Director of its North American Highway and Bridge Division today.

How She Knew When to Retire

In 2011, AASHTO elected Martinovich as its first female President. She is duly proud of that accomplishment. It is one of the goals she set for herself.

"When I became NDOT Director, there were several things I wanted to accomplish. First, I really wanted to open communication with our stakeholders and within the department. There was also leadership training for our folks, because we were going through a lot of changes. People were retiring and new people were being brought into positions after only a couple of years of experience. Then there was also financing and funding. And finally, that I become AASHTO President, which I succeeded in doing.

"When I finished with AASHTO, I sat down and I looked back at that list and felt that I really had accomplished the things I wanted to do. That's when I had to do a lot of soul-searching. I was also starting to become cranky. I was seeing projects over again and thinking, 'Didn't we just do that?' And people would say, 'That was 15 years ago.' So I thought, 'Okay, okay, it is time to go.'"

Though she accomplished her goals, it was not done without challenge. She relates a particular incident from AASHTO.

"When I became AASHTO President, my predecessor was Butch Brown from Mississippi. Butch was one of those people who would always comment on me being the Vice President. He would say sarcastically, 'How many people get a woman Vice President?' Even his final gesture, when he turned over the gavel to me, instead of just handing it to me he bonked me on the head! He's an example of someone who will never get it. He never will. But that was also so minor in my whole AASTHO career."

No, Sir, That Would Be Me

There were also tremendous rewards during her public service. She recounts one instance after her youngest son returned from his Marine service in Afghanistan. He had been severely wounded. Martinovich and her then-husband spent 39 days at his bedside during his recovery.

"In the hospital you get to know all of the nurses and people helping you. And we kept having important visitors, like Nevada Senator Harry Reid. One of the Navy guys said, 'How do you know all of these people?' And I said, 'I am the head of the Nevada Department of Transportation.' Then he said, 'You're one of the most Googleable mothers we've ever had!'"

Martinovich's son was slated to receive a Purple Heart. But he was in surgery the day the Marine Corps Commandant visited his ward. He was disappointed. His disappointment would soon be eclipsed.

"One morning my son calls and says, 'Mom, come to the hospital right now. They're giving me my Purple Heart today.' We rush over there, but things were . . . different. Before they would let us in we had to let them check our bags, which hadn't happened before. Then the Navy people said, 'That's the mom.' So they stopped and just let us in.

"Then in walks President Obama to present my son the Purple Heart! It was so cool. We're in a room with the President of the United States! It's just us. And the President was very respectful. He talked to my son and gave him the Purple Heart. He was at the head of the bed with my son and my then-husband, and I'm at the end of the bed taking pictures. Then President Obama looks at my husband and says, 'I understand you're the Director of the Nevada Department of Transportation.' And I said, 'No, sir. That would be me.' He goes, 'Oh, well come over here!' He puts his arm around me and he says to his photographer, 'We've got to get a picture.' So I've got this great picture that President Obama signed.

"Then he said, 'Well, how is transportation in the state of Nevada?' And I said, 'It would be great, sir, if we could get a transportation bill.' And in the back of the room you just heard a little intake of breath. And the President goes, 'Well, you just need to tell Harry what to do.' And I said, 'I'm working with Senator Reid.' And we had a really good conversation! The next day all of these people who were in the doorway say, 'We can't believe you told the President what to do!' But I thought, 'I'm going to take an advantage of the opportunity.' It was just cool!"

Martinovich made taking advantage of opportunity a hallmark of her career.

His Mom Didn't Work So . . .

Throughout her career, Martinovich defied many stereotypes. But there were some traditional roles that she found difficult to avoid.

"I got married very young. After about a year and a half of working, my first child was born. Two years later, I had my second son. My husband was a teacher. We were the reverse of a lot of couples. With many couples, the husband is the engineer and the woman is the teacher. We decided that I would work. He would stay home during the summers to take care of the boys. But I would have dinner made, because he came from a family where his mom didn't work and his sister didn't work. I came from a background where my mom did work. It was just the melding of two backgrounds. But it worked. And I'm very proud of my children and what we did together."

Traditional mores can have great sway with people. In the end, it was the undoing of her marriage.

Be Who You Are

Martinovich never shied away from the tougher road, even if the consequences were severe. Using her career as backdrop, Martinovich offers advice for younger professionals in that regard.

"You need to be who you are. In fairness to my husband, maybe I was something other than he thought, because I allowed myself to become who I needed to be. As a result our marriage didn't work after a while. We divorced after about 27 years of marriage. He retired when I was just starting the Director job. He wanted me to retire with him and I just wasn't ready to do that. I was still growing and he was ready for something else. But you have to do what your heart and gut guides you to do. So be who you are and really be open in communication and relationships and that's how you achieve work-life balance."

Her advice extends well beyond work-life balance.

"Don't be afraid to ask questions. Sometimes something is said in a meeting and you think, 'I don't understand that,' but nobody else asks the question, because they all *seem* to understand it. *Raise your hand and ask the question!* People will come up to you later and say, 'Thank you for asking that!' Don't be afraid. That is one of the things I really had to overcome. Also, I always feel like I shouldn't call someone because I don't want to bother them. Well flip that around and say, 'Would I feel bothered if they called me?' If the answer is, 'No,' then call them. People want to help. Sure, you'll come across some goofballs, but they provide the amusement in life. So just go for it."

Martinovich sees this formula as key to learning how to live a balanced, full life.

"A lot has happened in the last five years. My son was injured and he came very close to dying or not having a full recovery. A year after that I got a divorce and my mother passed away. But all of these life events have given me perspective. Everything that I get to do now is icing on the cake. I'm really learning to enjoy and not be stressed by life, because you don't know what's going to happen tomorrow."

DANA C. HOOK, PE

I knew there were people that were LGBT and afraid; I decided that was not going to be me. Chris was not my wife at the time because marriage was not legal in our state, but from my first job, she came to all of the events. I had colleagues, including my supervisor, come to our home. That was really something that I was going to share—even if it meant losing my job. They were either going to fire me or I was going to inspire other people to be out and not be ashamed.

Dana Hook possesses uncommon fortitude. She tackles problems head on. But that was not always the case. Though teaching was her first passion, Hook graduated with a degree in engineering. Then she took a job with the Indiana Department of Highways before her first child was born. Because her husband earned $200 a year more than she did, they decided she would be the one to stay home and raise their four children. While at home, she earned a master's degree in business and taught economics at Butler University She also realized she was a lesbian.

She and her husband divorced, and she started a new life with her partner. But her priorities did not change. With her children's four college tuitions on the horizon, Hook reentered the workplace as an engineer with the Pima County Department of Transportation. In 2001, she passed her professional engineer's exam 21 years after graduating from Purdue University. Next she joined Castro Engineering and discovered an issue with a contract, saving the firm a considerable amount of money. She got noticed.

Hook then moved to Seattle and joined a large consulting firm. In 2004 Hook joined HNTB Corporation in Seattle as a Project Manager. She rose through the ranks quickly, becoming a Vice President in 2010 and being placed in charge of their San Diego office. In 2013, she took a position as Vice President at CDM Smith, where she works today.

Hook also believes strongly in giving back. In addition to informally mentoring women at work, she currently serves as WTS International Board Immediate Past Chair, after serving as Chair. Dana Hook has applied her unique resilience to both her life and her career in the transportation industry.

This is her story.

My Passion Was Teaching

Dana Hook was not thinking about transportation when it was time for college.

"My passion was teaching. But my parents were adamant, especially my mother, that I would *not* be a teacher. She said she would not pay for my education if I went into education. You see, she had always wanted to be an engineer, and instead became a teacher."

Hook won a Society of Women Engineers Scholarship and joined her brother at Purdue University for engineering.

They Were Pretty Boring

School work came naturally to Hook, much more so than to many of her peers.

"Engineering is challenging, but I thought these guys were pretty boring. But I was friends with them. In fact, that's where I met my future husband; he was very good looking and the nicest person I'd ever met."

In addition to meeting her future husband, she achieved something that was virtually unheard of—she graduated in only four years.

"Almost everybody takes longer than four years. So I learned it, but never had a passion for it. I should have been more thoughtful and curious as to what my life was going to be. But that wasn't how my brain was working at that time. I thought: go to school, go to college, get a job. That's how I got through school."

My Husband Made $200 More a Year

Hook and her husband became civil engineers and Dana worked for the Indiana Department of Highways.

"I was 22 years old, married, and we lived in a little town in Indiana called Greenfield. I was the first engineering professional woman hired in the Greenfield district. In the interview they asked me what I would do if I had children, but I hadn't really thought it through."

She would soon find out. While working in a highways department in a small town in the early 1980s could be tough for a young woman, it wasn't tough for her.

"I didn't feel any resistance. I was 22 years old, practically a college student. And so 40-year-old men had no problem taking me under their wing. I wasn't a threat. It's not until you get to be experienced and an equal that you experience more resistance."

But resistance appeared in a different form when Hook got pregnant.

"We were deciding who was going to stay home and take care of the kids. But my husband earned $200 more a year than I did. That was really important because we had just bought a house and were going to be living on a one-income, shoestring budget. So I stayed home, because of that $200 a year difference in annual salary."

Hook did not sit idle at home.

"I got my master's degree. I went to night classes, and my husband would stay home with our son. Sometimes he had evening meetings that would conflict, but he had an intern whose mother thought women should be given the chance to excel. So she volunteered to babysit our son on those evenings. She believed that women should have opportunity."

She Becomes a Teacher

With her MBA in hand, Hook fulfilled her longtime passion. She taught economics until her third child was born. Looking for something to do while parenting, she volunteered at the kindergarten. It proved to be a valuable investment.

"I learned what a really bad teacher I had been. I didn't really understand how people learned. I thought you either knew things or you didn't. When I saw a gifted teacher and learned about communication and learning styles, I began to understand how to talk to people, how to present things in ways that are visual, auditory, or tactile, because people learn in these different ways."

Hook would use these tools throughout her career.

Looking for Adventure

Hook turned 36. By this time, she and her husband had four children. And they realized something.

"The experience we were giving our kids was idyllic, but it wasn't very adventuresome. So we moved to a little town in Arizona called Douglas along the border with Mexico. Arizona had always been one of those places that I had visited as a teenager and thought, 'This place speaks to my soul.' Douglas was much poorer than the community we were in, but we thought we could figure out how to educate the children. It was important that we bring a different experience to these kids for later when they go out in the world."

Douglas brought another advantage, a community college.

"My youngest was four years old, and it was time for me to think about what I was going to do. There was a community college there, and I knew that I could start my career again."

Douglas was a sea change from Indiana. But Hook would soon discover the changes were not only external.

The $300 Phone Bills Were a Clue

Hook taught math and computers. Her husband was the town engineer. But an issue loomed.

"We were there two years when I started to figure out more about myself. I really was attracted to women. My husband and I had a great working relationship, but I was 38, and I fell in love and thought, 'Oh, this is that really extra special part.' And it was with a woman I had known back in Indiana. When we moved to Arizona, I kept thinking, 'I miss this person so much. . . . '

"It took about two years before I could actually tell her that I thought I was in love with her. And she was having the same struggles back in Indiana. The $300 phone bills should have been a clue. I talked to my husband, and we decided we were going to move on and figure out how to raise our kids. One of the main things that helped me make that decision for myself was that he was the person I thought he was, the nicest person I had ever met."

Hook, her ex-husband, and their children all moved to Tucson. Her future wife, Chris, joined her there. Things were working. Then a harsh reality set in—paying for multiple college tuitions.

Omitting Her MBA

Paying for college education is not easy. Hook faced a fourfold challenge. Though she loved teaching, she needed to make more money and turned to engineering. But she had a problem.

"I had a 15-year gap in my résumé, and I was applying to positions in a city where I knew no one. I started removing my MBA from my résumé because I wasn't getting any calls. I thought maybe that was not appealing for these entry-level jobs. It took me two years to get that first full-time position. I was hired as a traffic-engineering technician with the Pima County Department of Transportation. Chris and I were so excited that I had a full-time job—even one that paid only $12/hour."

More importantly, Hook worked for a registered engineer, necessary for her to eventually earn her status as a professional engineer.

A Test 21 Years in the Taking

Hook prepared rigorously for a new engineering world, taking AutoCAD and other courses while working. It was not easy, but she had a goal.

"Twenty-one years after I graduated college, I sat for the professional engineering (PE) exam and passed it. I couldn't tell you whether I was happier when I got that first call about having a full-time job or when I passed the PE exam. I knew I brought a lot more life skills and maturity to the market, but now I would be considered an engineer and I could move into the management part of engineering, which is where I knew my future would be. I was a member of the club now."

Hook joined the county's flood-control department. Despite being a registered engineer, it was like starting all over again.

"I was back to being the first woman professional, but this time I did not have a supportive supervisor. He seemed to have an axe to grind in terms of making sure I was put in my place. I went to my first department meeting and they needed someone to take notes. There's always an administrative assistant at every meeting and she said, 'I'll take the notes.' At which point the supervisor said that one of the professional staff should do it. One of the younger junior engineers said, 'I'll take the notes!' The supervisor said, 'No, I think it should be a woman.' I was the only woman who was not the administrative assistant, so that meant me. I said, 'Okay, I'll do it this time.' Then I went and talked to him and told him I wouldn't do it again.

"It didn't take me more than a couple months to recognize that that was not going to be the only way that he was running an inappropriate department. I think it might have been the alcohol on his breath every day that could have been another clue. After I took notes at that meeting, I went to the consulting community where I knew people and said, 'I'm going to be looking for a job soon.' I only stayed in that department for six or nine months. I talked about my supervisor in my exit interview, and two months later he was fired. But I was already gone."

I Was Not Going to Be Someone People Didn't Know About

Work was not the only challenging environment. Hook was also learning what it meant to be out as a lesbian.

"In our first year in Tucson, we tried to find a community that extended beyond my four children, my ex-husband, and his wife. We went to a LGBT-friendly church and met people whose lives had been very different than ours, as privileged white married women. We met women who, when they fell in love, their husbands took their children away. We met young people whose parents had kicked them out. Their entire lives were fear-based in some way. And that was the great majority of the LGBT community that we met. In some ways, we couldn't relate to them.

"So I thought it was important to make sure that people *know*. I'm a strong person, a good person, and a leader. I wanted people to see that being LGBT did not make you a second-class citizen or mean that you could not achieve. So I was always out."

"I Think You'll Be a Manager"

After leaving the flood-control job, Hook went to work for a small consulting firm, Castro Engineering. Though a junior engineer, she had the ear of senior management.

"I hadn't been there very long and I heard them talking about a contract issue they had with the Pima County Department of Transportation. They thought they would have to pay a $50,000 penalty on one of their contracts, because they weren't going to deliver the project on time. I said, 'Can I see the contract?' I noticed very quickly that the county had added a lot more work. This was evidenced by the fact that they also added significant dollars to the contract to get the work done, but they hadn't added any more time. So I said, 'That's an important thing to tell the county. And because of that, you're not going to pay a penalty.' And the owner said, 'I think you'll be a manager.'"

Castro Engineering had just won the largest project Pima County had ever initiated, an arterial roadway. Castro named Hook as the Project Manager.

"I was in the club; I had my PE. And they said, 'You can really lead people.' So that's when I entered into the let's-figure-out-how-to-get-things-done part that I knew I was good at. I became management by finding a little thing in a contract that I thought was pretty straightforward, but saved them so much money that they said, 'You can do this.'"

Hook stayed with Castro for a couple of years, when the Pacific Northwest drew her urgent attention.

Words Every Parent Fears

Hook's second oldest child was a freshman at the University of Washington in Seattle. She called and said she wasn't coming home for the summer.

"And then we heard the words every parent fears, 'I've met someone, and I'm going to move in with him.' So my ex-husband and I, and his wife and my wife Chris, had to figure this out. And I said, 'I know somebody in Seattle, a friend of mine from Purdue. He always said he would hire me. Maybe I should see what the job market looks like there. . . .'"

They had a plan; their high-school-aged daughter would finish her last year in Tucson, and eighth-grade daughter would join Hook and her wife in Seattle. Hook went to Seattle and became a department manager for a consulting firm, which she did not name. With everything in place, it was time to talk to her youngest daughter.

"We said, 'We're thinking about going to Seattle, and we don't want to leave you behind.' And she said, 'I'm in.' Just like that. Evidently our moving to Arizona to make our kids more adventurous had worked."

An Ethical Divide

With her daughter settled in Seattle, Hook's focus returned to work. But once again, all was not happy in her world.

"This friend of mine at the firm was doing something I thought was unforgivable. He was directing staff in my department to bill to jobs they were not working on. In my world, that is fraud. It was all the same client. It was all in the same bucket of money. But it still wasn't right. You write down on your time card the project you worked on. That's the only thing that we can offer our client, that we are ethical on our invoices. So I knew I couldn't stay working for him. He never asked me to bill that way. And when I confronted him on it he said that it didn't make a difference to the client. It was his business, but I just knew it wasn't going to be my business.

"I stayed with that firm for just a year, as they had helped me with moving costs. In my exit interview, I talked to the company leadership about what I thought he was doing, and it was theirs to take care of it or not."

But many things with the firm were positive. Hook recounts a very important person that she met on her very first day there.

"I found a real supporter whose name was Hugh Fuller. And on my first day he said, 'We're going to a WTS meeting.'"

A Different World

Though she had attended WTS meetings in Tucson, Hook experienced a different world at WTS Seattle. There she gained access to transportation leaders, particularly women leaders. And her experience did not end there.

"Hugh introduced me to everyone. And when I decided I was leaving the firm we worked for, he took me to meet other consulting firms. I got two different offers. And in 2004, HNTB hired me as an entry-level project manager."

Hook liked HNTB because of their emphasis on ethics and values. But she did note that she was the only lesbian professional there.

"I never wondered whether or not I fit in. I just wanted to make a difference on the projects I was doing, while serving the clients, winning more work, and advancing my career. It was good to see women's leadership through WTS, and I started forming my opinions about the importance of women in leadership roles. Because when I eventually went down to San Diego there were limited women leaders. You say to yourself, 'Oh, now *you* are the woman leader that needs to point things out here.' But up in Seattle I was still forming those ideas about what that meant."

Leadership and San Diego

HNTB promoted Hook to Vice President and put her in charge of their San Diego office. It was a good promotion, but she had some concerns.

"When I became an officer at HNTB, I didn't know exactly what that meant or how I should behave. I didn't even know *men* that had become officers since I had been with the company. When I first became an officer, I hadn't ever met another woman officer. I didn't have a role model."

Unfortunately, she couldn't find any role models in San Diego at first.

"All of the consulting firms were led by men. Men also led almost all of the public agencies. I was the first office leader that was a woman. And there was a large job we had to compete for. I recognized that having a woman-led project was a risk for HNTB."

In addition, Hook had gotten wind of a demonstrated prejudice in the public sector agencies in favor of male project leaders. After informing HNTB, she pressed on.

"My job was to form relationships with the client. But I don't smoke cigars, drink scotch, or stay on the golf course, which is where men often form relationships. And I am no longer a 22-year-old coed, where they just like having me around. I had to form my own relationships based on respect, and people wanted to hear what I thought about things. People respected my opinion."

That respect carried over to her role in WTS. On the WTS International Board of Directors, Hook found that she was now a mentor and role model to young women in the San Diego chapter.

Talking to the Next Generations

Today many young professionals seek out Hook for advice and counsel.

"I tell them that it's about hard work. I want them to hear about all of the work I did to get back into this industry. *Not* because someone said they were going to give me tuition reimbursement, and *not* because someone said that I needed to learn this. This was *me* saying that I would not be limited by my own knowledge gap. I want them to know how hard that was."

Hook also wants them to know the importance of mentors and sponsors, and the difference between them.

"A mentor is someone you meet with on a regular basis that provides advice. I had a great mentor in Dick Page at HNTB. He did my reviews. And I'd be very blunt and say, 'What can I do to be better?' The first time he said, 'You could speak up more.' The second time I met with him he said, 'You're the first person I ever gave advice to that followed it.' So when someone gives you advice, take it. But a mentor is someone you know you can trust.

"Then there is a sponsor. That's not someone you meet with often. You might see them once or twice a year. It's someone that's at a higher level who is not really directing your career, but when the doors are closed and they're talking about next assignments, they bring your name up. I was very fortunate at HNTB to have such a sponsor in Division President Larry Davis, a retired General from the US Army Corps of Engineers. He shared with me that in the military it's always about mission, team, and self, in that order. And I keep that as a guide."

She also provides a specific example of how her sponsor boosted her career.

"He could only nominate one person in the West Division to become a Vice President. At the time there was a long-time HNTB employee who had been winning giant jobs, working on billion-dollar programs, which I don't really do. He was an engineer's engineer and a former Navy SEAL. We were both brought up as potentials for this vice presidency. And I was amazed when Larry said, 'I want this to go to Dana. She's an engineer. She's a leader. And she takes care of her people. She serves her clients so that they want her to come back and help them again.'"

The General's Missive

Hook offers further proof of the value of a well-placed sponsor.

"Larry wrote me a letter of reference for a position on the WTS International Board of Directors. In the letter he talked about his years of working with leaders both in the army and at HNTB and he said that he would put Dana 'in the top category of all of the leaders he had met in his career.' Kelli Burn-Roy, who's President of the Technical Service Unit for CDM Smith, read the letter because she was interviewing me for the WTS International Board Chair position. And she said, 'I'm going to hire you.' And that's who I have as a sponsor today."

Hook now serves as a Vice President at CDM Smith. She adds this.

"This is the first time I've ever worked under a woman. And it hasn't been different except that I know that she's there. I see someone ahead of me in the corporate ladder who is a woman, so I can say, 'That could be me.'"

Children and Your Career

When faced with the dilemma, Hook and her ex-husband wanted someone to stay home with their children, and she made less money. But she doesn't necessarily recommend that plan for everyone.

"I would never say that's it's the greatest career advice to stay home with your kids for 15 years. When I reentered the workforce, I was very fortunate to be in a position to show my skills and have a sponsor so that I could advance to a leadership position in a very short 15 years of working. I hope I'm setting an example for the employees that work for me and around me. And I can look at myself and say, 'There are a lot of choices out there that you're going to make. But those choices don't have to stop you from doing the next thing. You don't have to think that you'll never get to do—whatever—if you make these choices now.' I would never tell a young person to stay home for 15 years and then see how your career goes. But it worked for me."

And her choices continue to work for her today.

Chapter 20

THE NEXT CHAPTER IS YOURS

At the End, the Journey Begins. . . .

At first, we thought it was important. Then it became a passion. We began this project because we wanted to capture the stories of women who became leaders during our time in the transportation industry. At the outset, we had little idea of how it would go and what the stories would be like. We expected to learn a lot. But the reality of what we experienced far exceeded any expectations. When we interviewed these women, their stories brought us joy, resonance, understanding, sadness, and surprise. Hearing what happened to each woman firsthand was a unique experience. But after that we had to set to work and put those experiences into book form.

The Finer Print

We asked the women to be frank, and they delivered. They were also moving in ways we had not expected. In some cases, they were even shocking. But overall we wanted to make sure that the written stories truly captured each woman's voice. We wanted the words to accurately reflect and honor the integrity of the telling.

We believe we did that. In fact, we were relieved that the voice and the person behind the story emerged so clearly in each case. Once that process was completed, we were able to see in each person and each story many leadership lessons and valuable advice. We then took a moment to pause and reflect.

Yes, each woman was unique. Yet they all possessed many similar leadership traits. Still, some qualities seemed to better define certain women and their careers. We thought it would be helpful to point those out.

- *A singular focus on doing their job well and a vision of what that meant.* **Mary Peters** maintained that throughout her career, as did **Susan Martinovich**. They were able to rise to the top within traditional organizations.

- *A good working relationship with, and support from, a boss.* **Rina Cutler** established this with Boston Mayor Ray Flynn, Philadelphia Mayor and Pennsylvania Governor Ed Rendell, and Philadelphia Mayor Michael Nutter. They gave her great freedom and support to make change. **Ann Hershfang** spoke eloquently of working for Governor Dukakis and Fred Salvucci, great people to work for, people who inspired an entire generation of outstanding transportation professionals. Similarly, men like Mort Downey and Tom Downs assisted many talented women. These men and others mentioned in the book created environments that welcomed women, innovation, and change. The women in turn reached out and helped many women and men.

- *An ability to seize experiences and opportunities.* **Lillian Borrone** and **Anne Canby** both demonstrated that skill many different times in their respective careers. Lillian took on jobs in operations and in finance that prepared her for the Director of Ports opportunity at PANY/NJ. As Secretary of the Delaware Department of Transportation, **Anne Canby** saw how to "right the ship," including raising taxes. In all her jobs she found opportunity.

- *A penchant for risk taking.* **Shirley DeLibero** was the queen in this area. She strategically advanced while facing tremendous professional peril many times—often building new relationships in tough political environments, like Houston. **Rina Cutler** also showed this risk-taking inclination as she relocated for jobs and tackled tough issues.

* *An undeniable resiliency.* **LaVerne Reid** demonstrated this powerful trait many times throughout her life and career. Her strength resonates in her story.

* *An irrepressible fortitude.* **Jolene Molitoris** and **Nuria Fernandez** both showed boundless determination as they faced complicated political, institutional, and people issues. They figured out the contribution they could make and made it. Both women had many transferable skills that worked in the private and public sectors and in all modes of transportation.

* *A fearless authenticity. All th*ese women knew themselves well and shared who they were with others. It is a remarkable part of their success. **Dana Hook**, particularly, understood the power of authenticity and used it in traditionally male engineering organizations to create her own path.

* *An outstanding facility with people and communication skills, as well as a unique ability for building trust.* **Jane Garvey** took this to an art form in many instances, but one stands out. Turning doubters into champions, Garvey led the FAA at a very difficult time and gained the support of the federal air traffic controllers, the pilots, and Congress. Similarly, with her magical understanding of people, **Jane Chmielinski** won fans in whatever position she held. They knew she would serve them well.

* *A vision and drive for being a change agent.* **Dr. Beverly Scott** demonstrated that special capacity to join an organization in need of change, turn it around, and then move on to the next challenge. **Joan Claybrook**, from the time she was a young women, was always focused on creating change. Early on she chose safety as her lifelong interest. She achieved change through her extraordinary legislative and political skills. **Ann Hershfang** was a change agent through the

force of her vision for neighborhood-friendly transportation, whether it was an airport, a subway near her home, or streets. She introduced innovation and change wherever she worked.

* *Some women worked deftly within their organizations at a pace that didn't ruffle feathers, but made gradual, significant change.* **Mary Jane O'Meara** did that at Massport where she created an effective and loyal team.

Some of the women went into the transportation field because of a relative who was an engineer, like **Susan Martinovich.** Many of the women entered the transportation industry by chance, like **Jane Garvey.** Some women planned their careers strategically as **Shirley DeLibero** did. Other women followed their instincts and pounced on opportunity when it arose. Some women did a combination of both.

From a family perspective, the women represented a broad range of situations: single; single or divorced raising children; married with and without children. Some women stayed in one place and built their careers, like **Mary Jane O'Meara.** Other women were highly mobile, like **Nuria Fernandez.** A few of the women were stay-at-home moms when their children were little, like **Dana Hook** and **Jolene Molitoris.** Women currently married with a first or second spouse usually noted in the interview that their spouse was supportive. Marriages where they had non-supportive spouses often ended in divorce. All of the women made their situation work for them, no matter what it was.

We did not pry into their upbringings unless *they* brought it up and thought it integral to their experience. Yet we could imagine that they each displayed leadership qualities as youngsters and that they would have been successful in whatever field they chose. Many of these women showed transferable skills within their transportation work. They navigated well in both public sector and private sector jobs. They succeeded in operations and strategy roles. Many worked holistically in a number of different transportation modes. Overall, these women knew who they were and were willing to go on the record and share that knowledge with others. And for that we are grateful to them.

What struck us most about the women we interviewed was this. Each story, each woman represented a singular perspective, a unique set of challenges where an individual prevailed almost always against great odds. They all exhibited a strong sense of what mattered most to them in terms of who they were and how they contributed to the transportation industry and beyond.

So, read their stories, even study them. See how these successful women approached different situations, succeeded, or took a step back and then came back stronger. Reflect on what their stories say about leadership and life, success and failure, value and meaning. Reflect also on their advice to you. Then think about your own story in relation to theirs. Think about what your story says about you, who you are, where you are, and what you want to be. See how you can further develop your own style. Their stories are powerful. We hope they inspire you to look at your own story and make it what you want it to be. We hope you are the next chapter.

Moving Forward

The next decade should be a good decade for women. By sheer number, our stars are on the rise. And more women in high-level positions are reaching back to bring other women along. But it isn't enough. Only through real change to our institutions can we produce new organizations and change old organizations so that they are truly places with opportunity for everyone. Women are in a particularly good place to create that change: they are outsiders to the system and they can bring strong values and newer leadership styles that are desperately needed. We hope that each of you will learn from the examples of the women in this book and carry that work forward with your own signature path, creating a new example for those behind you.

LIST OF ABBREVIATIONS
AND ACRONYMS

AASHTO	American Association of State Highway and Transportation Officials
ADOT	Arizona Department of Transportation
APTA	American Public Transportation Association
ARTBA	American Road and Transportation Builders Association
BART	Bay Area Rapid Transit
BPW	Business and Professional Women's Foundation
Caltrans	California Department of Transportation
CMA	calcium magnesium acetate
COMTO	Conference of Minority Transportation Officials
CTA	Chicago Transit Authority
DCA	Massachusetts Department of Community Affairs
DelDOT	Delaware Department of Transportation
DOT	Department of Transportation
DPT	Department of Parking and Traffic
DPW	Chicago Department of Public Works
DPW	Massachusetts Department of Public Works
EIS	environmental impact statement
EOTC	Massachusetts Executive Office of Transportation and Construction
FAA	Federal Aviation Administration
FHWA	Federal Highway Administration
FRA	Federal Railroad Administration
FRH	Frederic R. Harris
FTA	Federal Transit Administration

Houston Metro	Metropolitan Transit Authority of Harris County, Texas
IBTTA	International Bridge, Tunnel, and Turnpike Association
ILA	International Longshoreman's Association
ISTEA	Intermodal Surface Transportation Efficiency Act
LGBT	lesbian, gay, bisexual, and transgender
M&E	Metcalf & Eddy
M/WBE	minority and women's business enterprise program
MARTA	Metropolitan Atlanta Rapid Transit Authority
MassDOT	Massachusetts Department of Transportation
MassGAP	Massachusetts Government Appointments Project
Masspike	Massachusetts Turnpike Authority
Massport	Massachusetts Port Authority
MBCR	Massachusetts Bay Commuter Rail Company
MBTA	Massachusetts Bay Transportation Authority
MMS	US Department of Interior's Minerals Management Service
MTA	Massachusetts Turnpike Authority
MTA	Metropolitan Transportation Authority (NY)
MWPC	Massachusetts Women's Political Caucus
NASTO	National Association of State Transportation Officials
NDOT	Nevada Department of Transportation
NFBPA	National Forum for Black Public Administrators
NHSB	National Highway Safety Bureau
NHTSA	National Highway Traffic Safety Administration
NJDOT	New Jersey Department of Transportation
NJT	New Jersey Transit
NYCTA	New York City Transit Authority

ODOT	Ohio Department of Transportation
ODOT	Oregon Department of Transportation
OMB	Office of Management and Budget
ORTA	Ohio Rail Transportation Authority
P3	Public/Private Partnership
PANY/NJ	Port Authority of New York and New Jersey
PATH	Port Authority Trans-Hudson line
PennDOT	Pennsylvania Department of Transportation
PMI	Presidential Management Intern Program
RFC	Road Finance Committee
RFP	request for proposals
RIPTA	Rhode Island Public Transit Authority
SDOT	Seattle Department of Transportation
SSA	Social Security Administration
STPP	Surface Transportation Policy Project
"T"	MBTA nickname
TBTA	Triborough Bridge and Tunnel Authority
TIGER	USDOT's Transportation Investment Generating Economic Recovery
TRB	Transportation Research Board
UMTA	Urban Mass Transportation Administration
USDOT	US Department of Transportation
VTA	Santa Clara Valley Transportation Authority
WCG	Washington Council of Governments
WMATA	Washington Metropolitan Area Transit Authority
WTS	Women's Transportation Seminar, now known as WTS International or simply WTS

CPSIA information can be obtained
at www.ICGtesting.com
Printed in the USA
LVOW10s1829230318
570973LV00014B/237/P